'Set Your House in Order'

God's Call to George Jeffreys
as the Founder of the Elim Pentecostal Movement

Frontispiece photograph was taken in 1947 during George Jeffreys' meetings in Copenhagen, Denmark, when he was 58 years of age.

PRINCIPAL GEORGE JEFFREYS

'Set Your House in Order'

**God's Call to George Jeffreys
as the Founder of the Elim Pentecostal Movement**

Albert W. Edsor

New Wine Press

© Albert W. Edsor
World Revival Crusade
17 Sumburgh Road
London SW12 8AJ

British Edition first published 1989

New Wine Ministries
P.O. Box 17
Chichester
West Sussex PO20 6RY
England

ISBN 0 947852 48 4

Contents

Preface

I HAVE called this biography by the title 'SET YOUR HOUSE IN ORDER' because George Jeffreys firmly believed it was God's command to him as the Founder of the Elim Foursquare Gospel Movement, subsequently to become known as "The Elim Pentecostal Church". He knew Elim was his 'house' in this context, and although the message came when he had everything to gain from disregarding it, at a time when he was held in the highest esteem by thousands in the Movement for his work's sake, he had no alternative but to obey.

Reform and change can be drastic, far—reaching and generate opposition which inevitably includes those who, having voiced their views, afterwards come to leave a Movement for reasons best known to themselves.

There is a new generation in the Elim Movement today, those 'which knew not Joseph,' many of them forging ahead, having a desire and zeal for God in their hearts and lives, and with its progress and affluence as a spur. Is progress as such the criterion whereby a Movement is tested and judged to be right? With some men, Christian and otherwise, the answer could be in the affirmative; but God, surely, has a more exacting criterion, that of His Word and its challenge and outworking in one's life, which so often calls for painful renunciation and a new beginning.

Those of this generation do not owe their 'Elim' to their present leaders, much as they may respect them as such, but to the Founder whose dedicated life and phenomenal Pentecostal ministry I have endeavoured to portray in these pages.

Writing in my former book entitled *George Jeffreys — Man of God,* published in 1964, Commander D.H. Macmillan, M.B.E., R.N.R., F.R.I.C.S., in enlarging on the free and self—governing principle in the ancient and primitive Church of the first centuries, and of its carnal obscurity for 1700 years since, went on to state: "To the great servant of God, whose life and ministry is portrayed in this book, was given the noble task of revealing this principle to the Faithful in Christ. The conflict wounded him, but the Truth he proclaimed must prevail despite misrepresentations, misunderstandings and betrayals, all tending

7

to cloud the issue and help error enthroned for centuries." He concluded: "God's Pattern of Church Government, as with every other phase of the Truth of His Word, is high and is attained only by the Scriptural holiness of Pastors and People under the Cross."

History testifies to 'battles' for causes believed to be right in the Christian warfare and to the fact that, if Christian reformers do not always live to see the fruits of their labours in their own day and generation, others ultimately do.

With recent publications propagating distorted views about Principal George Jeffreys personally and what he stood for, it is necessary I bring my former book up to date, to include dealing with these. I do so as a friend and colleague so closely associated with him for so many years, and that the facts may be on permanent record.

A.W. Edsor
28th February 1989

The above date, being the 100th anniversary of George Jeffreys' birth, this book is dedicated to his honoured memory.

Foreword

THE distinguished theologian D.R. Davies, who had been acquainted with George Jeffreys since childhood, when he reviewed my book *Fight for The Faith and Freedom* in 1947 for the magazine *The Bible Speaks to Britain,* said that George Jeffreys was a much greater man than I had portrayed him to be. This evaluation ought to be placed side by side with the more recent claim that George Jeffreys "died a nonentity." This new work on the revivalist by his long—term colleague, Albert W. Edsor should go a long way to set the record straight. It surely elucidates and validates D.R. Davies' claim, and exposes the falsity of the nonentity opinion.

I myself became closely associated with George Jeffreys. In my opinion he was the greatest crowd—compelling personality on the religious scene that Britain has produced during the present century. He had remarkable eyes and hands and voice which the Holy Spirit used to move the multitudes. And these gifts were combined with keen intuition and deep compassion. His preaching was strictly biblical and logical, the atmosphere of his meetings was reverent and devotional and his healing services were dignified, free from the questionable and sometimes bizarre practices of some more recent healing evangelists, yet powerful and effective in their impact.

A number of factors had combined to mould George Jeffreys into a powerful evangelist. He was born again during the Welsh revival. In his early years he received the Pentecostal baptism. He was a great admirer of Charles Finney, whose Systematic Theology was his guide. He was greatly influenced by biblical prophecy, and was an adherent of the National Historicist School of Interpretation. The theme of his crusades was threefold: Revival—Healing—Prophecy. Armed with this theme, his powerful Spirit—filled personality filled the largest auditoriums which the cities of Britain could provide. Thousands were brought to Christ, and scores of churches were organised, and many young people brought into the Pentecostal ministry as the result of these services.

I have many memories of this great evangelist, yet I feel indebted to him for one thing in particular. He continually

9

exalted Holy Scripture as the sole and absolute authority in the church. He constantly warned his followers not to place the gifts of the Holy Spirit either above Holy Scripture or on a level with it. Only the Bible is authoritative.

Whenever there have been fresh movements of a Pentecostal nature, as in the Latter Rain movement of the forties and fifties, and the Charismatic Renewal of more recent years, outbreaks of fanaticism have occurred. But also there has been something more insidious yet equally destructive of the work of God, the thing which George Jeffreys frequently spotlighted in his preaching and strove long and hard and successfully to keep out of his own churches, namely, the tendency to place too much credibility on 'messages in tongues,' interpretations and prophecies, to put them on a level with the Word of God, or even above it, to allow them to override and set aside the proclamation and exposition of the Word.

I am grateful in these present times of confusion that as a young Pentecostal preacher I learned this important guideline from this eminent Pentecostal pioneer. It has keep my feet in many slippery places. There is a place for tongues, interpretation, and prophecy in the church. But if we delight in them more than in the Word and the Sacraments, if we give them precedence or authority above the Word and the Sacraments, if we imagine they contain and communicate more of the presence and power of the Holy Spirit than the Word and the Sacraments, it is my deep conviction that we are heading for delusion and confusion.

The conviction that Scripture is supreme — not only supreme over the human reason and ecclesiastical councils, but equally so over every kind of charismatic gift and ministry, — controlled George Jeffreys' powerful ministry throughout his career. But in middle life his mind was gripped by another conviction which came to him almost with the force of a mystical insight but of which he found strong confirmation in the Bible, namely, that a local congregation of Christian believers is sovereign of its affairs under Christ. The supremacy of Holy Scripture and the sovereignty of the local church henceforth became the twin pillars of his ministry.

As the concept of local church sovereignty was quite opposite to the centrally controlled body of churches which he had hitherto been building up for many years, he felt compelled to make radical changes in that organization. His efforts to bring those changes about forced him along the painful path of controversy and conflict, even with life—long friends and colleagues.

In the year 1945, Dr. Vaughan Rees, who had recently returned from his work with the *Jesus Families* of China, was staying in our home. We were discussing the sad conflicts into which George Jeffreys had been thrust, when Dr. Rees asked: *"On which side is the Cross in this dispute?"* It is a highly significant question! As I look back through the years it is evident to me that there was a cross on both sides of the dispute, certainly for those engaged in it who had pure hearts and right motives. Yet, it surely must have been George Jeffreys himself who bore the heaviest cross of all. His deeply—felt conviction concerning the sovereignty of the local church meant (though in several stages over several years) severance from pioneer friends and colleagues, from large numbers of Elim ministers, many of whom were his own converts, and from thousands of his devoted followers who made up the membership of the Elim churches. Perhaps the most painful cross he had to bear was that some of those who had supported him and followed him into virtual ecclesiastical exile eventually drew back from him. No doubt they did so for a variety of reasons and motives, but there were some who did so because they had come to feel that their leader was going too far and had placed himself in an inflexible position, and that he ought to be satisfied with a more moderate stance on the vexed question of church government. I myself, who had followed him all the way, came to believe, though only by degrees over a process of time, that we ought to adopt a more eirenic attitude to those who differed from us, and perhaps seek a synthesis of the two extremes of centralization and local church sovereignty.

But to George Jeffreys and his closest associates (including the author of this book) this was unthinkable compromise. Perhaps it was a further mark of his greatness that George Jeffreys would not permit even friends and allies to turn him from what he profoundly believed was God's pattern for the church. He set his face like a flint to travel his increasingly lonely way.

NOEL BROOKS, B.D.
author of *Fight for The Faith and Freedom*
and other books

11

Introduction

IN chapter 2 I give Rom Landau's impressions of George Jeffreys' ministry in his book entitled GOD IS MY ADVENTURE, first published by Ivor Nicholson and Watson in 1935 and later by Faber and Faber (Ninth Impression). These appear under the chapter headed *Miracle at the Albert Hall.* This distinguished author could number amongst his books a life of Ignace Jan Paderewski, world—famous pianist and one time Premier of Poland.

Having met Rom Landau at his London home and country retreat in Sussex when he was engaged on the book, I talked freely with him as Principal Jeffreys' private secretary. I unwittingly confirmed the impressions he had already gathered as to his humility, coupled with his strong adherence to the Bible as the Word of God. Undoubtedly this is why George Jeffreys, together with the crowded Easter Monday demonstrations in the Royal Albert Hall (1926—1939), and the meetings in the huge Crystal Palace in London (1930—1936), again chiefly composed of thousands of converts won to Christ through his pioneer revival and healing campaigns, did more than any other British Pentecostal leader to bring, not only Elim, but the Pentecostal Movement as a whole to the forefront of people's attention everywhere.

1939 saw the passing of an era in the Pentecostal—Evangelical life of our country. Such gigantic meetings, with their world—wide witness to Divine healing (morning), baptism by immersion in water (afternoon) and the partaking of the Breaking of Bread (evening), each filling the vast Royal Albert Hall from floor level to top promenade gallery, have not been seen since.

The Press reported queues waiting as long as eight hours for admission. *Ristin Voitto,* Pentecostal periodical of Finland, reported of George Jeffreys:

"When before the war he had meetings in the Royal Albert Hall in London, with 10,000 seats, it was filled year after year to capacity. The Finns who attended have told that they have seen, neither in Europe nor in America, meetings so powerful and wonderful as these occasions in the Albert Hall."

In both this hall and the Crystal Palace he baptised converts in water totalling thousands (over 1,000 in one service alone at the Royal Albert Hall), spectacular achievements in themselves before wondering crowds, never to be repeated at the Crystal Palace now that Paxton's original 'Palace of Glass,' brain child of Queen Victoria's Prince Consort, is no more. A writer in the *Strand Magazine,* after the Crystal Palace had been destroyed by fire in 1936, wrote: "...if you chose your day with skill, you might see the handsome figure of Principal Jeffreys immersing his Foursquare Gospellers in a large tank of warm water."

As Revival Party pianist I was a witness from the platform of these gatherings in both these great halls from 1930 onwards.

When finally George Jeffreys left the Elim Movement in 1940 on what was to him a vital fundamental issue he could not ignore, i.e. Church Government, the last Volume of the *Elim Evangel* he received, the official magazine of the Movement, was Volume 20, completing the years from the first issued in 1920, to 1939. Go through these from beginning to end for an incredible story, supported by photographs, of a British Pentecostal pioneer's ministry unequalled in this the 20th century.

His revival and healing campaigns in the industrial centres of Great Britain and Northern Ireland, such as Glasgow, Belfast, Cardiff, Birmingham, Greenock, Dundee, Manchester, Liverpool, Bradford, Leeds, Sheffield, Halifax, Huddersfield, and of course London, in the 1920s and 30s, with unemployment to the number of two millions and more, brought hope and cheer to thousands of men faced in the great 'depression' with the hopelessness of no work and the dole queues, after having to undergo the Government's 'means test' before being in receipt of a pittance on which to keep themselves, their wives and families. In their need of daily bread God's servant brought them the Living Bread, the Christ who was able miraculously to change their lives, their homes, and their circumstances — and did!

If industrial towns and cities of our land responded in the way they did, the more sedate Cathedral/Abbey cities such as Exeter, Bath, Rochester, Carlisle and York, also saw ingatherings of souls and results in the healing ministry through the preaching of the Full Gospel message to crowded congregations.

It is generally conceded by historians that John Wesley, by his ministry of the Word of God in the 18th century, saved the country from revolution. In our day and age, cities and towns bordering on such a calamity because of the aforementioned conditions were saved through George Jeffreys' proclamation as an Evangelist and teacher of the same powerful Word. A report of a revival campaign was actually headed: "HAS WESLEY RETURNED?" One can rightly say, in accordance with Acts 19, verse 20: "So mightily grew the Word of God and prevailed."

Consider the many solid Pentecostal churches he created, by entering cities and towns without the support of outside church bodies and committees. He was often faced with much opposition from those in the denominations who were unable to accept the miraculous in the preaching of the Gospel. Usually the meetings in halls and church buildings and, in the summer in Evangelistic tents, went on for weeks, with himself preaching every night, except Friday, and three mid—week afternoons, with two on Sunday, afternoon and evening. The campaigns would begin small, but by the third Sunday, that is, within two weeks, the largest halls and places of worship would be unable to contain all those in the crowds eager to hear his powerful ministry. Then would come a great inflow of conversions and miraculous healings through God confirming His own Word with signs following. A disused church or some other building would be acquired by the end of the campaign to house the converts won for Christ, and a minister sent to take charge. So the Elim Movement was established and built up through the efforts of this dedicated founder and pioneer, sometimes many hundreds forming the nucleus of the new church after a campaign had ended.

In 1933 an extensive South Coast church tour was undertaken and again in 1936, which saw the Coming of Age of the Elim Movement, an even more arduous effort was planned and carried out, beginning at Liverpool towards the end of April and going right through day after day almost to the end of June, when some 36 churches in England and Wales alone were visited for meetings. Such tours as these saw the building up of these established places of worship by the adding of new converts and the spiritual blessing resulting from the ministry of Principal George Jeffreys. This tour saw the use of the 4-berth caravan specially made by Eccles, of Birmingham, and towed by the car in which we lived and moved as a Party from one end of England to the other, and into Wales, often parked in fields after permission to do so from farmers and others, then our going out to church centre after centre in each vicinity and back to 'lodge' for the night. The resourceful R.E. Darragh, George Jeffreys' first Evangelist in Ireland in 1915, had other capabilities besides those of song-leader and preacher — he did the cooking in the small tent which was part of our equipment, maintaining with his Irish humour he had 'Mrs. Beeton' to hand as well as his Bible!

Earlier that Coming of Age year George Jeffreys had further consolidated the Elim work by his ministry in Scotland, through a Scottish Church Tour commencing in Aberdeen and going on to preach in a number of churches. Then in the summer Northern Ireland saw amazing scenes when those brought into the Elim Irish churches, together with thousands of the general public, attended the services in Belfast for several weeks in the Big Tent, considered to be the largest Evangelistic Tent in the country, at 150 feet long, by 80 feet wide. The last three days of this campaign were held in the King's Hall, Balmoral, Belfast, the largest public hall in Ireland and used for religious services for the first time. This huge exhibition building was besieged, congregations of 10,000 attending, with Principal Jeffreys preaching from the boxing ring erected in the centre of the hall on the last night, a fitting 21st anniversary of the humble commencement of the Elim work in Ireland in 1915. The grand piano was raised up along the outside of the ring, a new experience for me as pianist, but not for George Jeffreys. Some ten years before he had preached in the Lime Street Boxing Ring in Liverpool, banner headlines proclaiming, "JEFFREYS IN THE RING AGAIN!" a clever journalistic allusion to the old—time heavy—weight boxing champion Jim Jefferies.

Hundreds were converted to Christ in this Belfast campaign, with miraculous healings recorded.

There followed the 21st birthday celebrations at the Crystal Palace in London, ending with a Breaking of Bread service in the centre transept in the evening attended by thousands of believers. Two months later the Palace was no more, otherwise I do not doubt George Jeffreys would have again been preaching there in 1937, such was the momentum created by the years since 1930.

As a minister from overseas wrote in 1962, on hearing that he had passed on: "The churches which arose out of his campaigns are a fitting tribute to his ministry, no other monument is needed."

The life's work of George Jeffreys did not end with Elim in

1939—40, as I shall show; on the contrary, it meant a further prodigious period of intensive labours and soul—saving activity, week after week, year in and year out, from 1941 to 1962.

This biography is the inside story of a phenomenal ministry; I cannot escape from alluding to myself here in detail and at some length, reluctantly but of necessity, by way of explanation of my background, and because of my long and very close association with Principal George Jeffreys, being so fully identified with him from 1928 until his sudden decease 34 eventful years later. I am therefore able to write authoritatively in the first person because 'I was there' throughout that period, beginning some 13 years after he had founded the Elim work.

This privileged position I held with George Jeffreys came about following my conversion to Christ at Brighton, Sussex, under his preaching of the Gospel in June 1927 when I was 17 years of age. Within fifteen months I had become a member of his Revival Party as pianist—organist, which in a short time led to my becoming his private secretary and secretary of his Revival Party work, to which he gave the name World Revival Crusade after his memorable meetings in 1935 in Palestine, Transjordan and Switzerland. As driver of the car which took us as a Party hundreds of thousands of miles, I was again in constant proximity to him.

A confirmed member of the Church of England and an apprentice to a music firm in Brighton, I attended the last two weeks only of that ten weeks' long revival and healing campaign, first in my case in the Royal Dome, and then on the last night which saw another stage in the varied use of the spacious and historic building in Union Street, The Lanes, Brighton, dating back to 1688, now acquired for the converts of the campaign. It was crowded to capacity with hundreds of newly—won converts and others sitting even on window—sills, stairs and on seats in the aisles, so that I found myself being invited by an usher to stand shoulder to shoulder with other young men on the platform owing to lack of room on ground—floor and gallery.

That God chose to set His seal on my future career cannot be doubted, because that last night which saw my conversion when the appeal for converts was made by Principal Jeffreys at the end of his address, I also responded to a request made from the platform for a pianist to accompany the Revival Party as they sang in quartet, complete strangers as they were to me then. Fred

17

Bell, of Bangor, Co. Down, N. Ireland, their pianist and car driver and soon to marry and leave the Party to live abroad, handed the music book to me as I went to the piano, whereupon he joined in song with the Principal, Pastors R.E. Darragh, incomparable song—leader, and James McWhirter, efficient campaign organiser and the one called to deal with newspaper reporters, both able preachers themselves.

I severed my connection with the C of E, with the prospects I had as assistant organist at the Church I had first attended as a choirboy, after my parents had left London in 1918 to live in Brighton, becoming pianist at the Elim Tabernacle in The Lanes, where my youngest brother Alfred and I were baptised together in water on the confession of our faith in Christ. Little did I know, as I entered into the activities of that local Elim church, what the future was to hold for me with God's so greatly—used servant.

My mother, a professing Methodist, also came to Christ in that Brighton campaign of 1927 and was baptised with hundreds of others by George Jeffreys in the Public Baths hall. She it was who, on returning from her first meeting in the Royal Dome, excitedly urged me to attend by exclaiming, "I have never seen anything like it," adding, "You must go!" Subsequently she was herself a witness of many of the revival campaign and convention meetings in Brighton, London and elsewhere, and remained a staunch member of the local church at Brighton until her death 25 years later. She kept copies of my letters to her over the years from 1928 on, in diary form, an incomparable asset; letters which tell of what I saw of the revival and healing campaigns, demonstrations and events in which I took part, not only throughout Great Britain and Ireland but abroad in France, Switzerland, Sweden, Norway, Denmark, Finland, Palestine and Transjordan.

Before I became a member of the Revival Party there is an account in these letters of my first visit to the Elim Bible College, known as "Elim Woodlands," in Clarence Road (later Clarence Avenue), Clapham Park, London, in February 1928. This was three years after it and the spacious grounds of approx. 4½ acres had been acquired for the Elim work, and the training of Bible students, through George Jeffreys' personal contact on the premises with 'Mother' Mary Philip Connelly, C.SS.R, of the then Roman Catholic Convent housing a closed Redemptoristic

18

Order of nuns, an astonishing business transaction to say the least! During this contact George Jeffreys walked the grounds with 'Mother' Mary and talked with her about the Scriptures, with particular reference to the Second Coming of Christ.

The sum paid for the property and grounds, some £6,000, was loaned by a Christian lady on interest, the monetary advantage to Elim being that when the Bible College was sold by them after 40 years, the price agreed with the Borough Council under the CPO for high-rise flats development on the extensive site was substantial as could be expected, resulting in the purchase of the property at Capel, Dorking, Surrey, as the New Elim Bible College. Such was the monetary difference after that long period, yet material values are not to be compared with the spiritual results accruing through the College over those years and since through a man's vision and faith. In 1987 the Bible College was transferred from Capel to Nantwich in Cheshire.

That weekend visit of mine to the Bible College in 1928, at Principal Jeffreys' invitation, was shortly after my 18th birthday, when he gave time in his busy life to interview me as to the possibility of my becoming a member of his Revival Party as pianist and car driver. The Party were then conducting simultaneous revival and healing campaigns in North and South London, at the massive Rink Cinema, Finsbury Park, one of London's largest cinemas, where I was at the piano for the Sunday afternoon service, then travelled across London to attend the equally crowded evening service at the Grand Theatre, Croydon.

My letters home go on to tell of the holiday week from my employment which I spent at Eastbourne, Sussex, in May 1928, three months after the visit to the Bible College in London. At Eastbourne I was at the piano for the campaign in the Music Pavilion on the Pier. Then in September of that year, at the promptings of a Christian gentleman who taught me to drive his car, I left my employment of my own accord under remarkable circumstances, in the fifth and final year of my apprenticeship, shortly before it was completed because my father, through an oversight on his part and that of the firm, had not signed the papers on my behalf as a 14-year old straight from school in December 1923!

I drove down with this gentleman to the Cathedral city of Exeter in Devon, from where I wrote in enthusiastic youthful fashion, "I am playing here for the campaign and last night we had a marvellous time...close on 2000 in the hall for the service." I added the momentous news for me personally, "After the service I had a talk with the Pastor (George Jeffreys) and I am going with him as his pianist." Thus was my life mapped out for me in God's work through these sequence of events right down to the present day.

Immediately following the Exeter Campaign in 1928 and my joining the Revival Party, Aimee Semple McPherson, of the Foursquare Gospel Movement in America, visiting Great Britain at the invitation of Elim, having filled the Royal Albert Hall in London, went on a successful tour of revival meetings in the provinces, presided over by George Jeffreys, which meant I was at the piano: at Glasgow, Carlisle, Leeds, Hull, Sunderland, Brighton (my home town) and Bristol. Her appearance at the Royal Dome, Brighton, brought her in touch with Sir Harry Preston, a notable Brighton character and owner of the Royal Albion hotel. He invited Aimee, Principal Jeffreys and Pastors Darragh and McWhirter to dinner at the hotel, another guest being Signor Marconi, the famous inventor who first put wireless telegraphy on a commercial basis, as patented by him in England in 1896. Aimee was heard saying to him that she believed he had been used to fulfil Bible prophecy.

I believe it would be difficult to find a longer serving evangelistic team than ourselves as a Revival Party, the first two being originally in the Elim Evangelistic Band in Ireland with George Jeffreys, viz. R.E. Darragh, from 1915 until his death in 1959: James McWhirter, from 1920 until his marriage in 1936, and ultimate resignation from the Party on the issue of church government in 1956, and myself, from 1928 to 1962, being therefore the last surviving member of the Party. George Jeffreys never married, neither did R.E. Darragh. I did not do so until both had passed on.

If George Jeffreys was an exceptional leader and preacher, R.E. Darragh was second to none when it came to song—leadership. We worked as one together, with the congregations singing the Gospel choruses and hymns from full hearts, bringing a lilt into the services which was irresistible. At the close young people by the score would gather around the piano to sing yet again and again, many of them becoming recruits to the Elim Youth Crusader Movement, comprising those between the ages of 14 and 35. Sometimes as many as 2000 formed the Crusader Choir at the Royal Albert Hall demonstrations, under the baton of Douglas B. Gray. The Elim Choruses pioneered by the Revival Party are today being sung in various denominations, Pentecostal and otherwise.

I suggest it was teamwork in the best sense of the word — preacher, song—leader, pianist/organist and campaign organiser working together in close co—operation, each in their own sphere of service contributing to the blessing experienced in campaigns and conventions.

It should also be said of R.E. Darragh, that he had that sympathetic touch, following on after George Jeffreys as he laid hands on the sick and quietly talking to as many as he could and thereby encouraging them to look to the Lord in their individual need. I would engage the congregations from the piano or organ in appropriate choruses and hymns during the healing sessions.

Such letters as these of mine home, if edited and published, would comprise a sizeable book of compelling interest. In point of fact I have refrained from delving into them with my limited space in mind, in case I should be caught up in a great number of the general individual incidents in the pioneer campaigns and other events over the years. I have sometimes surprised people by saying where we stayed in their particular city or town, even years before, simply because these addresses are on record.

I was ordained a minister in the Elim Movement at Kensington Temple (formerly Horbury Chapel), Notting Hill Gate, London, in 1934, having taken part in George Jeffreys' opening campaign in establishing an Elim Church there after it had been acquired in 1930. 23 others, including P.S. Brewster, also converted under George Jeffreys' ministry in the East End of London in the 1920s, and who was to become Secretary—General of the World Pentecostal Conference, and Douglas B. Gray, conductor of the London Crusader Choir, were also ordained that night.

I remained a fully accredited minister of the Foursquare Gospel Churches of the British Isles (afterwards of the Elim Church Incorporated) until my renewal certificate (credential) was withheld at the end of 1940 by the Executive Presbytery of the E.C.I., because I chose to stand with the Founder of Elim and others for what were considered to be much—needed reforms in Elim's legalised central government system of control. This division on Church Government leading to the Founder's resignation, saw the birth in November, 1940, of the Bible—Pattern Church Fellowship of free, self—governing churches.

I held ministerial credentials with the Bible—Pattern Church Fellowship following its recognition by the British Government, having been at its formation at Nottingham in November, 1940, being elected with others at times by the local churches to its Advisory Committee. I was also Editor for some 20 years of *The Pattern,* its official magazine, originally launched by Principal Jeffreys (as a pamphlet) in November, 1939. The subsequent history of the Fellowship and my association with it is given in chapter 8.

At George Jeffreys' decease in January, 1962, R.E. Darragh having predeceased him by three years, I became the Director, at his wish, of the World Revival Crusade, founded as a pioneer work in 1935 by Principal Jeffreys, together with the three members of his Revival Party, when we were in Elim and therefore in existence before the Bible—Pattern Church Fellowship, with its own Fundamentals, Constitution, Declaration of Trust and appointed Commissioners and Trustees. Having been in the work of the Crusade from the beginning and, as Secretary, in day to day touch with its outworking, I was in a position to ensure its smooth continuity from 1962 on.

This biography will show the consistent zeal of Principal George Jeffreys as a soul—winner, as founder of the Elim Pentecostal Church, the World Revival Crusade (his Revival Party work) and the Bible—Pattern Church Fellowship. That the reason for his resignation from Elim has been clouded by adverse propaganda, even up to the present time, is confirmed in the official history entitled *The Great Evangelists,* by Desmond Cartwright, published in 1986 by Marshall Pickering — Mr. Cartwright being an Elim minister since 1957 — and in another book called *Restoring the Kingdom,* by Dr. Andrew Walker (Hodder and Stoughton, 1985), with their intolerable misrepresentations and half—truths about George Jeffreys' labours and what he stood for, the myth of his ill—health which, it is implied, incapacitated him in the last 20 years of his life and even a base attack in the earlier volume on his godly character, all of which I have dealt with in a measure in a published *Open Letter* refutation dated July 25th, 1986, a response pro tem at what I considered as being outrageous — see Appendix 1 and 2.

22

Nowhere has it been unequivocally stated in these books why George Jeffreys resigned, or that his illness when in Elim towards the end of 1937 was brought about by the tremendous pressures upon him, and the "shock" (the word used by the surgeon to me as his patient lay at the point of death) of having examined for himself the position at Elim Headquarters. The illness of E.J. Phillips, the Secretary—General, had brought George Jeffreys away from his full life on the evangelistic field into Headquarters for some weeks, to deal with a situation of crisis proportions, with so much trusteeship responsibility on his own shoulders as the Founder and Leader. This but confirmed the ever—increasing realisation of the power of legal control being exercised over ministers, people, church property and finances under the rigid central government system which, he readily admitted, he had unwittingly helped to establish and consolidate.

It was from that sick bed in hospital he came back restored in answer to the prayers of Elim ministers, members and others all over the country, in 1938, to continue his ministry in Elim, including that of the three annual Easter Monday meetings in the Royal Albert Hall in which he addressed "vast congregations throughout the day, besides praying for the sick in the morning, baptising candidates in water in the afternoon, and conducting the communion service in the evening" — *Elim Evangel*. He was there again, Easter, 1939. Yet burning in his heart was the message he firmly believed he had received from God, to set his house in order, which, sadly, was the more bitterly opposed from then on.

He suffered from sugar diabetes for the rest of his life, which he called his "thorn in the flesh." Like the Apostle Paul, he rejoiced in the promise of 2nd Corinthians 12:9: "My grace is sufficient for thee: for My strength is made perfect in weakness." He could also add, "Most gladly therefore will I glory in my infirmities, that the power of Christ may rest upon me." This in no way curtailed his abilities nor his activities, any more than was the Apostle Paul hindered by his "thorn," and the staggering record of work undertaken by George Jeffreys in the 20 and more years after Elim until his sudden and unexpected decease is positive proof of this. Such can be assessed somewhat by dated items after 1939—40 in this biography and in my *Open Letter*.

Dr. Walker writes of Desmond Cartwright's book, as I have pointed out in my *Open Letter*, that it is "genuine history, not

23

hagiography," which brought a letter to me from Mr. Cartwright in July, 1986, asking of my biography, "Will it be critical of the Principal's faults? Biography and history are special arts, hagiography is another thing altogether." Who would deny that, apart from our Lord Himself in His humanity, any man is perfect in this life? George Jeffreys was no exception, but his virtues far exceeded his faults. Used as he was in such mighty fashion, with weighty testimony to his goodness from his own kith and kin and others, is sufficient reason for putting the emphasis where I have in these pages. I would ask: where do either of these authors in this context fit in with the old adage, that to really know a person one has to live with them? The last word is with the Bible itself, where we read in Psalm 37:37: "Mark the perfect (blameless) man, and behold the upright: for the end of that man is peace."

Desmond Cartwright never witnessed George Jeffreys' unforgettable meetings in the Royal Albert Hall and Crystal Palace, such as Rom Landau, a host of journalists, and I did with thousands of others, otherwise he could never write of them as he does in such a cursory fashion. This goes for much of what he has written in this respect, not having been a spectator.

His book has had a spin—off effect on at least one other book I have read published in 1987, *after* I had strongly remonstrated with the author over his manuscript relating to George Jeffreys.

Three important chapters in this biography are devoted to the division in the Elim Movement of almost half a century ago, dealing mainly with the salient points surrounding this traumatic event and down to the present day. If it is argued that, as such happened so long ago, should it not be forgotten? My answer to this is: *with the recent publication of the aforementioned books, with their prolongation of that which is false, coupled with the fact that the events I am narrating are a vital part of a man's life's work, the passing of time means nothing in the propagating of the truth for posterity.*

Reverting to the Elim Bible College (page 19): reference needs to be made to God-blessed missionary efforts through the work of the College since 1925.

If my part in this Introduction is felt to be inordinately long, I ask the reader to accept it as such on the grounds of my involvement in so much of what I have to tell.

Chapter 1
"A Ministry of the Miraculous"

GEORGE Jeffreys' miraculous healing *before* the days of Elim obviously had a significant bearing on his call of God into the full—time ministry, as he testifies in his own words:

"Upon entering one of the classrooms when studying for the ministry, I found the following sentence written on the blackboard, *'He that hath an experience is not at the mercy of him that hath an argument.'* When I read these words I could not help but say aloud, 'Yes, and especially if the experience carries with it the authority of Scripture.'

"I was first convinced of the Spirit's quickening power when, as a frail youth, I received the experience in my own body. My weak state began to manifest itself in facial paralysis, and I was heavily burdened, for I felt the creepiness of paralysis down one whole side. Being somewhat reticent I suffered in silence beyond measure, for I knew that unless a miracle was wrought in me, life was to be very short. When my mouth began to be affected, the one thing that distressed me greatly was the possibility of my not realising the one call and ambition of my life, the Christian ministry. From my earliest days of childhood there was the consciousness borne with me that I was called to preach the Gospel. When this affliction came it seemed as if the end of all that was worth living for had come, there was no other purpose for me in life if I could not preach.

"We were kneeling in prayer one Sunday morning and were interceding on the subject of the services of that day. It was exactly nine o'clock when the power of God came upon me, and I received such an inflow of Divine life that I can only liken the experience to being charged with electricity. It seemed as if my head were connected *to a most powerful electric battery.* My whole body from head to foot was quickened by the Spirit of God, and I was healed. From that day I have never had the least symptoms of the old trouble.

"Many times since then I have relied upon the Spirit's quickening power for my body. All who conduct prolonged

25

evangelistic campaigns will admit that a great deal of physical strength is necessary. This in many cases could never be found if it were not for Divine strength that is given. The body, tired and weakened by constant labour, needs a special inflow of Divine life. Sometimes towards the end of a campaign I have been confronted by monster congregations, and if it were not for the frequent quickenings of the body I would have been helpless. Even the voice is charged and changed as the result of the body being quickened by the Spirit."

I have heard him say, after facing such congregations, that beforehand at times, he felt as weak as a kitten, but once he stood there with open Bible before him, it seemed he could have held the congregation in the palm of his hand!

If his own healing and those of so many others in his ministry took place in the realm of the miraculous, he firmly believed that conversion according to the Scriptures was a mighty miracle, indeed the greatest, and would emphasise the paramount need of seekers to first accept the Lord Jesus Christ as their own personal Saviour.

In his book *George Jeffreys — A Ministry of the Miraculous,* published in 1928 by the Elim Publishing Co., Ltd., Pastor E.C.W. Boulton, of the Elim H/Q staff, had this to say of the days preceding Elim:

"It was in the year 1912 that the now famous Founder and Leader of the Elim work, the history of which this book records, came into the picture. George Jeffreys, a young man who had recently received a mighty baptism of the Holy Ghost, whose heart burned with holy amibition and throbbed with passionate purpose, lived and laboured away there in one of those Welsh valleys. He was brought up in the Welsh Congregational Church 'Siloh,' Maesteg, whose Minister, the Rev. W. Glasnant Jones took a decided interest in the young lad, privately coaching him for a future Ministry. The Rev. W. Glasnant Jones, writing of George Jeffreys eloquently testifies to the religious zeal that burned in the heart of the young disciple:

"'At the open—air revival services I always found young Jeffreys at my side. I was privileged to give him his early religious tuition and a splendid scholar he was. Superior to other lads, there was character in his face: I knew he was a 'chosen vessel.' When I left 'Siloh,' Maesteg, in 1907, young Jeffreys was in business, and had he remained in that calling, I am convinced he would have become a merchant Prince.'

"Although having reached a position of some responsibility and trust in the business world, he was conscious that the Divine call to be a regular minister of the Gospel of Christ was about to be realised. The conviction that God had called him to the Christian ministry had been his since childhood.

"How to enter the regular ministry seemed problematical as there were insuperable difficulties in the way. The few doors that seemed open began to close when his faithful testimony to the baptism of the Holy Ghost with signs following was maintained. Then again, as the only unmarried son, the responsibilities of the home began to weigh upon him, responsibilities which he has never shirked but gladly shouldered to this very day. Though often sorely tried along financial lines, yet God has, in most remarkable ways, provided the portion that was needed to send home to his mother. Only the Judgment Seat of Christ will reveal the depth of holy determination which has carried him over the tremendous obstacles which barred the way to the realisation of the God—given call. At what appeared the darkest hour, Mr. Cecil Polhill, one of the famous Cambridge Seven, came forward and supplied the financial support to undergo a course of Bible training under the auspices of The Pentecostal Missionary Union of Great Britain. Thus was the door opened through which George Jeffreys passed into a ministry and a work that is to—day world—renowned. In the furnace of trial he had borne within him an undying purpose to see doors opened into the ministry for other lads who were similarly placed as he himself had been. That this Spirit—generated desire has been amply realised is patent to all who peruse the chapters of this book...

"Within the heart of this Welsh youth were latent those qualities which, when properly harnessed and handled, make for powerful and successful leadership. Unseen and unknown, the hand of God was at work, moulding a vessel in which He could place the utmost confidence, and to whom could be entrusted responsibilities, the greatness of which are to—day but dimly apparent. Silently and surely Divine forces were in bearing upon the future of this 'Latter Rain' awakening in this country."

In common with Welsh people in general, George Jeffreys had a love for his own native land, particularly of the Llynfi Valley where he was born and brought up. Who better than himself to tell us something of his early life and aspirations. In 1929, at 40

27

years of age, he wrote a Christmas article for the *Elim Evangel* when he was seeing times of revival power and blessing through his ministry in the Principality. In it he re—lived something of his own boyhood and youthful days in these words:

"I am penning these lines in dear old Wales, the land of revival and song, where scenes that are reminiscent of the great revival of 1904 are being witnessed. Not very far from the two main Foursquare Revival centres, Cardiff and Swansea, is the place of my boyhood days. Now and again, when opportunity has presented itself, the boy George Jeffreys, resurrected from the past, has led me over the old familiar tracks, and boyhood life has been lived over again. The youth Jeffreys has taken me to Siloh Congregational Church, where the blazing light of regeneration broke in upon my soul. I have heard him talk to his minister, the lovable and indefatigable Rev. Glasnant Jones, who in turn gave him his paternal advice and able instruction. This minister is now in charge of a Congregational church some five miles from Swansea, and has attended my present Revival Campaign at the Central Hall.

"The youth Jeffreys guided my footsteps to the place where he was baptised by immersion in the rippling river of the Llynfi Valley. He has reminded me of the quickening touch of the power of God that healed his frail body, and the thrill of the Baptism of the Holy Ghost which he received according to Acts 2:4, in the old Duffryn Chapel building.

"I have seen young Jeffreys grappling with the seeming insuperable difficulties that lay in the way of his cherished hope to enter the regular ministry. I found him reasoning with himself, 'If you are going to stand true to the testimony of Salvation, Healing, Baptism of the Holy Ghost, and the Second Coming of Christ, you might be able to enter the regular work of the ministry, but it will have to be entirely on faith lines. Then again the responsibility of the old home is now upon your shoulders and you cannot be a true minister of the Gospel and not provide for your dear old mother. On the other hand, if you cut out some of these controversial subjects, such as the Baptism of the Holy Ghost and Divine Healing, it will be an easy matter for you to enter the ministry, for the door is already open, and the financial needs for yourself and home are assured.'

"I have been with young Jeffreys just as he takes the plunge

28

once and for all: 'Come what may, I will not be unfaithful to the whole Counsel of God, and will trust my heavenly Father to see me through.'

"Many Christmas seasons have passed since then, and if the question *'Lacked ye anything?'* was put to me as it was to the disciples of old, I would answer, *'Nothing!'* as they did. From the moment I uncompromisingly entered the open door of the Christian ministry right up to the present day, God has been faithful and His abundant grace has been lavished upon myself and the work entrusted to my charge..."

As we have seen, he would refer to the late Rev. Glasnant Jones with affection, and was particularly pleased to read the following headed "HIS CONVERTS BECAME REVIVALISTS!" in the *News Chronicle* (Welsh Edition) on October 20th, 1947:

"The revival of 1904 is the subject of Glasnant's reminiscences in the current Dysgedydd. He confirms the testimony of others that long before Evan Roberts' name became known, the devout in many parts of Wales were conscious that a great religious awakening was at hand.

"It was at his church Siloh, Nantyffyllon, Maesteg, that Pastors Stephen and George Jeffreys were brought 'into the net.' According to Stephen's biography a sermon by Glasnant was responsible. The two brothers were instrumental above all others, in perpetuating the Revival fire and carrying it to all parts of the earth. 'And here I am,' adds the veteran of Dunvant, 'like Goldsmith's old soldier who shouldered his crutches to show how fields were won. Without a doubt Stephen and George Jeffreys were the means of converting a great multitude of unbelievers, and perhaps I may have a mark or two to my credit in the 'grand inquest' for bringing the two brothers into the fold.'"

EARLY DAYS IN IRELAND

OF the early and humble beginnings of the Elim Movement in Ireland, the Minute Book of "The Elim Evangelistic Band" speaks for itself:

"First Informal Meeting of Christian Brethren at Monaghan Thursday, January 7th, 1915"

"A number of Christian brethren at a meeting which was held in Knox's Temperance Hotel, Monaghan on Thursday, January 7th, 1915, viz. Albert Kerr, Co. Monaghan; Geo.

Allen and Frederick Farlow, of Co. Fermanagh; Robt. Mercer and John Mercer, Co. Armagh; Wm. Henderson, Co. Monaghan; R.E. Darragh, Co. Down; and Geo. Jeffreys, South Wales; came together for the purpose of discussing the best means of reaching Ireland with the Full Gospel on Pentecostal lines...

"We believe it to be the mind of God that Evangelist Geo. Jeffreys, of South Wales, who was present with us, be invited to take up permanent evangelistic work in Ireland, and that a centre be chosen by him for the purpose of establishing a Church out of which evangelists would be sent into the country towns and villages, and that a tent be hired, for the purpose of holding a Gospel Mission during the month of July to commence the work in Ireland.

"We agree that God promises to supply the temporal needs of every Evangelist that would be called by Him into the work, and that through prayer and faith in His promises He would prove Himself to be to each one Jehovah Jireh."

(Signed)
George Jeffreys
Wm. Henderson
Fred A. Farlow
R.E. Darragh
A.S. Kerr

Later, we read:

"Second Informal Meeting of Pentecostal Workers at Monaghan on Saturday, July 3rd, 1915"

"At a meeting of Christian Workers who were interested in the Pentecostal work in Ireland, which was held at the house of Mr. Jack Wilkinson, Swann Park, North Road, Monaghan, on Saturday, July 3rd, 1915, we were delighted to have with us Evangelist Geo. Jeffreys to commence the Gospel Mission in the Tent at North Road according to previous arrangement. He informed us that God had already answered our prayers and had given a definite call to Mr. R.E. Darragh and Miss M. Streight, of Bangor, Co. Down, to work in connection with the Band of Evangelists which we had claimed by faith for the Pentecostal Movement in Ireland. Mr. Darragh had kindly accepted the invitation to act as Secretary pro tem."

The same five signatures are added.

On December 24th, 1915, came the "Third Informal Meeting of Pentecostal Workers," this time in Belfast. We are told:

"A number of Christian friends at a meeting held in the

Hall, Hunter Street, Belfast, on Friday, December 24th, 1915, were very glad to know that further answers to prayer had been given by God for the Pentecostal work in the land. We rejoiced to hear of the success that had attended the ministry of Pastor Jeffreys since he had taken over the pastorate of Elim Church in the city of Belfast; many souls had been saved and accepted into membership, while lives and homes had been trans—formed. Each one present at the meeting felt that God had given them the desire of their hearts — the formation of a good centre for sending out Spirit—filled workers.

"Second. That a tent had already been purchased for £20 from Mr. Ferguson, of Bangor, for the evangelistic work in the coming summer months. The missionary tour in Galway was also reported and hearts went out to God for blessings received and bestowed."

(Signed)   Fred A. Farlow
                                   Wm. Henderson
                                   R.E. Darragh
                                   George Jeffreys
                                   Margaret Montgomery Streight

According to the Minute Book, Pastors W. Henderson and F. Farlow were both received into the Evangelistic Band on April 24th, 1916, and not long after it was agreed that the Evangelists should be known as the "Elim Evangelistic Band."

One who figured prominently in the work then was the Rev. Thomas Hackett, M.A., Church of Ireland clergyman and brother—in—law of the Primate of All Ireland. He was baptised by total immersion in water by George Jeffreys at the Belfast Tabernacle and frequently ministered with the Elim Evangelistic Band, having been accepted with them in an advisory capacity.

Another honoured name associated with those early Elim days is that of Mr. John Leech, M.A., LL.B., K.C., who became President of the Elim Evangelistic Band, and who remained a staunch friend of Principal George Jeffreys right up until he also went to his eternal reward in 1942 at the age of 85. He was one of the reforming party in the division in Elim in 1939—40 and was Vice—President of the Bible—Pattern Church Fellowship until his homecall. It was Mr. Leech who suggested this name for the new movement of free, self—governing churches, in the desire to conform more closely to the Biblical Pattern. It was said of him, possessed as he was with a ready wit and Irish humour that, having presided as Judge on the Bench in the Dublin Courts, he would come up to Belfast for those early Elim Conventions singing the words of the old—time hymn, "Free from the law, O happy condition...!"

Pastor Robert Mercer, who was present at that first historic meeting in Monaghan on January 7th, 1915, and who became a member of the Elim Evangelistic Band in 1918, later married Miss Margaret Streight. Together with Pastor R.E. Darragh, Pastor and Mrs. R.G. Tweed and others, they took their stand with Principal George Jeffreys when he resigned from Elim after twenty—five years.

Pastor Mercer had this to say of those early pioneer days:

"My first personal contact with George Jeffreys was in Belfast, Christmas 1913 or 1914, at a Convention that was held in Dover Street Assembly (now Hopeton Street). He was one of the speakers. I had come to spend Christmas with my relations and went to the Convention with an aunt who was a member of that Church.

"At the close of the service George Jeffreys came down to Mr. Henderson and I for a chat. From the other side of the aisle Mr. Darragh walked over to join the little group. That was my first meeting with these two servants of God (George Jeffreys and R.E. Darragh). It was as though God was thus bringing us all together.

"There were three of us who were taking our stand for Pentecost in Monaghan, namely, Messrs. A. Kerr, George Allen, and myself. We invited George Jeffreys to Monaghan for a Gospel campaign in the Methodist Church, which did not then materialise. Later, in 1915, we invited him for a Tent Campaign which he conducted in Monaghan. Mr. William Gillespie came up for a week—end and it was then decided to open up the Elim work in Ireland.

"The first Elim Church was in Hunter Street, Belfast. Soon it was packed to capacity. Then we sought a larger building and my uncle told me about the church in Melbourne Street, Belfast, which was purchased."

The Hunter Street Hall was formerly a disused laundry!

It was Pastor Robert Mercer who, on seeing some of those pioneer workers on their knees in prayer so that the soles of their worn shoes were clearly visible, provided new shoes for them, such was the "all things common" spirit which prevailed amongst the members of the Elim Evangelistic Band, so dependent upon God were they in a very real way for their daily needs to be met. Pastor Mercer was minister of a number of Elim Churches, including the Portsmouth Church, and of others of the Bible—Pattern Church Fellowship. A stalwart to the end, he died in Belfast in 1970.

The *Elim Evangel* at the end of 1924 listed a total of 46 under "Members of the Elim Evangelistic Band in the regular Work of the Ministry," associate members, probationers and prospective missionaries. Some went out into another Pentecostal Movement (Assemblies of God) then newly formed. Of these originally named I know of three survivors only today, viz. Pastors R.G. Tweed, James McWhirter and Miss Alice McKinley who became the wife of Pastor Tweed in 1926. They are all now in their 80s. We find that the activities of the 'Band' were reported under "The Elim Evangelistic Band" up until 1927, then they merged with the ever—enlarging Elim ministry.

It can well be asked of those early days of the Elim Movement in Ireland, of which George Jeffreys was the recognised founder and leader, "For who hath despised the day of small things?" (Zechariah 4:10), resulting in other towns and cities besides Monaghan and Belfast, such as Ballymena, Bangor, Lurgan, Armagh, Lisburn, Portadown, and remote country farming districts, being moved for God; halls, Gospel tents, and churches being used for the revival and healing campaigns and conventions. The members of the 'Band' were well used in their respective ministries, and it has been truly stated "...the foundations of a work were being laid whose ramifications should, in days to come, stretch forth in beneficient, benignant ministry to thousands of souls then unborn."

In October, 1943, George Jeffreys paid tribute to Mr. Jack Wilkinson, of Monaghan, in these words:

"It was at his delightful home I stayed when, under God, I launched the Elim work in 1915. The news of his home—call brought sacred memories to me and I lived those early days over again. From the moment our beloved brother saw the truth of the Pentecostal message he never wavered, he stood solidly by me in the bitter opposition that came against me from every quarter. But truth prevailed and the stream of truth that found its source in Jack Wilkinson's home town has reached many people and places far away from dear old Monaghan."

He never tired of telling how an incident in those early days impressed upon him the power of the Name of Christ (I would mention that illustrations in his messages were mainly based on real—life experiences, not just 'stories'). At 8 o'clock one morning in Belfast he was urgently summoned to an address in Silvergrove Street. He would say how he took the cycle and on arrival at the house he saw a powerfully—built man obviously under the power of the devil, being held down by four others. He said to them, "Loose him, let him go." As they obeyed the man sprang at him as he stood there with Bible in hand. His testimony was that every bit of natural strength left him as he simply said, "In the Name of the Lord," whereupon the man fell back and lay on the floor staring up into the ceiling. He asked the men to stay with him, intending to return. For some reason he forgot all about the man.

That night there was a baptismal service in the Hunter Street Church, Belfast, and as he entered the building the people were singing from full hearts, in an atmosphere that was charged with the power of God, "He is able to deliver thee"! There was the man in the midst. He told a remarkable story, how that he lay there until 4 o'clock in the afternoon when he had a vision of Christ coming to him and touching him on the shoulder, saying "I am come to deliver thee." And delivered he was, such was the power of Christ's Name uttered that morning by God's servant.

Another remarkable story he would tell was that of Mrs. Bell, of Bangor, Co. Down, N. Ireland who became a walking miracle in 1915! Knowing almost nothing about the teaching of Divine healing at the time when she was practically helpless, yet such was her faith, that when family members returned from their work one day, she was walking about the house completely healed. No laying on of hands, no anointing with oil for healing, simply through her faith and trust in God's Word the miracle happened.

Obviously when George Jeffreys came to hear the story from Mrs. Bell's own lips he understood there were times when she was unable to use her hands and reverted to turning the pages of the Bible with her tongue, as he would recount. I have sought verification of this remarkable testimony and have come to the conclusion it was published as follows in the *Elim Evangel* of September, 1920, under the heading:

A VERY PRESENT HELP

In these dark days when so many are denying the Lord Who bought them with His Own precious Blood I feel I must give my testimony to His wonderful cleansing and healing power.

The Lord saved me early in life and I enjoyed a great measure of His presence and power. I had a very busy life and was very happy, but, as I can see, I was not at all concerned about how much glory God was getting through me. Years after my conversion the Lord spoke to me very definitely about my wasted opportunities and luke—warmness. I saw that I was bought with a wonderful price and I was therefore not my own. This was a new revelation to me and I was at once made willing to have all the hindrances removed. The result was that I wept my way back to a perfect obedience, praising God for His wonderful tenderness and love. This brought me to the place where I was teachable, and what a joy it was to have every fetter broken and to be fully yielded to His blessed will — every plan and purpose, wish and will surrendered to God.

About this time I became suddenly helpless in body through an attack of sciatica. I did not get alarmed knowing I was a child of God, and I had perfect rest in Him. I could speak, hear and think perfectly and I kept praising the Lord and enjoyed His presence all the time. Although I suffered great agony I could not help praising God. The doctor was called in and did everything possible to relieve me. I took everything he prescribed but with very little benefit. Perfect rest and quietness relieved my nerves greatly.

In a few weeks the doctor left. I continued to follow his instructions, but found myself very helpless. I could not stand upright nor dress myself, my nerves were shattered. I feared I was going to be a cripple, and I got in earnest with God about my condition.

I had been reading in the *Christian Herald* for years about Divine Healing, and yet it was only when everything else failed that I turned to God. My people insisted on having another doctor but I had perfectly surrendered my poor helpless body to the Lord. I did not doubt His *power* to heal, but I had some doubts about His *willingness*. I spent practically all my time alone with God, and being able to use my hands a little I could read my Bible. I prayed for His leading in everything, and having no help outside Himself I sought with all my heart to know His will. In the 103rd Psalm I read "Who forgiveth all thine iniquities; who *healeth all thy diseases.*" "Well," I said, "Lord, my iniquities are forgiven, now what about my diseased body?" I became so much in earnest that I wanted to be all alone. My visitors did not interest me and I even feared to speak to any of them on the subject of Divine healing, though they were Christians. I had a very blessed fellowship with the Lord and felt assured that He would supply my every need.

I took my medicine for some time and then began to think that this was not consistent as I wanted to prove the Lord's willingness and power *outside everything else.* I was much blessed by following His life on earth amongst the suffering crowds. I wondered if there were any turned away without healing, but found there was not one.

I put my medicine away, and surrendered my all afresh to Him. I had never known anyone who had been healed though I read of some in Mrs. Crisp's messages in the *Christian Herald,* and she helped me greatly. On July 15th, 1915, I read her message to some suffering one who had written for advice. It was God's message to me. She said, "You *will* be healed, but He will do it to glorify Himself, not for any selfish purpose of yours. Not to do your work, nor to make money, nor to look after your household, but *alone for His glory.*" I saw where I had failed, and I fell at His blessed feet and said, "Lord, I'll have it for Your glory or not at all." I could not utter another word. His power and glory filled and overwhelmed me. The very room was filled with His glory. I praised Him and knew the work was done. He made me perfectly whole. My nerves were settled. My body was perfect, and there was no more agony. I was so filled with His presence and power that I could not cease to praise Him and tell everyone of His wonderful power to heal. Many of my friends who regarded me as incurable wept for joy when they saw what the Lord had done for me. I was so blessed in my soul that I felt that I was completely separated unto the Lord and living in new surroundings. The Lord is *everything* to me, why should I not praise Him?

Earnestly praying that God will bless some suffering one through this testimony,
Yours for His glory alone,

M.B.

Mrs. Bell's story has reminded me that in his campaigns George Jeffreys would sometimes encourage those seeking healing to remain standing in their seats and to believe God for their deliverance without coming out to the front, whilst he would urge God's people present to pray with him on their behalf. Such was the outstanding case with Miss Edith Scarth, whom I knew and who, like Mrs. Bell, was healed without the laying on of hands. She had suffered for years from tuberculosis of the spine, having to wear a spinal jacket and splint, being wheeled about in a spinal carriage. As she herself has written: "By holding on to the seat in front of me I managed to stand, then Principal Jeffreys prayed, and as he prayed something happened. I felt as if someone lifted something right off me. My whole body was charged with new life and power. My head clicked back into place: I was healed. My mother looked on in amazement. I wanted to sing, to shout, to dance, I even wanted to run all the way home. When I reached home I ran up the steps, I could not take time to walk, I was so happy. I took off my splint and have never needed it since, bless the Lord. I was healed on 11th April, 1927. My doctor could find no trace of tuberculosis. My back was perfectly straight, and I was quite well."

It is noteworthy to recall that R.E. Darragh, George Jeffreys' first Evangelist in 1915, as long ago as 1912—13, read in the *Christian Herald* of the revival at that time at Cwmtwrch, in the Swansea Valley, South Wales, under the ministries of Stephen and George Jeffreys. This gave him a longing to see something similar taking place in his native Ireland. In 1913 he saw in a Belfast newspaper that George Jeffreys was to visit Ireland for meetings. He was in the opening meeting and through the laying on of hands and prayer was healed of throat trouble. This, his first contact with George Jeffreys, was two years before the beginning of the Elim Movement in Ireland. And how R.E. Darragh used his voice in song and song—leadership for the next 44 years!

In 1952, as a Party, we were ministering at the Pentecostal Church at Cwmtwrch for the 40th Anniversary Services, a Church which had been faithfully pastored by Pastor and Mrs. George Griffiths since its inception in 1912.

From those early beginnings in Ireland, in which both William and George Gillespie played a part, together with other Elders of that first Elim Church in 1915 in Hunter Street, Belfast, and those in Monaghan and subsequent centres, the Elim work grew and spread until the largest halls in this and other lands were too small to contain the crowds flocking to hear the Foursquare Gospel message from the lips of Principal George Jeffreys, a truly dedicated servant of the Lord.

Chapter 2
A Man of The Book

THAT this was the case is borne out by those early beginnings of Elim in Ireland, and in George Jeffreys' ministry in the years before that. It was so when he came over from Ireland to England where, in the summer of 1921, he conducted the official opening services of England's first Elim Hall in Leigh on Sea, Essex. In 1922 the first Elim Church was established in London, now known as the "Elim Central Church" at Clapham Common. Pastor E.C.W. Boulton, in his book already referred to, tells at length of the faith of the Founder and his followers, resulting in the once disused and derelict Methodist Chapel being so transformed that it seemed to "rise from the dead." He quotes an onlooker as saying:

"For the past month meetings have been held every night in the Park Crescent Church, Clapham, the preacher being Pastor George Jeffreys. Night after night the message of God is given to professing Christians. At one time the Hammer of the Word is brought with crushing and irresistible force upon empty profession, and at another the Word is opened up in such a marvellous way that heights of attainment, hitherto deemed impossible, have been made plain to many a longing heart, and never without results. Conversions, healings, and baptisms in the Holy Spirit have followed at every meeting. Souls have been saved even at the open—air meetings. The large hall at the rear of the building is frequently filled and sometimes overcrowded with anxious souls."

Pastor Boulton tells of the generous giving on the part of the Clapham Christians, nearly £2,000 in one evening, and concludes: "Ever since it was opened it has been a centre of blessing from which lasting good has streamed to other needy districts, until today it proudly claims the honour of being the parent of many another Elim church in London and its environs."

Rom Landau had this to say of George Jeffreys at the Royal Albert Hall in his book referred to in my Introduction:

"There was a quality in his delivery which I can only describe as biblical. The Bible was obviously the source from which he had derived his knowledge and his powers as a speaker. But the main feature of his style was not merely the right adaptation of biblical knowledge: there was in his words a natural persuasiveness which can be derived only from full identification with the Bible...It seemed that the Scriptures had become the very life—blood of George Jeffreys..."

Landau also gave these vivid impressions in the same chapter:

"The man whom ten thousand people from all over the British Isles had come to see and to listen to had mounted the platform quite unobserved. Though my eyes had rarely left the platform I did not see the entry of George Jeffreys, the founder and leader of the Elim Evangelists, and I only discovered later that he had been sitting for some time among his friends in the front row. He was wearing a dark suit, as were all the other men around him, and there was no mark to distinguish him from the others. I saw through my opera glasses a strong face with rather a soft mouth, dark curly hair and a fine presence in which there was nothing calculated to play upon the emotions..."

"I did not doubt that the strong and sincere tone of the voice of Jeffreys was responsible for much of the veneration in which his followers held him...

"When Jeffreys came up to the microphone to say another prayer I began to understand why ten thousand people had come to listen to him. He was not a high priest but simply one of the people. Between them and their God there stood no altar of mystery; there was no complicated ceremony. They communicated with God without the help of symbols that had no meaning for many. The man who spoke to God in their name did not address Him in Latin or in the archaic words of a centuries—old Church. God approached in that way did not seem very distant...

"While the organ played softly, the vast audience looked down on the stalls. There was none of the morbid curiosity that crowds generally manifest when confronted with something outside their usual experience. They were sitting quietly, many of them with tears running down their cheeks; some prayed to themselves with numb lips, others prayed aloud with clasped hands. The atmosphere of faith that pervaded the hall was beginning to overpower one's critical faculty. After all, Jeffreys would not be the first to give proofs of bodily healing through faith and grace. When I got home I found a passage in John Wesley in which he records a case of his own illness: 'I called on Jesus aloud to increase my faith...While I was speaking my pain vanished away, my fever left me, and my bodily strength returned, and for many weeks I felt neither weariness nor pain.'"

Of the Revivalist's Crystal Palace meetings, Rom Landau concluded his assessment of these with this eloquent testimony:

"It seemed as though the presence of God really filled the hall. And there was nothing miraculous in it. The people who were assembled round their leader had always known that God is everywhere and in everyone; but it had been a problem for them how to find Him. It had been difficult for them to hear His voice, to become conscious of Him. What Jeffreys did was to compress their consciousness of God, to vitalise it, to force it into a concentration that was more powerful than any state they were able to achieve by themselves. Jeffreys forced their God to emerge from the shadows of their longings and to manifest Himself in their conscious feelings. He made Him their living God...The faces of these people suggested that they were living at this moment with God and in God. The one great miracle of all religions seemed to have happened: God had descended into man and had become a part of his consciousness."

In attempting to convey something of the life and ministry of George Jeffreys one is well aware of the magnitude of the task. His was no ordinary life, for as Revivalist and Reformer he accomplished astonishing things for the work of God which have left their indelible imprint on the individual lives of countless men and women, as well as on the religious climate of our nation. He was, as one London newspaper justifiably called him at his decease, "The Last of the Great Revivalists."

Yet, as we have shown, they were very humble beginnings in Ireland in 1915 when he founded the Elim Foursquare Gospel Movement, subsequently to become known as "The Elim Pentecostal Church", which he was to build up and establish throughout the length and breadth of the British Isles over the next 25 years, mainly as the direct result of his phenomenal revival and healing campaigns. His stirring Scriptural proclamation of New Testament Christianity created some of the greatest mass evangelistic meetings ever seen in our land. As the Rev. R.J. Jones, J.P., wrote of the Birmingham Campaign of 1930, including the meetings in the original Bingley Hall:

"1875 saw the Bingley Hall, Birmingham, the largest hall in the Midlands full for the Moody—Sankey Campaign. 1904 saw it filled during the Torrey—Alexander Mission. On both these occasions practically the whole of the Christian Churches of the city co—operated, but miracle of miracles, the huge building is packed to capacity for Principal George Jeffreys' Foursquare Gospel Revival Campaign of 1930. There has been no blare of trumpets, no joint Church committee arrangements beforehand. The Revivalist came to the city being unable to count on one person to come to his services. Revival services during his campaign baffle description. In ten weeks it is estimated that 10,000 souls have been saved, over 1,000 have been immersed in water, and there have been hundreds of most astonishing cases of miracles of healing, many of which I have interviewed myself. The great Bingley Hall was almost filled for a communion service which finds parallel only in the Principal's Royal Albert Hall gatherings."

The Birmingham Gazette reported at the time: "Imagine Bingley Hall crammed with seats and every seat occupied. Imagine the galleries crowded and people wedged tight in doors left open to let in the air."

If D.L. Moody and R.A. Torrey, both Americans, filled Bingley Hall for revival campaigns, so did George Jeffreys, a Britisher, the only three evangelists ever to do so. The 1930 campaign saw 26 meetings in this great hall, the city being stirred so that even the evolutionist Bishop of Birmingham Dr. Barnes made comment upon it at the time.

It is not inappropriate for me to say here that the one who was to become my wife in 1963 was a convert of this great campaign at which I was the pianist. She was amongst those baptised by immersion in water in the Bingley Hall, becoming a member of the Graham Street Elim Church, Birmingham. This Church and other Elim churches were established in the city, with yet other Pentecostal churches, such as the well—known Birmingham Hockley Mission, having come into being through the campaign.

Wherever George Jeffreys went, at home and abroad, he

41

uncompromisingly declared what he termed as "The Foursquare Gospel" Message:— The Lord Jesus Christ the Saviour, Healer, Baptiser in the Holy Ghost, and Coming King — and he established churches for the converts believing these fundamental truths because, as a general rule, they were not preached wholly in other denominations. Hence the inevitable formation of the Elim Movement under his leadership in 1915, and later the Bible—Pattern Church Fellowship after he had severed his ties with Elim.

As one who was close to him for so many years, I can say he always remained a sincere and humble servant of the Lord. He was completely self—effacing for a man who had accomplished so much, not 'eaten up with pride' and with no 'side' whatever. He had great strength of character as a born leader of men and one knew when he had made up his mind. There was nothing slip—shod in his methods and he would do the most menial of tasks to give 'a helping hand' with the rest of us. He enjoyed an argument, but always with charity towards opposite views. At the same time he was uncompromising in contending for the Truth of God's Word, although such a stand, as always, meant the painful loss of some personal friendships. But with the Apostles of old he could say, "We ought to obey God rather than men."

As the chapter heading indicates, he was a man of one Book — The Authorised Version of The Bible, which he loved and treasured and from which he derived great spiritual strength.

A man of prayer, I have often heard him quietly lift his voice to God on behalf of others — even when travelling by car — and he never missed the opportunity of a personal word with someone in need, ever ready to point them to Christ. He prayed for such as we drove in London on the night of Thursday, January 25th, 1962. Little did we know it was to be the last time together in the car, so suddenly came the call to higher service the next morning.

Some of his own memorable sayings are still remembered by those who heard him minister, as "It is not your great faith that counts, but your *little* faith in a *great* God," and "The outlook is dark indeed," referring to world conditions, "but the uplook is exceedingly glorious," concerning the 'blessed hope' of the believer of the Coming of the Lord, (Titus, chapter 2, v:13). This was a favourite text he used when signing his letters.

Although he did spectacular things, George Jeffreys was never

42

flamboyant, upholding the dignity of his calling as a minister. In his public preaching he never attempted to 'play to the gallery', but pressed his messages home with power and authority. It was said that his very presence on the platform silently conveyed a spiritual influence which was most marked.

He exercised remarkable control over meetings, sometimes comprising thousands of people of varied backgrounds, meetings in which he laid hands upon hundreds seeking Divine healing. Occasions when fanaticism or extreme emotionalism took over in the congregations were rare, if at all, a clear indication of the power of God upon preacher and hearers alike.

A man of faith, he laid no great stress on the need for funds in his campaigns, simply taking up offerings or collections in the services, with a special thankoffering being asked for at the end. This would be given in envelopes and placed towards the expenses of the campaign and the furtherance of the work. Gifts, large and small, were duly acknowledged by a receipt and letter of thanks, including those gifts which came from grateful donors who remembered past blessings through his ministry.

He it was who taught me bookkeeping, and who insisted on accounts for work done to be promptly paid, a principle noted and commented upon by Christian firms and others.

George Jeffreys was a lover of his own native land and the form of relaxation he enjoyed best was to travel through the countryside by car. In fact he did most of his journeys at home and abroad in this way. He never went by air, as other prominent evangelists are apt to do in this modern age, yet for all that, he covered hundreds of thousands of miles in the preaching of the Gospel. Such journeyings often included all night travelling, at times by road, all of which I recall with thanksgiving to God in keeping us, apart from minor mishaps, accident free.

He was very fond of children who would be drawn to him by his gentleness. As an animal lover he was attached to his dogs, several of which I knew over the years; one, a Welsh corgi named by its master "Corgi," given to him in 1945, frequently went with us in the car. It lived to be nearly 13. Another of the same breed bearing the same name as its predecessor had the habit of coming upstairs first thing and was with him in his room that January morning just prior to his passing.

People could be tongue—tied somewhat on meeting him for the first time, but he would quickly put them at their ease. A shy man himself, yet having an unexpected and quite disarming sense of humour.

There are a few published pictures of him wearing a clerical collar, yet I never once saw him in such an attire.

I recently read that Herbert von Karajan had said of a woman violinist, Anne—Sophie Mutter, that she is one of the three greatest violinists in the world. "Audiences are the same the world over," she is reported as saying, "always there are people who are coughing." She effectively stopped a man when performing in Germany by pointedly looking around at him! This brought to mind that George Jeffreys had his own way of dealing with this prevalent habit in audiences, knowing how distracting it could be. He would stop and tell his hearers to take out their handkerchief, roll it up into a ball, then cough into it once and for all! In drawing attention to the habit in this practical way he was more often than not successful in at least curbing coughing in his revival meetings.

Principal Jeffreys was the author of several books, the best known of which, *Healing Rays* and *Pentecostal Rays,* have been acclaimed for their excellence by Bible students everywhere. The former shows he stood for healing in two realms, i.e. the natural, in which doctors and nurses work, and the supernatural, in which God works miraculously, God being the Healer in both. The latter book containing his teaching on the Baptism and Gifts of the Holy Spirit is also very convincing, clearly showing the Scriptural difference between being born of the Spirit and being filled with the Spirit. He himself had received a powerful baptism of the Holy Spirit, with the manifestation of the gifts of the Spirit in evidence.

He had his *Bible Students' Open Forum in the British Isles* feature in our periodical under which he wrote a series of informative articles on various subjects, some of which he broadcast over I.B.R.A. Radio (Swedish radio work). The gramophone recordings he made in earlier years are no longer available, but those who still possess these will value them the more.

Chapter 3
Bold Things for God

IN February, 1959, I was privileged as Editor of *The Pattern*, to write a Tribute on the occasion of the Principal's 70th birthday, under the heading "AN ASTONISHING RECORD OF MINISTRY AND SERVICE."

After commenting on the fact that Principal George Jeffreys was born in South Wales, of good Welsh stock, on February 28th, 1889, I continued:

He has crowded an immense amount into these three score years and ten, as this special commemorative issue of *The Pattern* shows, but only in Eternity will we know the full results of his labours for God at home and abroad.

We do know that tens of thousands have been saved through his clear and penetrating presentation of the Gospel message; that the miracles of healing given in his great revival and healing campaigns reveal his faith in God's power to heal the body to—day; and that much fruit has remained through his anointed expository ministry in the cities and towns of our beloved British Isles.

Pastors in the homeland and missionaries on the foreign field thank God for salvation and blessing received through his preaching of the Word, while others also give praise that through his faith and vision doors have been opened for them into the full—time work of the ministry. The Elim Bible College at Clapham, London, which he secured for the Elim Movement, as well as his efforts to help Bible—Pattern Church Fellowship students, are evidences of this...

The Principal, who was born—again in the Welsh Revival, has put the Lord first in his life and ministry and has uncompromisingly declared the whole Counsel of God without fear or favour. This has stimulated the faith of others and they in turn have been blessed through their own personal obedience to the Word.

It is also a cause for rejoicing to know that grateful tributes have been paid to his well—balanced presentation of the truth and method of conducting revival meetings, both so singularly free of fanaticism of any kind. These admirable qualities have been of inestimable value to the Pentecostal life and work of this country and elsewhere.

He is one of the last of that honourable band of pioneers of the teaching of Divine Healing and the Pentecostal Baptism in this the 20th Century, truths that were shunned in those earlier days but which are now gladly received even by many in different denominations. It is noteworthy, too, that he was one of the speakers in 1913 at the Annual Convention in the Convention Hall of All Saints, Monkwearmouth, Sunderland, Church of England Parish of the saintly Vicar, the Rev. Alexander A. Boddy. Here the great Pentecostal Outpouring of 1907 took place, the Jubilee of which was celebrated throughout the Pentecostal Movement in 1957.

He has attempted bold things for God, yet with a single eye to God's glory and the blessing of the people...

I went on to draw attention to an earlier article in which I had stated:

On Good Friday, 1928, he conducted the first Baptismal Service ever to be held in the Royal Albert Hall, when he baptised over 1,000 believers by immersion in water before a packed hall. The *Elim Evangel,* the official organ of the Movement reported the crowded Good Friday and Easter Monday demonstrations that year as follows:

"George Jeffreys, Founder and Leader of the Elim Foursquare Gospel Alliance, immersed in water the greatest number of converts in one meeting since the Day of Pentecost before the greatest crowd of witnesses since the days of the Apostles, and officiated at a Communion Service that finds no parallel in modern times...Hours before the meetings were announced to commence, long queues of eager and expectant folk could be found waiting for the doors to open, ready to pour through the portals and flood its vast seating capacity. Young and old, rich and poor, eyes all luminous with revival fire and faces wreathed in smiles. The Royal Albert Hall was surrounded by a joyous throng. Wherever you turned you were caught up in a stream of praise, for the huge auditorium was girdled with song..."

Thus I wrote in 1959, adding a reminder of the great Jubilee

Year in Pentecost (1957) when through the magnanimous efforts of God's servant the debts were cleared on Bible—Pattern Churches in the British Isles — not planned months ahead but as by a miracle in that Year of Jubilee.

Incidentally, in 1937—38 Principal George Jeffreys launched a debt—clearance fund in Elim so that the debts on Elim Churches were reduced by about £30,000 in a very short time, although as Dr. Wilson points out in his book, *Sects and Society* (page 49): "Reduction of debts in no way curtailed the power of headquarters."

In the Introduction and chapter 2 I name outstanding halls, viz. Royal Albert Hall and Crystal Palace, **London,** the King's Hall, Balmoral, **Belfast,** and the Bingley Hall, **Birmingham,** in which George Jeffreys fervently preached the Gospel before the Second World War. I now give an account of other outstanding halls, some of them magnificent auditoriums seating thousands and steeped in British history, including those used for religious services for the first time, in which he ministered to capacity crowds in those years in the building up of the Elim Movement. It is an unparalleled account of spectacular achievement and, as such, I feel it has to be placed on record:

London: Alexandra Palace; Queen's Hall, the birthplace in 1895 and 'home' of Sir Henry Wood's Promenade concerts (The 'Proms') until the hall was destroyed in the Second World War; and the Westminster Central Hall.

Birmingham: The Town Hall, scene of historic political meetings and musical events, and Sparkbrook Skating Rink, the largest in Europe. **Manchester:** The renowned Free Trade Hall, destroyed in the war and afterwards rebuilt.

Edinburgh: Music Hall and Usher Hall; **Glasgow:** St. Mungo Hall and St. Andrew's Hall. **Belfast:** Ulster Hall and Wellington Hall. **Paisley:** Town Hall. **Greenock:** Town Hall. **Dundee:** Caird Hall. **Aberdeen:** Music Hall and Capitol Theatre. **Southport:** Cambridge Hall. **Halifax:** Victoria Hall. **Bradford:** Olympia. **Leeds:** Salem Central Hall and Coliseum. **Scarborough:** Skating Rink. **Glossop:** Empire Theatre. **Brighton:** The original Royal Dome and Royal Pavilion, both of George IV fame. **Hove:** Town Hall. **Eastbourne:** Pier Music Pavilion and Winter Garden, Devonshire Park. **Southampton:** Central Hall and newly—built and opened Guildhall. **Portsmouth:** Guildhall and Coliseum. **Bournemouth:** Drill

Hall. **Bristol:** Empire Theatre and Military Drill Hall. **Cardiff:** Cory Hall, Drill Hall and Olympia Theatre. **Swansea:** Central Hall and Grand Theatre. **Guernsey, Channel Islands:** St. George's Hall.

York: Exhibition Buildings. **Ipswich:** Public Hall. **Exeter:** Civic Hall. **Plymouth:** Guildhall and Drill Hall likened to "A field with a roof on it"! **Carlisle:** The huge Military Riding School which the people helped to seat for the campaign by bringing chairs from their own homes! **Sheffield:** The newly—built and opened City Hall.

Some of these halls were used for days and weeks on end in the great pioneer campaigns.

In addition, during the summer months lengthy campaigns were held in the Big Evangelistic Tent seating thousands, often full to overflowing, with the canvas sides let down, purchased new and in use for the first time at **Hull** (1933), then **Barking,** in London's East End (1934). Large Tents were hired to suit sites available at **Middlesbrough, Scunthorpe** and **Lincoln** (1935), with the Big Tent again in use at **Belfast** (1936); **Southampton** and **Blackpool** (1937). **Colwyn Bay, N. Wales** (1938) where the Tent was damaged beyond repair in a gale and replaced by the Big Tent, followed by the Big Tent again in use at **Portsmouth** (1938) and **Worthing** (1939).

Before the advent of the Big Tent in 1933, other large Evangelistic Tents were similarly crowded at **Moordown, Bournemouth,** and **Everton, Liverpool** (1926); **Hastings** and **Southsea, Portsmouth** (1927); **Brixton, London** (1929); **Wandsworth** and **Ealing, London** and **Surbiton, Kingston—on—Thames** (1930); **Ryde, Isle of Wight, Blackpool** and **Sheffield** (1931).

To this list must be added cinemas, other theatres and public halls, and many churches including the famous City Temple, Holborn, **London,** the great Surrey Tabernacle, Walworth Road, **London,** and the equally notable Wood Street Congregational Church, **Cardiff,** S. Wales.

I have seen people queuing for the afternoon meeting, with the hall filling for 3 p.m., with those still outside queuing for the evening meeting announced for 7.30 p.m. Such were the crowds, that George Jeffreys finished the first meeting at 4.30 p.m., with the hall filling up again for an impromptu service from 5 p.m. to 6.30 p.m., followed by the third meeting at 7.30 p.m.

When one takes into account George Jeffreys' extraordinary ministry abroad in these years before 1939 (chapter 5) and of that at home and abroad, from 1939 to 1962 (see Appendix 1), plus his constant administrative duties, the whole must surely provide a record of ministry and service unequalled in scope and range by few other evangelists.

In June, 1929, he conducted two unique baptismal services in the grounds of the Elim Bible College at Clapham Park, London, when he baptised hundreds by immersion in water in a large tank which had been erected for the purpose. *The South London Press* reported:

"To anyone who has never seen the effects of a religious revival, the scene in the sunlit grounds must have been an amazing one. Thousands of people were crowded on the terraces and lawns; there were more at the windows of the college, even on the roof of the college itself."

Again, in May 1934, he held yet another baptismal service in the beautiful grounds of the Bible College.

The establishment at Clapham in the early 1920s of the first Elim Church in London, the Elim Publishing Co. Ltd (Victory Press), and the Elim Bible College, is an indication of how the work was growing under his leadership and through his ministry.

Besides the many disused buildings acquired for the converts of his pioneer campaigns, including those discarded by various denominations, and for which he shouldered heavy financial commitments to secure, he laid foundation stones of Elim Churches he had founded in three of our capital cities — **London, Belfast** and **Cardiff** — as well as in other places in the British Isles. He also preached at church—opening services far and wide and presided at the ordination of new ministers, giving the charge to ordinands and congregations.

He was indeed a man 'on the go,' sparing very little time for rest and recreation.

BRITISH PRESS COVERAGE

Generally speaking, the Revivalist had a good Press through the whole of his remarkable career. All the great British national dailies and many of the provincial newspapers, as well as the illustrated journals, reported him and his meetings. From the Press 'cuttings' I have from England, Ireland, Scotland and

Wales, I quote from a few selected at random as being representative of the four countries:

London — The Royal Albert Hall: Amazing scenes of intense religious fervour were witnessed at the Albert Hall last night, when Principal George Jeffreys, the leader of the Elim Foursquare Gospel Alliance, baptised 200 members of the movement in the presence of a gathering of some 11,000 people. — *Daily Mail,* 22 April, 1930.

Birmingham — The Bingley Hall: The vast barn—like building which has housed all the city's greatest gatherings — has never been the scene of a meeting as remarkable as that held there last night...during Principal George Jeffreys' revival and healing campaign...Imagine Bingley Hall crammed with seats, and every seat occupied. Imagine the galleries crowded, and people wedged tight in doors left open to let in the air. — *Birmingham Gazette,* 5th June, 1930.

Belfast — The King's Hall: Huge congregations thronged the building. For the first time since it was constructed the King's Hall, Balmoral, Belfast, Ireland's largest hall, was used last night for a religious revival meeting...The ground floor and the balconies of three sides of the building were filled with an immense congregation. The number of people who attended the service on Sunday night was estimated at nearly 10,000. — *The Northern Whig,* August 31st, 1936.

London — The Crystal Palace: One hundred and fifty men and women were plunged in a tank of cold water at the Crystal Palace, London, on Saturday, while something like 15,000 sat watching in a state of almost hysterical happiness...The congregation was a mixture of young and old, rich and poor, crippled and healed, but every one shared in the religious fervour. — *Daily Express,* September 14th, 1931.

Glasgow — The St. Andrew's Hall: A wave of evangelism is sweeping Glasgow. More than 1,400 people have been converted, hundreds have testified to faith healing, and thousands have taken part in the revival campaign which is being conducted by Principal George Jeffreys. The series of revival meetings which have been held by Principal Jeffreys during the last four weeks here will conclude this week—end with a final rally which, it is expected, nearly 10,000 people will attend...Scenes in Glasgow and the surrounding towns during the past four weeks rival the most emotional incidents in Scottish

50

history. Vast crowds, moved by the passionate pleading of Principal Jeffreys, have risen in a body in reply to the evangelist's request to "stand up for God." Scores of people, blind, paralysed, deaf, suffering from all forms of "incurable" maladies, have been brought to the meetings to join in prayer for healing. Crowds have been lining up at the doors to the hall each night, and hundreds have been turned away when the place was filled. — *Daily Express,* March 24th, 1927.

Liverpool — Boxing Stadium: Using the roped enclosure of the boxing ring as his pulpit, Principal George Jeffreys, whose revival and healing campaign has been attracting immense crowds at Liverpool recently, conducted two immense services in the Liverpool Boxing Stadium yesterday. The evening service was attended by close on 3,000 people. Over a hundred men, women and children spoke of their own individual "cures." — *Liverpool Post and Mercury,* March, 1926.

Cardiff — The City Temple: It was in October, 1929, that the Principal first visited Cardiff, and for nearly seven weeks conducted one of the most sweeping campaigns ever held in the city...The Church is now over four years old and is attracting, as it has done from its inception, one of the largest congregations in the city...The story of the Cardiff campaign and its results is simply a repetition of what has followed the many other campaigns conducted by Principal Jeffreys. — *Western Mail and South Wales News,* March 24th, 1934.

London — The Royal Albert Hall: Thousands of men and women attended a revival meeting — the seventh annual Elim Foursquare Gospel Demonstration — conducted by Principal George Jeffreys, at the Albert Hall yesterday...Before the service many present had testified that they had been cured of cancer, tumour, and other growths, blindness and rheumatoid arthritis. — *The Times,* March 29th, 1932.

Brighton — The Royal Dome: The Foursquare Gospellers, led by Principal George Jeffreys, thronged the Dome on Whit—Monday. Almost to a day, twenty—five years ago, Mr. Jeffreys was in the Dome, and his first revival and healing mission at Brighton concluded with remarkable scenes of religious fervour...The Revivalist's successful campaign resulted in the acquiring of the historic chapel in The Lanes; the building of the Elim Tabernacle, at Hove; and the establishment of other district missions for people who had rediscovered the joy of religion. The fact that Jeffreys' followers, after twenty—five years, could fill the Dome on a Bank Holiday was quoted as the answer to those who wondered, a quarter of a century ago, whether the work would stand the test of time...Principal Jeffreys remains an able, humble and sincere preacher of the Word, who is completely unspoilt by success. — *Brighton and Hove Herald*, June 7th, 1952.

London — Albert Hall: Great dome of Albert Hall nearly lifted by ten thousand—voiced vibration...Foursquare Gospeller hymnsinging at 12th annual meeting.

Gospellers' sect came of age last year. Welsh preacher, George Jeffreys (he's now Principal of headquarters at Clapham Common), founded it 22 years ago. Building was convent till they took it over in 1925.

Outsize faith demonstration yesterday...people were healed in the morning; baptised in the afternoon; converted all day long.

Last night was biggest communion service in the country — 10,000 communicants.

Impressive sight. Servers (150 of them) — at a signal — rose from all parts of the hall, queued up at centre table (transformed from afternoon's baptismal tank). Table was covered with white cloth and 150 chalices, silver and glass, and 150 bread patens. Ten thousand people waited in breathless silence for day's great moment...Thirty thousand (10,000 at each of three services) passed through that hall since the morning. — *The Daily Sketch*, March 30th, 1937.

In some cases bold newspaper placards appeared on the streets proclaiming: "RELIGIOUS REVIVAL SCENES AT CARDIFF;" "SHEFFIELD RELIGIOUS REVIVAL SCENES;" "AMAZING REVIVALIST SCENES IN NOTTINGHAM;" "AMAZING SCENES AT ABERDEEN'S NEW CHURCH." *The Morning Post* put out the placard: "LONDON AUDIENCE MESMERISED!" and went on to report: "Hours before the doors were opened thousands of people queued up seeking admission. They stormed the great hall and soon every seat from the top of the Albert Hall to the bottom was occupied. Independent observers must have been struck by the extraordinary hold which the young revivalist exercised over his monster congregation. There was none of that sheepish half—attention; for an hour and a half the young revivalist held his audience enthralled." — April 19th, 1927.

I am repeating part of A.L. Lloyd's tribute to the self—effacing attitude of George Jeffreys in his *Picture Post* magazine article of May, 1946 (Appendix 2), something which struck so many on hearing him or meeting him. Describing him as "a slight dark, curly—haired man in his fifties," the journalist goes on to write of him: "Every spring for years his face has been familiar on the London hoardings. On the poster he looks quiet and modest enough, and in the flesh that quietness and modesty is what strikes you first. The fanatic's gleam is not there. If you go to a Jeffreys' meeting expecting the Bible—thumping and the conventional capers of the hot—gospeller you will be disappointed. Even when he is preaching, Jeffreys speaks quietly and with restrained gestures. His appeal, say his followers, is to the will, not to the emotions…"

This report in the *Brighton & Hove Gazette,* August 7th, 1954, bore the bold heading "BRIGHTON SEES ANOTHER BILLY GRAHAM," reading: "Echoing through Brighton's Lanes came the sound of fervent hymn—singing…and visitors hunting bargains or just window—shopping among the antique shops, stood and stared. A *Gazette* reporter found the church packed on Thursday. The usual bookstall had to be removed to make room for visitors — many of them holiday makers." It is true to say that Billy Graham has had the support of denominations of all kinds, whereas George Jeffreys chose to plough a lone furrow, preaching what he believed to be the whole Counsel of God. What was said of the Birmingham campaign of 1930 could be said of his campaigns in general — no joint Church committee arrangements beforehand. He preferred to be entirely free in his ministry, yet having ministers of various denominations in support on his platform.

The Armagh Guardian, of May 20th, 1955, reported: "The founder of the Elim churches, Principal George Jeffreys, drew a capacity attendance when he spoke in Armagh City Hall on Monday. The audience was made up of people from Lurgan, Portadown and even from Monaghan, as well as those from Armagh and surrounding districts…In the course of his uplifting address Pastor Jeffreys dealt with bodily healing, miracles, the outpouring of the Holy Spirit and Bible Prophecy."

I recall talking with Bernard Gray, a *Sunday Pictorial* reporter, who was impressed by the ministry at Colwyn Bay in the summer of 1938 and who reported fully on the campaign for his newspaper, writing of healings which had taken place and photographing a baptismal service of newly—won converts held in the Evangelistic Tent. He heard the Gospel as did so many other newspaper reporters over the years. In his case he was soon to be one of the first war correspondents to tragically lose his life at sea early in the Second World War.

If George Jeffreys no longer received national press coverage in his later years on the scale hitherto experienced, he certainly did not die as a 'nonentity.' Many notable evangelistic meetings have been held by others in Britain's public halls with no mention at all in the newspapers, a common omission in these post—war years. A classic example is that of the 11th World Pentecostal Conference in London in 1976, when the *Elim Evangel* reported: "From all over the world they came," comprising some twenty—one meetings in the Royal Albert Hall and the Westminster Central Hall, with an estimated 30,000 different people being present during these services. The magazine commented in bold type, **"World Event not noticed by Fleet St.,"** the news—black—out, it seems, having been total. Was it therefore a gathering of 'nonentities'?

Not only do I have the envelope uniquely addressed in 1946 to Principal Jeffreys from Greece, referred to on page 5 of my *Open Letter,* but I also have others from those at home and overseas which reached him through the ingenuity of the British Post Office. These, and the scope of obituary notices and tributes as given in chapter 10, clearly indicate he was constantly in the public mind. Here is a selection:

One from Rainhill, Liverpool, was simply addressed to him at the "Church of the Great Physician," London; that from Rivaz (Vaud), Switzerland, posted 15 days after the Crystal Palace had been destroyed by fire in 1936, was addressed to Monsieur Principal Georges Jeffreys, Palais de Cristal, Londres, Angleterre; from Misdroy, Germany, came this given as "England," Principal George Jeffreys, London Tabernacle; another from Stockholm, Sweden, in 1952, reads: Pastor Jefferies, "Head of Pentecostal Movement," London; from Louisville, U.S.A. came this addressed to him as "Superintendent of the British Jeffrey Churches; one from Owen Sound, Ontario, Canada, had no name at all, simply "The London Faith Healer," England; another from Bussum, Holland, in 1949 was addressed: George Jeffries, Esqr., Elim Foursquare

Reveilligten, London; from Tunis came a letter in 1954 c/o Royal Albert Hall, Kensington; another in 1948 reads: Monsieur Georges Jeffreys, Ecole biblique, Royal Albert Hall, Londre; and that from Guthrie Center, Iowa, U.S.A. in 1943 merely gave his name, London, England, with a message to the postmaster on the envelope, reading: "Principal Jeffreys is a prominent Full Gospel minister of England who is well known through his healing meetings." Whatever way his name was spelt when in Elim and after, and however obscure the address given, these along with thousands of other letters reached him throughout his long ministry.

To close this chapter I give the published thoughts and feelings of a lady present at Bank holiday meetings in a famous public hall in the provinces, which are, I feel, expressive of Principal Jeffreys' campaigns and conventions in general:

"The call was given for all who needed a touch of healing to come forward, and as well—known choruses were softly sung, hundreds left their seats and filed quietly on to the platform, kneeling among the beautiful flowers which had been placed there by loving hands earlier in the day. Others knelt around the platform and still others knelt in the aisles while Principal George Jeffreys prayed, anointed and laid his hands on them.

"We were softly singing, 'Breathe on us, Breath of God,' when a strange hush fell on the great congregation. The singing ceased — the silence deepened and increased — a heavenly wave of God's own compassion — the very breath of God it seemed, swept over the meeting. It was as if the Master were weeping, not only for the sufferers present, but for all the sorrow and suffering of the world. The Principal himself was deeply moved, as also the other helpers, many being melted to tears with the same deep compassion. The wonderful moments passed and then the silence was broken by the Principal softly starting a chorus, and the great never—to—be—forgotten healing meeting came to an end.

"Eagerly we looked forward to the evening meeting, and after snatching a hasty meal in the town, we joined the great queue already lined up outside the hall.

"At last we were once more inside…Then the Principal spoke in his clear forceful way on the gifts of the Holy Spirit, proving beyond a doubt that those great gifts are still with us to—day, even as in the beginning of the Pentecostal dispensation, with outward signs and manifestations; but I must leave that speech to be described by some abler pen than mine — I only know I felt, here is a man speaking under the immediate influence and power of the Holy Spirit.

"How we sang and waved our yellow hymnsheets (glory sheets, the Principal called them) and praised God for all the wonderful things that He had done — healing and saving many precious souls. How we praised, till the last minute...we felt indeed 'heaven has been down our souls to greet.'"

Chapter 4
Twentieth Century Miracles

PRINCIPAL Jeffreys never claimed to have the power to heal, but he did claim to obey the Scriptures in the laying—on of hands on those seeking healing. Astonishing cases of healing have been witnessed throughout his long ministry, as is evidenced in his book, *Healing Rays,* and elsewhere, yet he was always careful to give God the glory for all such deliverances.

Another book entitled *In Defence of His Word,* compiled by R.E. Darragh and published by the Elim Publishing Co. Ltd in 1932, gives selected testimonies of much suffering healed by the power of Christ in this ministry. The index of names of those testifying number 141 and the diseases cured include 26 cripple cases, those of cancer, blindness, deafness, dropsy, growths, rupture, heart disease, paralysis, and other infirmities. It was said that these testimonies were not published in book form for about three years after each had been healed, in answer to the critics who ask, "Do these healings last?" Many others have been miraculously healed over the years since.

If *In Defence of His Word* is no longer available, the four amazing testimonies, abridged, as given here, and which took place in 1927, are published in full with others in *Healing Rays,* a fourth edition of which was issued in 1986. Although George Jeffreys witnessed so many healings through prayer and the laying on of hands, he believed there were certain years when God wrought special miracles, 1927 being one of them.

HELPLESS CRIPPLE WALKS OUT OF WHEELED
CARRIAGE AT SOUTHAMPTON
Miss Florence Munday

"Fourteen years ago I fell, and tubercular trouble set up in my knee. During these years I had never been able to stand or walk. Together with this I suffered from a dreadful skin disease, which started when I was a tiny child, twenty—nine years ago. At times I had both arms from wrists to shoulders covered with bandages.

I used to faint when the dressings had to come off and the hot fomentations put on. The knee became worse as time went on, and I suffered agony from the various splints and bandages I had to wear...The doctor gave no hope and advised amputation; worse still, it would have to be taken off so high up that no stump was to be left, so that I could not wear an artificial limb.

"On Wednesday, 4th May, 1927, my sisters came home after attending one of Principal George Jeffreys' revival meetings at the Weslyan Central Hall, Southampton. They brought the news that a lady had stepped out of her bath chair that very day in the service. They asked me to go, and I nervously agreed to do so. I was pushed there in my bath chair and wheeled right up to the front of the service. It was a service I shall never forget. The missioner came to me and asked me if I believed God could heal me. I said, 'Yes! but I am in a splint.' I was anointed with oil, and as he prayed my whole body vibrated with life. I was under the power of God. My leg moved up and down three times in the splint, and soon I was able to sit up. All pain was gone. I was healed. I stood up and stepped out of my bath chair without aid. I was on my feet for the first time after fourteen years. I walked around that big building three times. My leg was like that of a frail baby's when the splint was taken off; and altogether the leg was 4½ inches shorter than the other. Now they are both the same size, quite normal. You can understand how I feel, when I tell you I want to sing all day, 'Jesus, Thou art everything to me.'"

SLEEPING SICKNESS, BLINDNESS AND SEIZURE HEALED AT PORTSMOUTH
Miss C. Jardine

"For twenty years I suffered from internal paralysis caused through a fright. During these years I suffered terrible agonies of pain, and had three serious operations. After the second one the surgeon told me I could never work again. I lay at death's door in hospital for weeks, but I never lost faith in the Lord Jesus Christ. I also had a tubercular knee and nearly lost my leg, but I praise and thank God he spoke to my mother, and she would not consent to the operation; but the surgeon removed a piece of diseased bone, and left me with a stiff joint...

"I was then put into an iron splint, and an extension to pull the leg down; but it gradually got worse, and I was put into an iron splint and cork boot, which I had to wear night and day...

"My trouble did not end here, for three years ago I took sleepy sickness *(encephalitis lethargica)*. I was unconscious for three weeks and I went totally blind. The sight came back into my right eye, but the left one was eaten away, and the doctors said I could never see again with that eye... Then I had a seizure which twisted me up, and I shall never forget the agony I went through when the doctor came and stretched all the muscles of my body. When I got to my feet I discovered I could not straighten myself, and my left leg was twisted right around, while my head almost touched my knees.

"On 22nd September, 1927, I was wheeled in my bath chair to Principal George Jeffreys' healing meeting, was prayed for and anointed by him in the Name of the Lord and was healed. I felt the power of God go through my body. My spine is quite straight now, and the sight has come back to my blind eye. Glory to God! Hallelujah!

HELPLESS CRIPPLE HEALED AT LEEDS
Mr. James Gregson

"I was an iron—maker by trade. On 2nd February, 1922, I met with a serious accident. I fell from a height into a coal—box, every bone being shifted out of place. My spine was also injured. I was taken to the hospital, where I received every treatment that the hospital could supply, but I became a helpless, hopeless cripple. I had to creep along the ground; my legs were twisted and I dragged them along in a crossed position. I could not sit, but had to lie. My life was a misery.

"My wife on the Wednesday evening read in the paper an account of a woman who was blind receiving her sight in Principal George Jeffreys' campaign meetings. As she read, I was convinced that I could be healed if only I could go to the meeting. I went on the Saturday on my crutches, dragging my legs behind. That night I was saved: He forgave all my iniquities. I then went again on the Sunday to the Coliseum. God alone knows how I got there, and when I got there I had a great struggle to get in, but some of the people took pity on me and dragged me round to the back. Then the attendants carried me in and laid me in front of the platform.

"One of the revival party came to me and said: 'Brother, you don't look comfortable; can I make you more comfortable?' and I answered, 'I am never comfortable,' for I was in pain night and day. I was prayed for by the Principal, and when he laid his hands upon me I felt as if a dozen hands were placed all over my body and I felt every bone going back into place. I was instantly released and I was completely healed. I was only skin and bone, my eyes were sunk in my head. Inside two weeks I had gained two stone five pounds, and I continued to put on flesh. I was able to go back to my work as strong as ever. I have never lost a day's work since through ill—health. To God be all the glory! Praise the Lord!"

BAPTIST MINISTER'S WIFE HEALED OF CANCER AT BRIGHTON
Mrs. Algernon Coffin

"For twenty years I had been a great sufferer. In June, 1917, I saw a specialist, who diagnosed my trouble as cancer; and on June 9th, 1917, I entered a nursing home for an operation. Twelve months later, the same specialist saw me again, and declared there was a recurrence of the trouble, and that I could not live longer than five months. But in answer to the earnest prayers of many, my life was spared. For many years I had been taking the strongest drugs to alleviate my pain and enable me to sleep...By this time dropsy had set in, also heart trouble, and my nerves were in such a state I could not bear the least sound.

"Just at this time God sent His dear servant, Principal George Jeffreys, to Brighton, and after much prayer I decided to go to the Divine Healing meeting on the afternoon of May 19th, 1927, in the Royal Pavilion. I was prayed for; I felt an inward thrill go right through my body, and was instantly met with healing, the evidence being that all my pain ceased, and I was able to sleep; I also regained my normal size, and never felt anything from the sudden leaving off of the drugs.

"Two doctors called to see me during the week, and were witnesses to the marvellous change in me. One doctor was amazed when I answered the door to him myself. Coming in, he said, 'What has happened, Mrs. Coffin? Is it really you?' 'Yes, doctor,' I replied, 'I am healed and quite well, after you told me there was no hope. In my helplessness and distress I appealed to a higher One, whose power is not limited. I did not appeal in vain.' The doctor answered, 'Well, it says, "If you ask in faith you shall receive"; and you certainly have: it is very marvellous. I cannot understand it, but I rejoice with you.' Praise the Name of the

Lord, I felt like singing as never before. I have walked miles and travelled about to convey this glad news to others. I have had occasion to praise the Lord, for that terrible disease has never returned. The Lord has been and ever will be my Great Physician, praise His wonderful Name. I touched by faith the hem of His garment and was made perfectly whole. His power avails today."

It is a joy for me to relate the sequel to these miracles of answered prayer: On Good Friday, 1928, the year after their healing, Miss Florence Munday and Miss C. Jardine had stood together with George Jeffreys in the baptismal tank at the Royal Albert Hall in London, when he baptised them and a thousand others by immersion in water before a congregation of ten thousand. Miss Munday was a lay preacher in an Elim Church for many years.

I knew each of these four personally. Miss Munday spoke in the Bradford revival campaign towards the end of 1928 (my first as pianist in the Revival Party) and referred to how she had walked into a ministers' fraternal meeting on the premises immediately following her miraculous deliverance at Southampton's Wesleyan Methodist Central Hall, where her own minister, the Rev. Boyce, had marvelled with his colleagues at what they saw. The Bradford Press took this up as Mr. Boyce had recently been transferred to that city, whereupon he confirmed the truth of her testimony.

Miss Jardine, four years after her miracle, came and kept house for us as a Party during the revival campaign at the Cambridge Hall, Southport, in 1931. Mr. James Gregson used to attend the Royal Albert Hall demonstrations at Easter, stand on the platform like a guardsman and leap several feet into the air before the rejoicing congregation as a proof of his complete restoration. Mrs. Coffin's deliverance from cancer took place at the Brighton campaign, my home town. I still count as one of my friends her nephew Eric Gibson—Smith, retired Pastor, who today lives at St. Leonards—on—Sea, Sussex, and who was present on the night I was converted in that campaign, in which his aunt was healed.

Each of these four lived to a good old age, Miss Jardine until she was 90.

In 1987 I received a letter from a Mr. M.W. Dyson, of Australia, requesting a copy of my *Open Letter* of July 25th,

1986. He wrote he was converted in the Leeds campaign of 1927, that he remembered Jim Gregson and his wonderful healing and had attended George Jeffreys' great demonstration at the Crystal Palace, London. He was now in charge of the Full Gospel Business Mens' Fellowship in Australia, having retired from his work with the South Australia Board.

Glyn Thomas' testimony of 1929 appeared under the title, "A SWANSEA MIRACLE" in R.E. Darragh's book:

"I was a sufferer from birth, having the deformity of a lump on the back. Five years ago I went under an operation for rupture. I suffered such pain I could not walk. This added to my deformity. I went to the Revival and Healing Campaign held by Principal George Jeffreys in the Central Hall. He prayed and anointed me with oil in the Name of the Lord, and I was miraculously healed. The coat I was wearing hung in folds on my shoulders. The lump had disappeared, and I was made perfectly straight."

Mr. Thomas, from his humble station as a newsvendor on the streets of Swansea, became a minister of the Gospel and Bible teacher of note in the Church of the Nazarene. I was there when he was healed in 1929 and knew him as a personal friend until his Homecall in the 1980s.

In more modern times Mrs. Margery Steven's testimony telling of salvation and healing which came to her father and mother in 1926 through George Jeffreys' ministry at Bournemouth, had a remarkable sequel in 1960. Her father, after the laying—on of hands and the anointing with oil in 1926 received a miracle of healing which enabled him to return to his engineering job for the next 18 years. This established in Margery, as a child, a faith in God and she sincerely believed, as she does today, that Jesus Christ is the same yesterday, and today, and forever. The one thing that lived for her out of the Bible stories she heard at Sunday School was the raising of Lazarus from the dead (John's Gospel, chapter 11).

Some 5½ years before 1960 she had a most trying illness so that her nursing career was interrupted. Eventually multiple sclerosis, or creeping paralysis, attacked her before she realised it. Gradually she got worse, until she became so helpless, with her legs useless, she had to be lifted from bed to wheelchair, like a baby, and be strapped round with belts to keep her from falling forward. She had to be fed by her parents. She had no power in her left arm. Her left eye was completely closed, her right eye often had trebled vision needing the use of dark glasses to try to help the sight of that eye. She would lose consciousness for hours, but with all this she would say to her Christian friends, "What my Lord could do for Lazarus, He can do for me if it is His Will."

Things got worse for her. On February 4th, 1960, she dreamed during the night she was sitting in a chair by her bed (as when she was fit enough her parents would lift her there from her bed so that her mother would be able to wash her more easily). As she dreamed she thought she put out her left leg, then awoke to find it was a dream. Then a voice sounded through her room — it was her Lord's, she testifies, in these words, "Tarry a little longer."

In the next few days she told several of her praying friends about the way she had received this message from Jesus in the night whilst she was alone with Him. Her faith became stronger, although physically she worsened, with her speech so badly affected that at times she could not make herself understood. But in all this suffering was the realisation — what Jesus could do for Lazarus He could do for her; and His message to "Tarry a little longer" meant that in His own good time He would heal her, however long or short a time this might be.

On Monday, July 4th, 1960, exactly five months after God had spoken to her, she goes on to say:

"My Lord healed me, in the very chair of which I had dreamed! I had said goodbye to my husband at five minutes to six on that Monday morning — a helpless woman. At 6.15 my mother gave me a cup of tea. At 6.20 my father and mother lifted me from my bed, strapped me in the chair beside the bed, put a bell in my good hand, to summon aid if needed, and left me alone. Mother went to get my washing water and my father had gone to get a towel from upstairs. *Then in a matter of seconds, when I was all on my own, my Lord Jesus healed me!* I felt a warm glow go over my body. My left foot, which was doubled up, straightened out; my right foot, the toes of which were pointed towards my heel, came back into position. I grasped the handle of my bedroom door which was beside me, undid the straps which were about my body, and said, *"By faith I will stand,"* which I did.

"With that I thought of my mother and the shock it would be to her if she came back to find her daughter standing after so many years, so I sat down and called for her. With that, both my parents came running to my room, thinking I was in need of them. I said, 'Mum, dear, take my hands, please don't be afraid, something wonderful has happened.' I put out my right arm and as I did so my left arm came out from behind me and joined the other! It was so wonderful, a few minutes afterwards to find I could wear my own wedding ring which I had not been able to do for years, as my fingers of that hand had got so thin. My mother said, 'Darling, how wonderful, your hand is warm, and it is well again.' I said, 'Mum, dear, it is more wonderful than that, *I can stand.*' With that, holding her hands, *I stood once more on my two feet.* Then, gently putting my parents aside, I said, 'Dears, I do not need your help any more, I'm walking with God.' Unaided I then walked from my bedroom, through the small dining room to the kitchen, my parents following mutely behind me. When I reached the kitchen I turned and went back into the dining room and, taking off my glasses, I said, 'Mum, I can trust God for my hands and feet. I can trust Him for my sight.' *With that, in a moment, my left eye opened and my sight was fully restored.* In fact Jesus made such a perfect job I do not need the glasses I had before I was ill, and I am now writing dozens of letters a day! To Him be all the Glory!

"I felt that I wanted this testimony to be such that people would forget Margery Steven and think of and thank her Lord only, for the great things He has done.

"We told no one until I had been examined by my doctor and he confirmed the miracle on Tuesday, July 5th. Since then several doctors and nurses have been to see me, and they have gone away knowing that only God has wrought this wonderful miracle: so please, forget Margery Steven and remember WHAT JESUS ALONE CAN DO."

On the Sunday following her healing Margery walked with her husband and parents to St. John's Church, Wimborne, their church, where at the morning service they heard the Vicar (Rev. R.E. Garrard) publicly thank God for her miraculous healing and preach from the text, *"We have seen strange things today."* (Luke 5:26)

Mrs. Steven wrote Principal Jeffreys a letter which came as he was about to leave London to conduct meetings at the Jubilee Temple, Blackpool. At his request I read the good news of the miracle to the meeting that night, having seen Mrs. Steven before her healing. Some three weeks later, accompanied by her parents, she testified at the People's Church, Clapham Common, London, expressing her joy at Principal Jeffreys' presence, in that he had lived to witness her restoration. One can well understand souls deciding for Christ on that memorable occasion.

Mrs. Steven was again present in 1961 to testify at George Jeffreys' last Easter Monday meetings at the Westminster Central Hall, London.

She has travelled far and wide here and abroad giving her story, to the encouragement and blessing of so many others seeking healing. It has also been broadcast over IBRA Radio. Three years after her healing she was at the marriage service of my wife and I at the People's Church at Clapham. At the reception afterwards she gave personal testimony to two doctors and others who were present as our guests. She and her mother still live at Wimborne in Dorset, the town which first saw her healing, her husband and father having passed on.

In my own case, I had an operation for mastoid in 1922 when 12 years of age, being desperately ill, with the specialist subsequently telling my parents, "In another week he would have been playing a harp, I don't know if they have any pianos up there yet!" My life was spared but I was left with both ear drums perforated and the membrane of one almost gone. My prospects, according to medical opinion, were of my becoming stone deaf.

Following my introduction to the teaching of Divine healing at Brighton in 1927, and the Scriptural laying—on of hands, I had a gradual recovery and have carried out my work unhindered since by any such catastrophic defect to this day. Whether healings are gradual or instantaneous (John 4:52 and Luke 13:13 for example), all the praise and glory for such belongs to God.

Chapter 5
Amazing Campaigns Abroad

IN the years 1933 to 1936, and those after the Second World War, 1946, 1947, 1948 and 1950 George Jeffreys also conducted some of the greatest revival and healing campaigns ever held on the Continent, particularly in Switzerland and France. Not only were many thousands converted to Christ through his ministry, Protestants and Roman Catholics alike, but great numbers testified to having received bodily healing.

We give a summary under the year dates, beginning with:

1933 CONCERNING THE REMARKABLE MEETINGS AT CAUX, SWITZERLAND, Dr. Emile Lanz, of Neuchatel, wrote: "The visit of Principal George Jeffreys and the Revival Party to Regina Hotel, Caux, from June 10th to 19th, will leave a permanent mark in the history of Swiss revivalism." Surely this was prophetic!

1934 LARGEST HALLS IN SWITZERLAND BESEIGED, covering Bienne—Macolin, Geneva (the famous Reformation Hall), Berne, Zurich and Basel. Nearly 6,000 souls saved. Converts baptised in Lake Geneva. Dr. Emile Lanz, who was one of George Jeffreys' able interpreters, especially in German—Switzerland, again wrote: "A mighty wave of Foursquare Revival has just rolled over Switzerland, sweeping thousands of precious souls into the kingdom of heaven and bringing encouragement and bodily healing of all kinds of disease and infirmity to thousands of stricken folks, while many converted and sanctified believers received the blessed baptism in the Holy Spirit for service, and last but not least, vast congregations were filled and thrilled anew with the blessed hope of the soon return of our beloved Lord and Saviour Jesus Christ...

"We are firmly convinced that Switzerland has never before experienced such a spiritual revival — not even in the days of the bygone Reformation enkindled by the God—sent Reformers, Zwingli, Farel, Calvin and others. In our eyes a manifest miracle has been wrought in that we

66

had the greatest trouble to find, in the prominent cities of Switzerland, halls large enough to contain the masses which thronged the meetings."

1935 A YET MORE ASTONISHING REVIVAL TOUR — Berne, Bienne, Baden, Zurich, Wald, St. Gallen, Schaffhausen, Basel, Lausanne, La Chaux—de—Fonds, Neuchatel and Geneva, during which National State Temples, great Exhibition Buildings, grand Theatres, were all thronged by teeming crowds. Reformation Hall at Geneva again packed daily, crowds standing in gangways, failing to gain admission. 12,000 conversions registered in five weeks and miracles of healing confirmed the preached Word. "The greatest religious awakening since the days of the reformers has taken place in Switzerland," was the considered judgment of a well—informed Swiss friend.

Crowded revival meetings also held in FRANCE, in the great Town Theatre, Le Havre, and at Rouen. At both these centres the congregations and converts consisted chiefly of Roman Catholics.

1936 THE LARGEST EXHIBITION HALL IN SWITZERLAND — COMPTOIR SUISSE, LAUSANNE — TAKEN TO ACCOMMODATE IMMENSE CROWDS. Between 6,000 and 7,000 gathered around the Lord's Table for the 9.30 Sunday morning service, at which 34 nationalities were represented. Over 2,000 souls were saved during this visit to Switzerland which included 'Deepening of Spiritual Life' meetings in the Kursaal—Casino of the famous spa centre of Baden, German—Switzerland.

1946 AGAIN ON THE CONTINENT FOLLOWING THE WAR—YEARS, Nice, Cannes, Marseilles visited in the South of France, and Lisieux, Evreux, Rouen, Le Havre, Dieppe, Lille and Calais in the North. Thousands received blessing in these inspiring revival meetings and 821 conversions were recorded.

1947 SWITZERLAND — Geneva, Zurich, Montreux and Yverdon. Crowded meetings and a further 574 souls saved in eight days.

1948 SWITZERLAND AND FRANCE — Neuchatel, Lausanne and Saint—Etienne. Over 1,100 decisions for Christ. Full Gospel message broadcast over Radio—Lausanne.

1950 FRANCE AND SWITZERLAND — Le Havre, St. Etienne, Evreux, Paris, Lausanne and Bienne. Further crowded meetings in Public Halls, including the famous Pleyel Hall, Paris: in Churches and Evangelistic Tents. Over 1,500 decisions for Christ. Mention must be made of Pastor Tom Roberts, a native of Wales, who had ministered for many years in France. He, with his excellent knowledge of the French language, proved to be an able interpreter in many of the meetings in France.

Memorable meetings were also held in other lands, such as U.S.A., Canada, Belgium, Sweden, Norway, Denmark, Finland, Palestine and Transjordan. In the U.S.A. — Canada meetings in 1924, the Principal was accompanied by his brother Stephen Jeffreys, R.E. Darragh, James McWhirter and E.C.W. Boulton. They travelled about 15,000 miles over sea and land, meeting with many Pentecostal brethren, when as a party they ministered in such centres as Montreal, Ottowa, Toronto, Winnipeg, San Jose and Fresno. They visited the splendid Angelus Temple in Los Angeles, opened the year before by its Founder, Mrs. Aimee Semple McPherson, where they met her, this being their first contact with this great woman evangelist.

Besides baptising in Lake Geneva, Switzerland, and in the icy waters flowing down from the Alps, George Jeffreys conducted baptismal services elsewhere abroad.

The meetings in France in 1946 included preaching in the Casino Theatre night after night at Nice, where compulsive gamblers gathered daily to satisfy the urge to gamble in the various forms available. What a venue this proved to be for the Foursquare Gospel message as preached with power by George Jeffreys! No wonder the Pastor at Nice later testified to how many of the converts, mainly Roman Catholics, he had baptised in water on the confession of their new—found faith!

We crossed over to Monaco and visited Monte Carlo Casino. An official there who had attended the meetings in Nice, told Principal Jeffreys he wished he could hear him preach his message in the Theatre in the Casino, into which he took us. Such public Protestant meetings, he said, would not be permitted in Monaco.

When leaving Stockholm for Finland by ship in 1947 we were advised not to take the car in case it should be commandeered, because of Russian domination, an aftermath of the initial

Soviet—Finnish war of 1939. This proved of benefit in two ways: the petrol tank of the car was re—galvanised in Stockholm, by courtesy of the Filadelfia Church, and ready on our return — a necessity owing to gathered sediment which sometimes prevented the free flow of petrol — and we took with us on the ship much needed goods supplied by the Filadelfia Church for the Finnish Pentecostal people in great need. During our stay in Finland, greatly blessed as it was, there were limited food supplies and we used paper towels and sheets. Russian guards were on the trains on which we travelled, with blinds drawn at times to prevent passengers from seeing Soviet building projects.

Pastor F. de Rougemont, also of Neuchatel and a State Church minister of Switzerland, another able interpreter, had this to say in tribute on the Principal's 70th birthday in 1959:

"Principal George Jeffreys celebrated on 28th February his 70th birthday. *Trait d'Union* and all its readers send him a message of great affection and deep thankfulness, and they pray God to grant him the fullness of His peace and joy, and to renew his strength as well, physically and spiritually, for a new period of service to the glory of his beloved Master.

"Innumerable saints in French—Switzerland and in France have their hearts filled with blessed remembrances. His visits on the Continent, from the first one at Caux in June, 1933, till the last in 1950 (Le Havre, St. Etienne, Evreux, Paris, Lausanne and Bienne) have been fountains of new life in body and soul for many, and are marked in the history of French Protestantism. George Jeffreys has been indeed one of the most (if not the most) powerful witness among us to the Foursquare Gospel.

"Let us only remember the glorious Lausanne Campaign in 1936, where nearly ten thousand people listened to the captivating messages of the evangelist, where hundreds were healed of all sorts of diseases, where hundreds answered to the Lord's call, and where more than 6,000 took part in the Communion Service on Sunday morning.

"What a vigour, what a fullness in his messages, perfect as to style, rich in content, alive and full of the unction of the Spirit. There are few evangelists who would know, as he does, how to bring the souls to a clear comprehension of the new birth. And how carefully he takes pains that no mis—understanding be left and that each one really receives Jesus in

69

his heart. And then, what a power in the laying—on of hands to the sick! We have seen miracles with our own eyes and the glory of God being manifested.

"We often meet people who say, 'I have been healed, or I have been saved at such and such a meeting of Principal Jeffreys...' and their faces shine with holy joy. Praise be to the Lord for this faithful servant!"

On October 2nd, 1960, Pastor A. Hunziker sent him the following telegram from Geneva, in acknowledgment of the Pentecostal Church founded through his ministry in that historic city:

FOR ITS 25TH ANNIVERSARY OUR CHURCH REMEMBERS AND SENDS YOU, DEAR PRINCIPAL, OUR GRATITUDE AND LOVE.

(Signed)   Hunziker.

I now draw attention to the Middle East Tour of 1935, in which we saw remarkable scenes of revival power and blessing amongst Jews and Arabs, with both crowded together in the same meetings. Writing in the Special Palestine—Transjordan Number of the *Elim Evangel* in 1935, under the heading "Ye shall be witnesses unto Me...in Jerusalem," Pastor R.E. Darragh reported:

"This glorious promise was graciously fulfilled every step of the way, God giving many opportunities of service, and contacts were made which brought about grand results...

"Long before the announced time of meeting the halls were packed. Everything was so different from a meeting at home, for in the services were Jews and Arabs of different creeds, members of the Greek Orthodox, Greek Catholic, and Roman Catholic Churches. In all the meetings men were in the majority. What an overwhelming joy it was to see hands raised in every service for salvation! During the meetings in Jerusalem, Haifa, Es Salt, and Amman, hundreds accepted the Lord Jesus as their Saviour. In Es Salt so many hands went up it was impossible to count them; as we looked out of the doors and windows we could see hands raised.

"Before six o'clock in the morning the dear people were waiting outside the house to be prayed for. After the Principal ministered to them we were called to the home of a C.M.S. minister, and there we found his drawing room full of those needing healing, seven of whom were gloriously saved that morning. On the way to the minister's home the people were calling to the Principal: 'Pray for me' — 'Come in my home, and pray for my son' — 'On the house—top my father lies sick; do pray for him.' A woman cries: 'I am losing my sight through carrying heavy weights on my head.' A father beseeches us to pray for his little boy. The same thing takes place on the way back as the people line the sidewalk. No wonder one of the Christian Arabs said to me: 'It's like the days of the Lord Jesus again.'

"We have heard of many healings. A cripple was delivered; a little boy who was paralysed was healed. A young man with rupture had a remarkable deliverance. Other healings were gall stones, kidney trouble, dysentery, and other have felt the touch of the Master that has set them free from pain, making life worth living. One man who had a remarkable healing, discarded his sticks, ran through the city of Amman telling everybody how he was healed and showing himself to many who knew of his sufferings. His testimony stirred those who heard it and some have become believers through it.

"On the whole tour we have found open doors and the people eager to listen to the old story of a Saviour's dying love. We returned to our own beloved land with our hearts full of praise that He fulfilled His Word unto us and made us witnesses unto Him throughout the whole journey."

On this tour of some seven weeks we saw the fulfilment of Bible prophecy in the outstanding developments taking place in Palestine, the British being in occupation then and helping to keep the peace between Jews and Arabs. We also visited Alexandria, Cairo (The Pyramids and the museum housing the fabulous Tutankhamun collection), Petra, the astonishing rose—red city of the East where we had to leave the hire—car and ride in and out on horseback (somthing I found more hazardous than being on the back of a leisurely—walking camel at the Pyramids), Constantinople (Istanbul), Cyprus, Athens, Naples (Vesuvius, Pompeii, Herculanean), and Lebanon (The Cedars, Baalbeck and Beirut).

George Jeffreys had invitations from others countries across the world. I think particularly of U.S.A., India and New Zealand, and indeed plans were afoot for the first two to be accepted. The call of his own country and its spiritual need was ever insistent with him and these plans did not materialise.

I now give his views on an organisation which claims the attention of the old—time Pentecostal Movement of this 20th century, world—wide, and begin by saying:

Having been one of the leading Pentecostal speakers at the first "World Pentecostal Conference" at Zurich, Switzerland, which we attended as members of the British party, in 1947, afterwards established to meet at three—yearly intervals in various countries, it was not to be wondered at that George Jeffreys would be invited as a speaker at what had become known as 'The World Conference of Pentecostal Churches,' held at Toronto, Canada, in 1958. He courteously declined the invitation and gave his reasons for so doing as follows, under the sub—heading "FACING THE FACTS" (*The Pattern,* June, 1958):

"The World Organisation designated 'The World Conference of Pentecostal Churches' has announced its 'Fifth' Conference, to be held from September 14th to 21st, 1958, at Toronto, Canada. Although kindly invited by the officials to be one of the speakers, I have had to decline the invitation because I cannot conscientiously support the Conference as it is at present constituted.

'Speaking the Truth in Love,'

"Bearing in mind these words of the Apostle Paul in Ephesians, chapter 4, verse 15, let me state some of the facts concerning 'The World Conference of Pentecostal Churches':

"(1) It has a false designation, because the Pentecostal Churches of the world have no assured right to elect delegates to represent them at the Conference.

"(2) It is a permanent World Organisation, *having come into existence without the sanction of the Pentecostal Churches.* It has an Advisory Committee, a World Secretarial Office, and the equivalent of an official World Magazine called 'Pentecost.' The members of the Advisory Committee, their Secretary, and the Editor of 'Pentecost' all hold key positions of influence in the Organisation.

"(3) It is a mystery World Organisation, in which groups of free Pentecostal Churches that stand for the Scriptural sovereignty of the local church are herded together with groups of bound Pentecostal Churches whose pastors, people, property and finances are under legalised central control. How the officials can be true to both free and bound groups of

Churches in the one and the same Organisation is indeed a mystery.

"*Now let me sound a warning note:* In view of the foregoing facts, what is to prevent 'The World Conference of Pentecostal Churches' from being stealthily merged into a larger World Organisation *without the sanction of the Pentecostal Churches?* THE SUBTLE TREND IN RELIGIOUS CIRCLES TOWARDS ONE WORLD CHURCH OF ALL KINDS OF DENOMINATIONS AND CHURCHES IS EVIDENT EVERYWHERE, AND IS A GRAVE DANGER WE IGNORE AT OUR PERIL."

With the gathering momentum of the false Ecumenical Movement of the present day such a warning note calls the more urgently for attention.

He then went on to suggest what he called "THE REMEDY," and wrote:

"As it is impossible to convene 'The World Conference of Pentecostal *Churches*' at Toronto on a strictly administrative basis, with delegates duly elected by the Pentecostal Churches of the world, *such as its present designation demands,* this false designation should be changed to 'The World Conference of Pentecostal *People.*' This would bring to an end the permanent World Organisation, with its Advisory Committee, its World Secretarial Office, and its equivalent of an official World Magazine. Pentecostal believers from all groups would then gather together at Toronto, and at subsequent World Conferences, *on a true individual basis;* each World Conference would decide where the next is to be held, the Host making the necessary arrangements; and all Pentecostal magazines would be on an equal footing to freely publish its activities."

It is noteworthy that the officials at Toronto *did* change the name according to their own Resolution:

"RESOLVED that in the interests of advertising convenience and for general expediency, we reduce the name to PENTECOSTAL WORLD CONFERENCE, but that we continue to follow the principle of recognising churches and groups of churches as heretofore."

Principal Jeffreys commented (*The Pattern,* April, 1959):
"This Resolution, our readers will note, disposes of the false designation 'World Conference of Pentecostal Churches', but

73

it perpetuates the same mystery World Organisation of Pentecostal churches and groups of churches under the veiled designation 'Pentecostal World Conference.' Yet it is impossible for free, self—governing churches and those under totalitarian central control to be proportionately represented at such a Conference.

"How much better it would have been had the Advisory Committee at Toronto resolved to change the designation to 'World Conference of Pentecostal *People.*' They would have rendered great service to the Pentecostal churches of the world, by not only disposing of the false designation but in two other ways as well:

"(a) By leaving no room for any veiled designation.

"(b) By establishing the Conference on a true individual basis, so that the members of the Body of Christ from all Pentecostal churches and groups of churches could conscientiously support it."

In the light of Principal George Jeffreys' warning note it is not without significance that the following appeared in the magazine, *Pentecost,* September to November 1961 issue:

"The Editor of *Pentecost* wishes it to be known that he will not be attending the forthcoming third assembly of the World Council of Churches in New Delhi in any capacity whatever.

"The Lord has been baptising in the Holy Spirit many hungry hearts in the historic churches, and there is a widespread desire to know more about the Pentecostal revival. For this reason the courteous invitation to attend New Delhi was welcome and accepted.

"But some large sections of the Pentecostal Movement have very strong conscientious objection to the World Council of Churches on theological grounds. One American leader has said they are 'miles apart.' The fear has been expressed that the presence of a well—known personality within the Pentecostal Movement, who also holds an official position, as an invited observer at New Delhi would be wrongly interpreted. This could be so, and for that reason the Editor of *Pentecost* feels that no other course is open for him but to decline the invitation. He does so with apologies.

"Purely private attendance at meetings of the W.C.C. is a matter for the individual conscience. The Lord has made some contacts very fruitful in the personal sphere, and we trust that

Pentecostal grace and power may be increasingly bestowed throughout all sections of the Church of Jesus Christ to meet the desperate spiritual need of the hour."

My own comment on this as Editor of *The Pattern* was as follows:

"In our Fifth 'Ecumenical' article published in our July Number (1961) we drew attention to the fact that Mr. Donald Gee (Editor of *Pentecost*) hoped to accept the above—mentioned invitation to New Delhi, and also that, according to a report in *The Baptist Times,* Mr. David J. du Plessis (another prominent leader in the Pentecostal Movement and former Secretary of 'The World Conference of Pentecostal Churches') had accepted. We are glad to publish Mr. Gee's statement, as now given in *Pentecost,* and trust that Mr. du Plessis will follow his example and for the same reasons."

As with the larger "Pentecostal World Conference" so with the lesser "British Pentecostal Fellowship," Principal Jeffreys' appeal was consistently the same, that membership should not be established on the recognition of formal Pentecostal organisations and churches but on that of believers from all Pentecostal churches meeting together on a true individual basis as members of the Body of Christ.

That there are significant moves in State Church and Nonconformist circles today towards "ONE WORLD CHURCH," in which the Church of England is playing a leading part in its relations with the Church of Rome, with the year 1988 being an avowed 'get closer together' target, cannot be denied. Rome's interest in the modern Charismatic Movement, capable of being confused with the old—time 20th century Outpouring of the Holy Spirit, makes George Jeffreys' warning note more and more urgent.

In the early 1960s, being fully supportive of George Jeffreys' views, as the reader will have gathered, I wrote a series of articles entitled *The Ecumenical Movement — The False and the True.* These were published in *The Pattern.* In the second one I drew attention to what the Chairman of the Keswick Christian Convention, held annually in England's Lake District, had to say about it, i.e. that the Convention from the beginning had ever been truly ecumenical in character, with the motto, 'All one in Christ Jesus.' I went on to comment:

"A clear lead is here given by the Evangelicals at Keswick to us as Pentecostals emphasising the characteristics of the *true* Ecumenical Movement, viz. the coming together of *believers,* not as formal organisations, but on an individual basis as members of the Body of Christ, having this same glorious motto.

"The centre of unity among true Christians is Christ, The Head of the Church, and Him alone. The World Council of Churches and general trend towards organising a false Ecumenical grouping lead inevitably to that ill—starred centre of unity that has for so long dogged the footsteps of Christendom — Rome! That way leads to substituting a formal visible Church unity for the very office of Christ Himself and is therefore Anti—Christ."

Chapter 6
The Nine Points of
Dr. Lewi Pethrus

I NOW come to the period leading up to Principal George Jeffreys' resignation from the Elim Movement in 1939—1940, followed by the formation of the Bible—Pattern Church Fellowship. Before enlarging on this I would draw attention to the academic thesis contained in the book, *Sects and Society,* By Dr. Bryan R. Wilson, and published in 1961 by William Heinemann, Ltd., with particular reference to the first part on the Elim Movement. A review of this section by the late Commander D.H. Macmillan is given in chapter 8.

We see in this penetrating study a complete vindication of George Jeffreys as the "charismatic leader" of all the phases of this intense Christian Revival, which is made all the more remarkable by the fact that he himself knew nothing of the book until *after* it was published, a few months before his call to higher service on January 26th, 1962. This is borne out by the following letter from Dr. Wilson to Commander Macmillan, which we gratefully publish with the writer's kind permission:

Leeds, 16
7th November, 1961

Dear Commander Macmillan

May I thank you very much for your letter and for the copies of the pamphlet reprint from *The Pattern* with the review of my book. It was very kind of you to send these to me; I had not in fact seen the review, and I am delighted to have it.

As you will see I was attempting to be completely impartial in the studies I pursued, and I am very pleased that you consider that in this my object was achieved. My comments on the humble origins of the early leaders of the movement was not made in any sense of superiority — and, of course, I agree with you entirely that the early Christians themselves appear to have been drawn overwhelmingly from humble stations in life. In its direct scriptural form, Christianity is hardly calculated to appeal to the world's wealthy people.

I think your remarks (in the pamphlet) about the British—Israel controversy are thoroughly judicious. I did not attempt to acquaint myself with the complete British—Israel position, but sought only to discuss the way in which this theory entered into the dispute with Elim. I found it necessary to briefly give the reader some idea of the type of theory about which the dispute was concerned, without wanting to undertake a major departure from my field of study by making too long a diversion into British—Israel exegesis. I have from time to time read articles of your own elucidating particular aspects of the British—Israel position, and I am certainly aware that my own passing references to it were no more than a superficial impression — but this was all which my enquiry demanded at that time.

It is more than likely that I am completely unknown to the various people involved in the Elim schism. I did at one time, in 1953, attempt to make contact with Principal Jeffreys and with Mr. Phillips, but at the time Mr. Jeffreys was busy, and instead of Mr. Phillips I met a young man who had an executive position in Elim, but who was too young to have been involved in any way in the dispute between 1934—40. Subsequently I regarded my failure to make contact as in some way providential — since, although it probably meant that I had less first hand information, it also meant that my study was left without the possibility of undue influence from either side.

If my book is in any way useful in the settlement of the difference among the people involved, I shall certainly be pleased: I had certainly no idea that it would receive such notice from the people concerned when I wrote it.

With kindest regards.

Yours sincerely,

(Signed)   Bryan Wilson.

The publishers of *Sects and Society* state that Dr. Wilson, then Professor of Sociology at Leeds University, has "lived for a long period with each sect (the three dealt with in his book), accepting its discipline and its pattern of behaviour. The result is a first—hand study of concern to all who are interested in religion, sociology, politics or psychology." With my own intimate knowledge of Elim and of the division in the Movement, I have found Dr. Wilson's meticulous presentation and documentation of absorbing interest, as did Principal Jeffreys. It is noteworthy that the Principal always had before him the reality of the Universal Church and was in no way a sectarian.

In 1983, and more recently in 1986, I had correspondence with Dr. Bryan Wilson, now of All Souls College, Oxford, and engaged in compiling for Macmillian, the Publishers, *A Dictionary of Minority Religious and Spiritual Movements in Britain*, a work he hopes would become a standard reference work for scholars, the Press, and the interested public. He kindly alluded to my book entitled *George Jeffreys — Man of God,* and sought information about the World Revival Crusade which I supplied.

George Jeffreys' serious illness of 1937, when so heavily burdened over the work in Elim, left its mark upon him, yet the occasions when a substitute had to take his place in his announced meetings were rare indeed. This in itself is a tribute to God's gracious care of His servant throughout the long years of his ministry.

He has movingly written of the remarkable experience he had at that critical period in his life, of foreseeing something of the hard and difficult road he would have to travel in his efforts to reform Elim's rigid central system of government: of the mis—representations, the half—truths, coupled with the undermining of his influence, which appears to be the lot of all true reformers. Those of us who have been with him in the struggle have seen these things come to pass. I give it in his own words:

"Nothing less than the sudden illness of Pastor E.J. Phillips, the Secretary—General of the Elim Movement, followed so soon by my own sudden illness in 1937, could have given the shock that was necessary to stop the machinery of the Elim organisation.

"Out in the evangelistic field God was certainly blessing my ministry with the Revival Party, and we were experiencing one long trail of revival triumph. Wherever we went cities and towns were falling before our Foursquare Gospel Message; multitudes were weeping their way to the Cross; regular church congregations were being established; students were continually entering the College, to be trained for the ministry; abundant literature was coming forth from the printing and publishing works; church buildings and manses were being acquired throughout the country; and new sources of finance were being opened up for the Movement as a result of our campaigns.

"In the Elim Headquarters' Offices Pastor E.J. Phillips was giving full time and much energy to the multifarious duties of the ever—expanding organisation, and one felt that as long as he was there all was well.

"Though one was on the evangelistic field and the other in the Offices, it seemed that as long as we two were united in purpose nothing could stand against us. No one inside the Headquarters' Offices or on the campaign field could offer effective resistance to our plans.

"Then came the sudden illness of the Secretary—General followed closely by mine, and I believe that under the circumstances it had to be, in order to bring about the opportunity for an exacting examination of ourselves and the rapidly growing organisation.

"In my illness I had an experience which revealed the things I would have to suffer in the oncoming struggle to free the churches from the legal system that had bound them and which had made it impossible for them to obey the Word of God. There was the cunning misrepresentation, the half—truth propaganda, and the delusive reasonings of those who would seek to undermine my influence and even try to blot out my name as founder and builder of Elim. The dangers of the system were many, and what I saw made me determined, regardless of cost, to reform it or to renounce it and to deliver as many churches as possible from its Babylonish bondage.

"To fully explain the experience I had would be difficult; all I can say is, 'whether in the body or out of the body I cannot tell.' It seemed as if the Elim organisation was judged before the bar of God and condemned. That experience showed me how very wrong it was to be a leading governor in a legal clique of clerical governors over Elim pastors, people and property. I was only too glad to get back to the Bible for church government, in which there were no legal central governors!

"Nine years have passed since that remarkable experience, and strange though it may seem to some, many of the things and much of the suffering that was foreshadowed in it for my future have actually come to pass.

"Within the secret constitutional walls of the Elim Executive Council, the Governing Body, I had also heard the command, 'Set your house in order,' and regardless of consequences, my one desire was to live to reform the Movement. God, I believe, raised me up from the gates of death to witness against all such systems, and to warn students, pastors and churches of their subtle dangers.

"If, after our illnesses, the Secretary—General had stood with me for the reform policy, things would have been different. We would have been as powerful a combination in reforming the system as we were in building it up. But Pastor E.J. Phillips came back determined to fight with legal weapons for a continuation of the system, whereas I could do no other than return to fight with the Word of God against the system."

With reforming zeal in heart, mind and labour, ever seeking the way ahead, came the practical challenge to George Jeffreys in 1939 of the Pentecostal Movement in Sweden, comprising hundreds of Pentecostal churches with their decided stand against any central organisation over their churches in the Movement. As the well—known British Pentecostal writer, Donald Gee, pointed out some years ago, they hold a regular weekly church meeting, exclusively for members only, and he added: "In this lies their greatest strength."

Pastor Lewi Pethrus became the Pastor of the Filadelfia Church in Stockholm on January 8th, 1911. This Church was founded as the seventh Baptist Church of Stockholm on August 30th, 1910, by 29 believers from different Baptist churches. Lewi Pethrus was their first regular pastor. In 1913, he was, together with his church in Stockholm, excluded from the Swedish Baptist Convention because his church practised open Communion for all who had been baptised as believers, besides by then being fully Pentecostal.

In June, 1939, just a few short weeks before the Second World War, Pastor Pethrus and the Filadelfia Church, now with its adult membership of thousands housed in a beautiful building seating thousands, organised the greatly—blessed European Pentecostal Conference.

This Conference in Sweden, of which Pastor Pethrus was the Chairman, saw a gathering of Pentecostal people from twenty—one European countries, including those of us from the

British Isles in Elim, Assemblies of God, etc., all brought together *on an individual basis.* It was therefore truly ecumenical in character, as is the annual Keswick Christian Convention in our own country. It included ministers and other brethren from centrally—governed Pentecostal churches, as well as those locally—governed, and "Church Government" was one of the main subjects under deep discussion.

Principal Jeffreys was one of the speakers at the Conference sessions held daily in the fine Stockholm Filadelfia Church. The measure of his evangelistic stature can be seen, however, in the fact that he was the only speaker chosen, out of the many present, to preach the Gospel each night to the thousands gathered in the three great Tents erected as one on the Military Parade grounds in the city. Again, on the Sunday morning, he was the speaker at the communion service in the Tents attended by Prince Bernadotte, the King of Sweden's Christian brother, and his Princess wife.

At the end of this soul—stirring Conference we visited the well—appointed and beautifully situated "Kaggeholms" on the lakeside, the Swedish Pentecostal Free Churches Bible School, after which Lewi Pethrus took George Jeffreys further afield to see other aspects of the Swedish Pentecostal work, *the emphasis ever being on local ownership and control of church and house properties, church funds, administration, and support of its own ministry and missionary efforts.*

Later, *Redemption Tidings,* official organ of Assemblies of God in Great Britain and Ireland, published a summary by Donald Gee of what Lewi Pethrus had to say on the subject of "Church Government" under 1 to 9, as follows:

"1. Brother Pethrus introduced the subject by stating that it is obvious that in any society like the Church there must be some organisation. The question is — of what kind?

"2. In answer to this we can take as our model *(a) The New Testament, (b)* Other existing denominations, *(c)* Examples from history.

"3. It is a fact that Pentecostal people accept the New Testament wholeheartedly for their doctrine concerning the Baptism of the Holy Spirit, and for the Gifts of the Spirit, and believe that it contains all we need of revelation of God's will on those matters. It would therefore appear very illogical and dangerous to take the position that the New Testament contains no revelation for us as to essential organisation for our Assemblies.

"4. Accepting the New Testament as our guide it is clear that it contained nothing about highly organised Missionary Societies, or Central Boards of Government for the Assemblies. It was affirmed by Brother Pethrus that the Scriptures reveal no organisation beyond the Local Assembly.

"5. Our brother then dealt with the matter of definite Church Membership in the Local Assembly, especially quoting Gal. 2:4. He made a helpful distinction between *invisible* membership of the Church of God, and a *visible* membership of the Church before men. The former was all that we required for purely personal salvation and spiritual fellowship; but the latter was needed for our collective testimony before the world, and for properly ordered ministry and necessary discipline as a body. He described the Local Assembly as of 'indescribable importance', and stated that it is the one all—essential unit of the Church's corporate life and testimony.

"6. Coming to details, it was made clear that the Local Assembly should own its own buildings, should support its own ministry, and send out its own missionaries. Testimony was given as to the success of the last point in Sweden, seeing the Pentecostal friends there now support 233 missionaries, whereas the next largest Swedish missionary body only numbers 185 missionaries.

"7. Turning to the claim that organisation will create unity, Brother Pethrus spoke very strong words to the effect that in actual experience it was proved that organisation beyond the Local Assemblies only destroyed unity. He spoke movingly of their experiences on this line in Sweden.

"8. Referring to the subject of Leadership, he said that history proves that God, not men, chooses leaders for Revivals, and instanced such cases as Wesley and Booth. In picturesque language he described how God—appointed leaders always come floating upon the river of Revival. In solemn language he warned the Conference that it is at the point where men elect leaders of their own choice that the Holy Spirit withdraws from any Revival. We can always recognise God's leaders, because of their spiritual gifts and ministry.

"9. Lastly, Brother Pethrus dealt with the claim that

denominational organisation helped the Pentecostal Revival before governments, and he repudiated any such suggestion. He considered from experience on this point that all that the governments looked for was dependable people whom they could trust, and that in moments of grave national crisis all respect for mere denominational organisation was swept away in any case. As evidence of the confidence that Pentecostal people could win from the authorities through well—governed local assemblies, free from fanaticism, he showed the marked friendliness of the city of Stockholm to the present Conference. Personal contacts with Ministers of State accomplished more than any other method to smooth away difficulties."

In connection with this last point, the civic authorities had all the flags of the nations represented at the Conference, i.e. Sweden, Norway, Denmark, Finland, Holland, Britain, France, Germany, and the other thirteen, flying outside the main Stockholm railway station.

As to point 5, the Scripture referred to by Pastor Pethrus in Gal. 2:4 was obviously given as a warning against those who would attempt to exercise an unscriptural control in the local church.

Then regarding point 6, it should be noted, as I wrote in 1964, that the Swedish Pentecostal Churches then had more than 450 missionaries in twenty—three fields. (I give the latest statistics of this and the work in general towards the end of this chapter).

I went on to comment: The fact that the Bible—Pattern Church Fellowship of the British Isles is a duly recognised denomination in no way interferes with the Scriptural sovereignty of each local church, based on Christ's Charter for His Churches in Matthew 18, verses 15 to 20. In all matters relating to the control of each local church, its property and finance, the registered members are the governing body, whereas the Advisory Committee, which is elected every three years by the members of the Churches as a whole, deals with matters appertaining to the Fellowship in general.

Whatever the shortcomings of the Advisory Committee members have been since, these seven Fundamentals are embodied in the Constitution of the Bible—Pattern Church Fellowship, the Local Church Constitution, the Declaration of Trust, and the Model Trust Deed:

(1) The whole Bible as the Inspired Word of God.
(2) The Tri—Unity of the Godhead, Father, Son and Holy Ghost.
(3) The Moral and Physical Depravity of Human Nature.
(4) Full Salvation through the Death and Resurrection of the Lord Jesus Christ.
(5) The Lord Jesus Christ as Saviour, Healer, Baptiser and Coming King.
(6) The Faith, with Miraculous Signs following, according to Mark 16:15—18.
(7) Government of the Local Church Members, by the Church Members, for the Church Members.

It is No. 7 which so exercised and challenged George Jeffreys from the Scriptures, in keeping with what he believed to be God's command, "Set your house in order," and which caused such a furore at Elim Headquarters and amongst the Elim Foursquare Gospel Alliance ministers.

He has himself written of that European Pentecostal Conference in Sweden:

"The sum and substance of the reason for my resignation from Elim on December 1st, 1939, was the refusal of the majority of my fellow—governors in the Executive Council to move with me towards *establishing the sovereignty of the local church in all Elim Foursquare Gospel Alliance Churches.* Earlier that year the great European Pentecostal Conference at Stockholm and what I saw of the Swedish Pentecostal work, helped to open my eyes to this vital truth.

"In 1940 I called a conference of Elim Ministers and Church Officers who shared my conviction. At this gathering the Bible—Pattern Church Fellowship was founded on the basis of the sovereignty of the local church."

The foregoing is from an article entitled "ELIM — 'Then and Now,'" written in 1956. In the same article Principal George Jeffreys stated:

"It was 'Then' — back in 1915 — that we in Elim made the big mistake that shaped the destiny of the Movement. *We did not establish the Scriptural sovereignty of the local church in the first Elim Church.* This mistake was repeated every time a new church was added to the Movement through our pioneer campaigns, consequently the Elim Churches had no assured voice in anything and came under centralised control.

"In 1934 nine leading Elim Ministers, including Mr. Phillips (Elim's Secretary—General) and myself, were so blind to the sovereignty of the local church that we legally entrenched ourselves by Deed Poll in an all—powerful Elim Executive Council, having complete control over the Elim Foursquare Gospel Alliance Church people, pastors, property and income throughout the country. This was done without consulting the Churches. *Had the sovereignty of the local church been established in Elim Churches from the beginning, the Movement could not have possibly developed along these Babylonish lines.*

"Nevertheless, in spite of our blindness, God did not cease to make us fishers of men. He did not withdraw the evangelistic gift from us. He did not allow love for the lost and perishing to wane in our hearts. Our Revival Party Campaigns continued to be demonstrations of Holy Ghost power throughout the country. Multitudes continued to turn to the Lord for salvation, to pass through the waters of baptism, and to gather at gigantic communion services. Mighty healings, signs and wonders still confirmed the preached Word. New churches were being founded all the time through our pioneering campaigns, and students continued to pass through our Bible College into the regular work of the ministry in our every—growing Elim Movement.

"The volumes of Elim periodicals, and books that have recorded the history of our twenty—five years' vigorous pioneering ministry are a lasting testimony to what was achieved.

"It is not to be wondered at that people sometimes argue: Seeing God so mightily blessed your ministry throughout the years in Elim, does it not show that He attaches little importance to the question of church government? To this I reply: God blessed us in Elim in spite of our blindness in this matter. I have come to see, however, that the Scriptural sovereignty of the local church is of paramount importance. *Christ is not only the Saviour of sinners, He is also the Architect of His Churches.*"

On August 15th, 1960, he addressed the following letter to Dr. Lewi Pethrus who had retired from the Filadelfia Church Pastorate in 1958:

"Our beloved Brother in Christ,

"I understand that the Filadelfia Church at Stockholm is celebrating its Golden Jubilee this month. I send you, Pastor Willis Säwe, the Church Officers and members my Christian love and greetings, praying God's abundant blessing upon you at this very special season and in the days to come.

"I shall always be grateful for the invitation to the ever—memorable European Pentecostal Conference in Stockholm in June, 1939, as convened by yourself and the Filadelfia Church. It was this visit to Sweden that convinced me that the centralised system of church government in my own Elim Movement was not in accordance with the New Testament pattern for the churches.

"By today I am thankful that I am a minister of the Bible—Pattern Church Fellowship of the British Isles which recognises, as you do, the Scriptural sovereignty of each local church.

"We can indeed say of you and the local churches of the great Swedish Pentecostal work what the Apostle Paul said of the Church at Thessalonica: 'For from you sounded out the word of the Lord not only in Macedonia and Achaia, but also in every place your faith to God—ward is spread abroad; so that we need not to speak any thing' (1 Thessalonians 1:8).

"With heartfelt praise to God for the Scriptural example set by the Swedish Pentecostal work to the Pentecostal Movement of the world as a whole, from 1910 to 1960, and again assuring you of my earnest prayers for His richest blessing upon you all,

> *Yours,*
> *A servant of Jesus Christ,*
> *(Signed) George Jeffreys"*

It was Lewi Pethrus, having their own Swedish free—church work in mind and in thinking of what might have been accomplished in and through Elim, who said to him that he had been "putting his results in a bag with holes."

The friendship between these two remarkable servants of the Lord over many years was based on a mutual respect, and Dr. Pethrus invariably stayed with Principal Jeffreys when visiting London. He was a man of many parts, living to the age of 90. He launched numerous enterprises including 'The Ark,' a refuge for the destitute and deprived, on the waterfront which we visited in

1947 in company with Lewi Pethrus when George Jeffreys was again in Stockholm ministering at the great annual Summer Bible School meetings.

Lewi Pethrus started the Filadelfia Publishing House in 1912, being himself a prolific writer as well as a gifted musician. In 1945 he founded *Dagen,* a Christian daily newspaper, of which he was editor—in—chief until his death in 1974. He was the leading figure in the setting up of I.B.R.A. Radio, the Swedish radio work, which transmits the Gospel in many languages to many countries. He also saw that a Banking institution was established for the needs of the Pentecostal work in Sweden.

In response to my enquiry about the Swedish Pentecostal work I had these statistics kindly given to me in September, 1987, by the Secretary to the senior Pastor of the Filadelfia Church, Stockholm:

There are 852 missionaries working in 49 countries.

The Filadelfia Church in Stockholm is still the largest with 6,887 members.

The largest of the Pentecostal Churches have regular weekly church meetings, exclusively for members only, but most of the churches have this church meeting once a month.

There are today 527 Pentecostal Churches in Sweden with together 100,674 members.

This great united Pentecostal work has gone on from strength to strength in Sweden over the years, with its relatively small population compared with ours in the British Isles. It is grievous to think that the message as given to George Jeffreys, and as embodied in Lewi Pethrus's 'Nine Points,' was rejected as it was. Its acceptance could have led to an even greater united Pentecostal work in our own country by today. Instead, we still have the divisions in Pentecost, with their differing views on 'Church Government' and consequently no strong united vision and purpose so needed in our day and generation.

Another valued friendship was that with Pastor T.B. Barratt, of Great Britain, who became the outstanding Pentecostal pioneer in Norway. He also renounced central control and took a strong stand for the Scriptural sovereignty of each local church. Today's splendid Pentecostal work in Norway, with its many churches and missionary enterprise in foreign lands, is a lasting tribute to him and those who have his vision. When writing to George Jeffreys in July, 1947, Mrs. Barratt paid him this tribute: "I know the Lord has led you through many deeps, from light to light, and you have been willing to follow on."

Pastor Barratt, whom I remember ministering in Elim in the late 1920s, was born in Cornwall, England, and was closely associated with the Pentecostal Movement world—wide from its early days this century, being in touch with Evan Roberts, Canon Alexander Boddy, W.J. Seymour, of the Azusa Street Mission, Los Angeles, and others of those years. He had this distinction: University Professors would send their students to his fine Pentecostal Church in Oslo to hear him preach in Norwegian. A pupil of Grieg, he became an excellent pianist himself, as well as composer, and was often to be heard improvising on the piano as the people gathered for his church services. A letter to Pastor Barratt from Grieg, after his decision to become a minister of the Gospel, reads:

Troldhaugen,
12th September, 1885

"Bedste Hr. Barratt (My best Mr. Barratt),
"In answer to your letter, allow me to send you my warmest wishes for your future. May the position you now have chosen be the means of making you and others happy.
"With friendly greetings,
"Yours respectfully,
(Signed)   Edvard Grieg."

The last time we saw T.B. Barratt was at the European Pentecostal Conference of June, 1939. Norway was over—run by the German Army in 1940 but not before he had passed on to his eternal reward, January 29th, 1940, aged 77 years. Some seven years later, together with George Jeffreys, we stood at his grave in Oslo, a granite stone effigy of him clasping an open Bible to his chest.

Both Lewi Pethrus and T.B. Barratt, in their own spheres of service and countries, heard the equivalent of the call "Set your house in order," according to the Scriptures, and despite opposing forces lived to see their efforts crowned with success, one reason being, that unlike Britain, the Scandinavian countries are not hide—bound to any great degree by organised religion.

As Noel Brooks rightly states in his book *Fight for the Faith and Freedom,* published by the Pattern Bookroom in 1948: "Elim's Founder and Leader came back from the valley of the shadow (1938) with that command ineffaceably impressed upon his consciousness. However others would appraise it, to him it was a Divine Imperative. It was a new 'heavenly vision' and he vowed tio obey it as implicity as he did his vision of former years. Henceforth he was not only to be a Revivalist, but a Reformer also."

He continues: "It must not be assumed that George Jeffreys fathomed the full significance of his new vision all at once, and that he came back to health with a comprehensive plan of campaign. In his spirit he knew that the command meant Democratic Reform, but how radical God wished it to be he had not yet perceived. Paul was to spend three years in the solitudes of Arabia learning the full implications of the vision he had seen and the voice he had heard. But he did not tarry until all was clear before he went to work: 'Straightway he preached Christ in the synagogues, that He is the Son of God.' George Jeffreys, Reformer, likewise went to work 'straightway,' obediently seeking to 'set his house in order'; and amidst the heats of dispute and the ruptures of friendship that ensued, his vision took shape, and God's real plan became evident in all its radical simplicity."

This, taken together with being torn between the love he had for the Elim Movement and that of God's command, explains his prolonged endeavours in seeking to conscientiously resolve the situation before and after December 1st, 1939. But he was faced with strong opposing factions within the limited confines of, first, the ministers only, then of ministers and laymen, with the churches in ignorance of the situation. Other considerations were his personal position in the Movement, his responsible trusteeship of much church and house property held in trust in the *interests of the Elim Alliance,* and, not least, the respect of the thousands he had won for Christ who highly esteemed him for his work's sake.

Yet the forces arrayed against his righteous message of reform were such, that Dr. Bryan Wilson could shrewdly observe in *Sects and Society,* pp.49, "...the concentration of power in the hands of the Secretary—General, who had the normal channels of distribution and transmission of information at his disposal, made it increasingly apparent that the leader had little chance of carrying through the reformist ideals which now inspired him."

The 'channels' or 'agents' of Elim Headquarters in the churches were the ministers, thus the churches in general were not made aware of what he was striving for *in their interests*. There are people I know well today who have told me that their Elim Church was deprived of the information they should have had, even to the tearing up of pamphlets sent to enlighten them. These circumstances, coupled with the interrupting of his public meetings, designed to prevent free speech (at each of which I was present), is indicative of the bitter prejudice manifested.

Chapter 7
Resignation from Elim

I CANNOT avoid dealing with *The Great Evangelists,* a book noticeable for important omissions in connection with the above, if I am to put the facts on record. In it Desmond Cartwright portrays George Jeffreys as seeking to "impose" the Lewi Pethrus form of church government in Britain, even in "trying to thrust the Swedish pattern on the Elim work (which) had disastrous consequences" (page 158). *No mention, mark you, of what Lewi Pethrus stood for, as clearly embodied in the Nine Points to which I have drawn attention in the previous chapter.* Undoubtedly George Jeffreys came to see the Biblical Pattern after what had transpired in Sweden and through his personal study of the Scriptures, gradual in its unfolding as it was. As the Founder of Elim he had every right to try to bring about what he believed were much needed reforms in the Movement. One can very well lay Mr. Cartwright's charge of "disastrous consequences" at the door, not of George Jeffreys, but of those who rejected, not just the "Swedish" pattern but the "Biblical" pattern!

Desmond Cartwright goes on about this issue: "There were many other factors that had to be considered, not only biblical, but sociological and even psychological." I suggest that this is a dangerous doctrine *seeing that the Swedish Pentecostal people possess and believe the same Bible as we Britishers possess and believe.* Such a doctrine, with its sociological and psychological nonsense in this context, if propagated in Elim, will be more "disastrous" than what George Jeffreys discovered through the Scriptures, as well as being a pretty poor justification for Elim's rejection of its Founder and his beliefs.

In 1985, before Mr. Cartwright's book was published, Pastor D.J. Green, of the Elim Executive Council, gave a glowing account in the *Elim Evangel* of what he had lately seen of the great Pentecostal work in Sweden. I wrote him on July 1st: "What you yourself have seen in 1985 of the Swedish Pentecostal work we saw 46 years ago, a solid Scriptural foundation having been laid by Pastor Lewi Pethrus and the Filadelfia Church in Stockholm in

92

1910...Now that you have seen something of this for yourself in Sweden, and your new—found zeal, should make you deplore these lost years when things could have been so different in Pentecost in our own country."

That *The Great Evangelists* gives a false picture of the life and ministry of George Jeffreys in resigning on December 1st, 1939 from the Elim Movement, and that of the months and years following, cannot be denied. Mr. Cartwright was not there in 1939, and did not come into the Christian experience until some 10 years later, yet as a historian he chooses what he wishes to include or omit in justification of Elim's opposition to the Founder's agonising struggle for reform. But even Mr. Cartwright has to concede of the report sent out to the ministers by Elim Headquarters after the 1939 Conference, that it was "not strictly honest" (page 155,), viz.

"Principal George Jeffreys, who for some time has intimated his desire along these lines, has resigned from the Executive Council, and is thus released from the business side of the work. This will free him more fully for his spiritual ministry in the work of the Lord, which God has so signally blessed in the past."

Mr. Cartwright then goes on himself to state the half-truth, "The Principal had resigned as a minister, and, consequently he was no longer a member of the (Executive) Council." The whole truth being, he was out of the Elim Movement entirely, not only as a minister and member of the Elim Executive Council, but as Elim's President and Principal of the Bible College, and as a member of the several other boards on which he served. I had typed out for him his notice of resignation from each, and he handed these to the ministers in charge of the respective departments, after which he knelt down and prayed for the ministers and the Movement before leaving the Conference hall, for me to drive him back to our home at Clapham.

Shortly after, Pastor W.G. Hathaway, of the Elim Executive Council, brought him two resolutions which had been passed by the ministers as soon as he had left the Conference:

"RESOLVED that this Ministerial Conference of the Elim Foursquare Gospel Alliance, on learning of the resignation of its President, Principal George Jeffreys, wishes to place on record its deep and heartfelt gratitude to him, under God, for his untiring and loyal service to the cause of Christ during the twenty-five years of his labours as Founder and Leader of the Alliance."

"RESOLVED that the Ministerial Conference wishes to record its earnest desire that Principal George Jeffreys should forthwith accept office as Moderator or Spiritual Leader of the Alliance and remain Principal of the Elim Bible College."

Two Resolutions which testify in no uncertain way to George Jeffreys' honourable life and ministry to say the least.

Whilst being grateful for these, he intimated he was unable to accept office again in the Elim Foursquare Gospel Alliance unless radical changes were made, the reasons for his resignation being given and issued in December, 1939, under the heading *Why I resigned from the Elim Movement:*

"(1)   Because the Ministerial Conference had made the possibility of the local churches electing lay representatives on the Governing Body and on the District Presbyteries, on a fifty—fifty basis with ministers, so remote.

"(2)   Because the local churches have no Title Deeds or Model Trust Deeds to give them control over the church property they have paid for, over assembly procedure in the churches, or over the finance that is handled in the churches.

"(3)   Because the churches in Ireland are to be allowed Elders or Deacons or both in each church, while the churches in England, Scotland and Wales are to be allowed Deacons only.

"(4)   Because I could not be bound by a resolution which prohibited me from writing a circular letter to the Elim churches, or printing anything that would make an effective protest against the Elim Alliance Constitution, should I ever consider such to be necessary."

In his introduction to the foregoing we see the measure of the man in wanting to deal with policy and not personalities. He wrote: "The story I have to tell is simple and you will find nothing of a personal nature in my explanation, for I have no quarrel with anyone. I trust no person shall be able to say that I have taken advantage of my position to prejudice the situation or cloud the vital issues."

He concluded: "God had graciously blessed the Elim work throughout the years, but the time is overdue for a more

94

democratic Elim. My one regret is that from the commencement of the work I did not establish churches more in keeping with the revealed New Testament pattern, under a more balanced oversight of ministers and qualified lay brethren from the churches."

His attitude is borne out by the late Principal P.G. Parker, who testified: "It was my privilege to be in closest consultation with Principal Jeffreys during the whole trying period of the 1939 Conference. The circumstances were extraordinarily difficult, but not once did I hear him utter a word of personal bitterness against anyone. His constant attitude was that we must maintain a Christlike spirit whatever happens — that we must fight for policy but have no personal bitterness."

"A REPLY" was issued to George Jeffreys' pamphlet in the same month of December by the Executive Council of the Elim Foursquare Gospel Alliance, supporting the Deed Poll, as set up in April, 1934, by which they held their autocratic central government authority over the affairs of the Movement, as still being in the best interests of the work.

So the months passed, with the 'battle' still joined, and with attempts made to resolve the situation, until in May, 1940, the Elim Conference, now consisting of ministers and laymen, saw him accepting the office of President of the Elim Church Incorporated, an honorary title with scarcely any authority or responsibility, in his earnest desire to achieve unity. It should be stated that the Elim Church Incorporated is a "Fellowship of Pentecostal churches each having its own form of government within the broad lines of the Constitution," which sounds reasonable enough, until one realises that by far the largest and most powerful section in it is that of the Elim Foursquare Gospel Alliance!

None of this is referred to by Mr. Cartwright as he nears the end of his book, apart from a brief reference to the two Resolutions and with only a mention of the *headings* of the Principal's pamphlet *Why I resigned from the Elim Movement* and that of *A Reply,* followed by a garbled account of the facts, which is why George Jeffreys' second letter of resignation dated November 12th, 1940, addressed to the Elim Executive Council is not mentioned either. He wrote:

"It is nearly six months since I accepted the overwhelming invitation at the May Conference (1940) to become President and I have conscientiously worked hard to bring about unity in the Elim Alliance, as the churches that are in touch with me will testify, but the task is becoming increasingly difficult under present conditions.

"It is nearly twelve months since I resigned from the largest and most powerful section in the Elim Church Incorporated, namely, the Elim Foursquare Gospel Alliance, and conditions are practically the same in the Alliance today as they were then...

"There is no safeguard against a small Governing Body exercising powerful legal control over the Ministers, Churches, Diaconates, District Presbyteries, Church Buildings, House Properties, Publishing Company, Bible College, Finance and Propaganda of the Alliance throughout the British Isles.

"There is no freedom of expression on Church Government or Church Reform without running the risk of being regarded as an agitator or a disturber of the peace."

Later, in analysing the revised Constitution of the Elim Alliance, of 1942, George Jeffreys referred to it as a "Make-Believe Constitution," and wrote: "If anything, this amended Constitution is worse than the original, because it can lead so many to believe that they have many assured rights in the government of the Movement, whereas in reality they have few, if any." He went into much detail to show that the *laymen half* of the Elim Conference is denied certain vital legal rights assured the ministerial half, so that the latter is a *separate* Governing Body, and commented: "In view of these facts no honest person can maintain that the ministers, congregations and properties of the Elim Movement throughout the British Isles are governed by a joint Conference of Ministers and Laymen on a fifty—fifty basis." I bring this up to date by saying Mr. Cartwright does not deny this. In fact he chooses not to go into it, which is surprising, seeing it is a vitally important part of the Elim work.

The revised Elim Constitution of 14th January, 1942, which defines the Conference as consisting of a "Representative Session" (Ministers and Laymen) and a "Ministerial Session" (Ministers only), also states:

"The Governing Body of the Alliance shall be the Conference constituted and meeting at least annually as hereinafter provided with the Executive Council as its instrument for giving effect to the decisions of the Conference and for administrative purposes."

The Conference, it is claimed, having been the final authority since 1942, it is therefore the duty of the Council to carry out the wishes and directions of the Conference. Good enough, one may think, on the surface, even allowing for a Conference which meets once every twelve months, leaving the Executive Council to direct the denomination during the other fifty-one weeks. But with such power in the hands of this small hierarchy at Headquarters, and with the *ministerial half* having a *separate* session in the Conference from which *the laymen are excluded,* there is inevitably the danger under such a class system of a block vote carrying the day on an issue in the Conference as a whole. To say therefore that the Conference as the Governing Body consists of Ministers and Laymen on a fifty—fifty basis, whilst being an admission that the former rigid system of central government needed reforming, is still palpably untrue as pointed out by George Jeffreys many years ago in his day.

Reverting to another of Mr. Cartwright's omissions, viz. the Elim Conference of September, 1941, concerned with the 'disfellowshipping' of its Founder, it had also resolved "during which Bibles were open and many scriptures quoted," we are officially told, "it is not contrary to the Scriptures for Trustees to take legal proceedings where necessary to protect the interests of charities, and it approves of the Executive Council taking such proceedings at its discretion in order (1) to enforce the relinquishing by Mr. George Jeffreys of his trusteeship of Elim properties, and (2) to prevent certain Elim Church buildings being used for purposes other than those of the Elim Foursquare Gospel Alliance." No mention that "Mr." Jeffreys should be properly indemnified. Most of these properties had been procured through his God-blessed ministry, with doors having been opened for many to enter the regular Elim ministry, plus offices for the services of paid officials being created at Elim H/Q.

Following this, the Portsmouth Church was arbitrarily taken over without warning on "Pearl Harbour" Sunday, December 7th, 1941, not by the instituting of legal proceedings, as threatened in the Conference of three months before but with *Elim H/Q taking the law in their own hands* and thereby forcing the minister and congregation to the road, as I have shown in my

Open Letter. Subsequently, the congregations at Southampton, Nottingham and Barking in London's East End were also forced out of their church buildings. Noel Brooks, in his book *Fight for the Faith and Freedom,* made these pungent comments on the lamentable situation:

"It is grievous that Christian men and women should be compelled to leave the place of cherished memories and sacred associations, purchased by their own love-gifts, and be made to search for 'rooms' in a blitzed city and to save once more in order to build anew. The claim that, because an invitation was extended to the people to stay under Elim auspices, the church was not forced out, is puerile. How could people honestly be driven out as a community and welcomed back as individuals? Was not the conviction of the community the sum of the consciences of the individuals?

"Moreover, these churches were not heretical, neither from the Christian faith nor from the Elim Fundamentals. They were evangelical Christians giving allegiance to exactly the same creed as the Elim Alliance. This one thing they claimed, the right to a voice in the control of their own church affairs. For this one thing they must suffer the loss of property.

"If we put the best possible construction upon the matter by admitting that the Elim Governors had no choice but to act thus because of their Trust obligations, it only confirms what we have been saying continually in this book — viz., that despotism is implicit in all clerical central control. If a system is such that the sincere men who rule it have no option but to perform actions so out of harmony with the gracious spirit and principles of the New Testament, what a menacing thing that system must be! If insincere men should rule it what depths of tyranny may not be the issue? At any rate the incidents serve to show that systems of clerical central control in Great Britain still possess at least one effective weapon with which to punish dissent — they have the legal power to make dissenting pastors and congregations forfeit church property."

Under the heading "A JUST SETTLEMENT" Mr. Brooks shows that the secessional churches were prepared for such a settlement of the controversy under "Four safeguards for the Movement as a whole" and "Four safeguards for our church," as outlined which, as he goes on to state, "proved unacceptable to the Elim Governors."

In June, 1942, George Jeffreys addressed a statement in leaflet form to "The Diaconate and Congregation, c/o The Church Secretary" of every Elim Alliance Church in the country, as follows:

"I hereby give twelve months' notice, as from July 1st, 1942, that, with the exception of any Church whose congregation passes a Resolution requesting me not to sign over their Church property, I will relinquish my Trusteeship of Elim Alliance Church and house property at the expiration of that period in favour of the Elim Trust Corporation, provided of course that cost of transfers is paid and that I am fully indemnified against all liability and financial commitments."

Either this conscientious notice of intention was withheld in concealment of the facts, or else it was ignored. Sufficient to say that he published the long lists of the properties involved in this operation in *The Pattern* of mid-April, 1944, under the heading "SIGNING OVER" He wrote by way of Introduction:

"After careful and prolonged negotiations with Elim Headquarters, my solicitors expect soon to secure a satisfactory Indemnity, and to be ready to advise me to sign the various legal documents. By this signing over of the Elim properties to the Elim Trust Corporation I am severing the remaining legal links between myself and the Churches I founded throughout Elim.

"The signing over will be done with mixed feelings of gladness and sadness. Gladness, because I shall be released from a legal position I have disliked intensely; that of being a Trustee of many Elim Churches and houses so completely under the legal control of the Elim Governors. Sadness, because the Elim people who have paid for the Church buildings, out of hard-earned incomes, are not to have any assured right to worship God freely in those buildings..."

The matter was completed on August 29th, 1944.

George Jeffreys would say: if the Romish system is a government *of* the people, *by* the priests, *for* the Vatican, such is the case in certain Protestant circles, viz. a government *of* the people, *by* the ministers, *for* the central dictatorship. Who is to say that this is not the case? When writing in 1943 he expressed it like this:

"The Pagan Babylonish form of central government soon

99

found its way into the Christian Church, and it has more or less remained in different sections of the Church to this our day. It is a government OF the people, BY the priests, FOR a central dictatorship, a system that is against the rights and liberties of the people.

"The Biblical Pattern for the Christian Church is a government OF the people, BY the people, FOR the people, a system that protects the rights and liberties of the people.

"When as Leader of the Elim Movement I was faced during latter years with the vital question: 'Is the Elim system of church government Biblical or Babylonish?' I concluded that it was more Babylonish than Biblical."

The matter of "SIGNING OVER" was in the much wider context of Elim church and house properties in general, but together with other Bible-Pattern ministers at the time of Principal Jeffreys' death in 1962, I stood by the Bible—Pattern Churches worshipping in three special trustee church buildings, i.e. Kensington Temple, Notting Hill Gate, London, of which I was a member, the Elim Tabernacle, Union Street, The Lanes, Brighton, and the City Temple, Bath Street, Glasgow. These valuable properties had been acquired by the Revival Party, namely Principal George Jeffreys, Pastors R.E. Darragh and James McWhirter through their revival campaigns of 1927 and 1930 respectively. They were personally responsible for their purchase without recourse to Elim H/Q for a penny of the purchase money, on the principle that as they had been the means in God's work of providing so many churches for others — and what properties they brought into Elim! — these three buildings would be their ministerial charges in after years when campaign days were no more, as governing trustees. Meanwhile, they were mainly responsible under the deeds to see that a Pastor was appointed to the Church, that they kept the buildings insured and in repair, etc., and that they paid all current expenses, including mortgages (where applicable) on the buildings, out of the offerings, with the surplus, if any, going towards their livelihood.

This was all very well under central government control when the churches were known as Elim Churches, but the situation was drastically altered when George Jeffreys, fully supported by R.E. Darragh, came to see the Scriptural sovereignty of each local church, backed by the command, "Set your house in order."

There was cause for regret that the reversionary clause in the deeds, made in all good faith as between themselves as trustees and the Elim Alliance Executive Council in 1936, meant that the buildings at the death of the trustees would legally become the properties of the Elim Trust Corporation, with the church members thereby coming under Elim's central government rules.

George Jeffreys fought long and hard with the Executive Council for separate Trust Deeds to be granted to these churches, incorporating vital Scriptural rights which would mean that the Bible-Pattern people who had been worshipping in them in freedom, in co-operation with the majority of the three trustees since 1940, and who had seen to the upkeep of the buildings, would continue to do so in freedom in perpetuity, even allowing for them still to be Elim Churches, but not under Elim's rules. All this was to no avail with those in Elim who held the whiphand under the original legal arrangements. Consequently with George Jeffreys and R.E. Darragh now gone and with James McWhirter as the sole surviving governing trustee of the Kensington and Glasgow church buildings, determined to run these two churches himself, the situation in which I was fully involved resolved itself under most distressing circumstances. He refused to come to terms with the Bible-Pattern ministers and people worshipping in them, and instead co-operated with Elim Headquarters. Thus the church members lost these valuable buildings (Kensington, Brighton and Glasgow) to Elim, by methods which can only be deplored.

A fourth church building, known as the Jubilee Temple on Waterloo Road, Blackpool, which was built as a result of the Principal and Party's revival campaign, and held under a special Trust, was signed over to the Elim Trust Corporation under the original deed, because Pastor R.G. Tweed, as the governing trustee, and having personal responsibilities, was unable to alter the legal position in favour of the Bible-Pattern Church people worshipping there without the co-operation of those in Elim.

With the people compelled to leave these places of worship under the legal system, to meet in other halls, the World Revival Crusade, working in conjunction with the Bible-Pattern Church Fellowship, became a timely benefactor in these difficult and trying circumstances not only to a number of Bible-Pattern Churches but also to those at Glasgow, Brighton and Blackpool, as well as to my own Church in London following the loss of Kensington Temple.

Such was the drama surrounding the events described in this chapter, yet it cannot be denied that supporters of central government of churches can point to failures in the local church government system, made easier to do so by turning a blind eye to the like in their own organisations. Churches have been dissolved for various reasons — divisions on certain issues, a dwindling membership, a dictatorial oversight — leading to their buildings being sold sometimes after long years of Gospel witness. That of a Pastor holding on rather than honourably resigning, until he presides over the liquidation, not only of such a membership but of the place of worship itself, with himself and co-trustees subsequently being legally responsible for the disposing of the enormous sale funds of the church building, is not unknown and might well bring forth an opposer's comment, 'So much for free-church government.' I answer a challenge of this kind by claiming *that such a situation makes no difference whatever to the truth of God's Word as to local church government,* grievous as such is through the vagaries of human nature.

To the very end of his life George Jeffreys still strove for unity, showing his readiness to forgive the past as late as five weeks before he was so unexpectedly called to higher service in 1962. It makes his efforts the more poignant when in 1958 he addressed a letter to the Elim Executive Council, making an Offer and an Appeal, in which he wrote:

"The need of the suffering world today loudly calls upon every church member in the God-indwelt community of the local church to fear God and keep His commandments. Obedience to the Word of God makes the local church a permanent centre of practical holiness, a centre of supernatural power to bind and to loosen, and a centre for the training of men and women to go forth in the warfare against spiritual forces in high places.

"Time is short, earth is receding and Eternity is coming on, so may we be prepared to blot out the past and stand together in these last days for these righteous principles."

Both this, and the unity call in Commander D.H. Macmillan's Review of *Sects and Society,* given in the next chapter, went unheeded.

Chapter 8
Sects and Society

APROPOS Dr. Bryan Wilson's letter to Commander Macmillan (chapter 6), there now follows the Review of the Elim section of *Sects and Society,* first published in 1961, derisively dismissed by Desmond Cartwright in his *The Great Evangelists* (page 138) without a single fact having been challenged by him. Mr. Cartwright's measure can be assessed when he refers to Dr. Wilson as "an inexperienced student."

The Review was published in *The Pattern* in October, 1961, under the heading:

THE TAKE-OVER TECHNIQUE IN MODERN CHURCH HISTORY : TRANSITION FROM CHARISMA TO LEGALISM

By Commander D.H. Macmillan, M.B.E., R.N.R., F.R.I.C.S.

Nothing is more lamentable than schism in the Body of Christ, but it is interesting and profitable for Christians to study the mechanism and spirit that leads to an event that must be regarded as a tragic crucifixion of that Body, considered collectively, within the historical process.

The Roman Church, claiming that she alone is the Mystical Body, has to admit the schism of the Greek Church in her manifestly false and carnal conception of Catholicism.

Luther, when asked to define the True Church, replied: "The 'Consensus Fidelium'", meaning with our Lord Himself, and the Apostles, the sum of regenerate souls in whom is the Spirit of Christ. Certainly all those who have honestly and finally responded to the Saviour's call to the "Whosoever will" belong to the Mystical Body in the sight of God, and human organisations can at best provide temporary scaffoldings for this Divine Building.

When the last of the Elect is numbered the scaffoldings will be removed and finally discarded, with all their various designations, thus revealing Her in Her resurrection likeness to Her risen Master and Lord.

Dr. Bryan Wilson, a lecturer at Leeds University and the writer of this remarkable social study, has considered three "Sects" — two of them, Christian Science and Christadelphianism, by their formal denial of the Divinity and Godhead of the Lord Jesus, being outside the traditional Christian Faith of the Apostles.

The remaining Christian body discussed is The Elim Foursquare Gospel Church with which this review is particularly concerned as it reveals and illustrates in modern times familiar tendencies and patterns of power previously manifest in Apostolic, Primitive and Medieval Church History.

The author has apparently spent considerable time in intimate contact with each of these groups in turn to enable him to make his survey of each of them as accurate as possible.

One remembers St. Paul's prophetic injunction to the elders of Ephesus concerning those who would disrupt the self-governing charismatic (Spirit-indwelt) communities he had so lovingly founded whom he describes as "grievous wolves...not sparing the flock"; it is probable that as a Roman citizen he used the word "wolves" cautiously but designedly to indicate the later usurpation of Christendom by Roman legalism, for the symbol of the seven-hilled city was the she-wolf that supposedly suckled its child founders — Romulus and Remus (Acts 20:28-29).

Early in the third century the Latin father Tertullian of Carthage left the Church of Rome because it had "exiled the Spirit", and joined a charismatic (Pentecostal) group called the Montanists who were at first orthodox and even rigorous but later exhibited excesses with which he was not associated.

The early father Hippolytus had also at this time been outwitted by the clever legalism and committee procedure of Callixtus who, by sharp practice, had worked himself by lobbying into the seat of the Roman Bishop, carrying within him the seeds of the false penitential system and ecclesiastical domination that was to flower in a sinister medieval tyranny that only a Luther, under God, could challenge successfully with the hammer of the Word.

Yet under all this swaggering counterfeit of the Truth, the Faithful of the True Mystical Body, always a minority, witnessed often even unto death, as the Roman legal experts exploited Church politics and the votes and alms of the humble faithful towards papal tyranny, and one day Bishop (later Pope) Damasus had the satisfaction of having his supremacy established over his rival Ursinus by leaving the defeated corpses of 160 of his opponents in the basilica of Sirinicus — a church where the ambitious ecclesiastics and their followers had been in conference! (Vide *Decline and Fall* — Gibbon; also *Ammianus*).

The charismatic (*Spirit-indwelt*) Faithful were again outwitted by the worldly-wise of this world in the Visible Church — aptly named "Nicolaitans" in the mystical Greek language of Revelation 2:6, the word meaning "Lords of the people".

Just before the Reformation it would seem that the sons of the Holy Ghost Charisma had been erased and their witness silenced forever. John Huss, despite a "*safe-conduct*", had been burnt at the Council of Constance in 1415 by order of a totalitarian Church with full legal approval, and the bones of John Wycliffe were soon afterwards dug up and burnt at Lutterworth by a further unanimous legal decision of the same conference. What could men of the Spirit do except rely solely on the Written Word of God as did their Master?

So with Luther and the Word, the monolithic legalism of the Medieval Church was destined to come to a shattering end, and when the Reformer bravely cried before the glittering and fully legal assembly of Bishops and Princes,

"Here I stand, I can do no other!"

her doom was sealed, her system broken, and her grip over the Faithful — once her prey — smashed open forever.

"Sic Semper Tyrannis!"
"Thus ever with Tyrants!"

Dr. Wilson, in his study, reveals an unwitting recapitulation of this age—old contention between men of the Spirit and Word only, on the one hand, and men who seek bureaucratic control over the Faithful by legal instruments and secular procedures on the other. He outlines this age-old pattern with great precision in his purely scientific, factual social analysis and historical sketch of the Pentecostal origins and later development of the Elim Foursquare Gospel Church admittedly founded by George Jeffreys almost half a century ago.

Dr. Wilson's thesis is completely objective, and to the best of my knowledge he himself is unknown to the various leaders involved in this tragic story of schism in a Bible-loving Christian community.

He depicts George Jeffreys as a very intense Christian young man who received his call by the Holy Spirit and the Word to build a work for God in what he believed to be the last days of the

105

Christian era. The writer portrays him from first to last as earnest and transparently honest, never doubting for a moment that his associates were, like himself, enthusiastic, mutually loyal and zealous for the glory of Christ alone.

Again and again the writer illustrates the earnest desire of George Jeffreys that his charismatic (Spirit-indwelt) community should never become a "sect of perdition" (claiming to be the *only* way of salvation), but a movement destined to bless the *whole* Universal Church and prepare Her for the Second Appearance of the Lord at the end of Gentile history in this century. Jeffreys definitely restored the characteristic doctrine of Luther and Calvin that the believer could have the *assurance* of his salvation.

Wilson writes (p. 16): "...there is here a liberality which is *alien to the typical sect*...In a sense, Pentecostalists regard themselves as a specially privileged order *within the body of the church, which is the collectivity of all true believers"* (Luther's 'Consensus Fidelium' — reviewer. Italics also the reviewer's).

The writer's statement on page 19, i.e. "The partaking of wine and bread is understood simply as a memorial..." is inadequate, for in truly Pentecostal meetings the bread and wine are effectual signs and pledges of the benefits of the Passion of Christ *to the believer,* and the real Presence of Christ, whilst not in the elements, *is specially present in the souls of the faithful celebrants.* Its theology is not Zwinglian.

Dr. Wilson shows elsewhere throughout his thesis that George Jeffreys is a genuine son of the Reformation and, through its medium, an inheritor of the doctrines of the Early Scriptural and Primitive Church. The author is, however, mistaken in asserting that he (Jeffreys) had no adequate historical knowledge of Early Church history in dealing with the Gifts of the Holy Spirit in the Primitive, Medieval and Reformation Churches, as a reference to his work *Pentecostal Rays* will show. Indeed no modern teacher has presented the need for the Pentecostal endowment in as scholarly a manner as he.

Dr. Wilson then describes the gradual process — unrealised by the Evangelist — whereby his spiritual enthusiasm was being overtaken and even exploited by the lesser personalities surrounding him at headquarters who were obviously much more earthbound than he, and accordingly we read: "...by degrees organisation was developing" (p. 36).

The later statement of his former colleagues, after they had disloyally manoeuvred him out of the Movement he had founded, is an interesting comment on the "double-talk" of which the ecclesiastically minded are capable: "'In the early days of the Elim Movement, the government was entirely an autocratic one...When the Elim work commenced it was under the absolute control of Pastor George Jeffreys...'"* (p.44). What this ingenious statement does not reveal is that, as the Movement grew and progressed, the Evangelist had clearly delegated in trust to the Secretary-General, E.J. Phillips, and others, the general administrative oversight of the Movement, never for a moment foreseeing that lesser minds, obsessed with legal power patterns, would organise an actual usurpation of his leadership and scorn any conception of a "gentleman's agreement" in loyalty to their undoubted leader.

George Jeffreys was not concerned with a desire for administrative power over his converts, as his whole attitude shows, *but for the glory of Christ alone in their conversion and sanctification.* It is therefore supremely unjust to present him as an autocrat, when the desire for power and legal control must obviously be located and identified in his accusers, as is shown by this remarkable objective study.

As Lord Acton has well observed: "All power corrupts but absolute power corrupts absolutely".

Dr. Wilson states: "His (Jeffreys) charisma was a derived charisma, resting on his achievements as an evangelist, and his *actual control* (reviewer's italics) may never have extended to all departments of the movement, and no doubt became increasingly limited as the bureaucratisation of the movement began" (p.39). Incidentally, his control was effectively paralysed at the very time when he needed loyal support for the constructive reforms he saw to be necessary in the interests of his converts.

Again: "It has been men of natural talent — George Jeffreys, with evangelising ability, and E.J. Phillips, with administrative ability — who have led the movement" (p.41).

History will judge which of these men have used the gifts God has given them in humble obedience to His Spirit, and *in the service of the body of believers committed to their care,* in the freedom of Christ who bought this for them on His Cross.

Dr. Wilson shows how, just before the outbreak of World War

* *Elim Evangel* XXII, 25 August, 1941.

II, no less than 280 congregations had been formed, and also how George Jeffreys was by no means the "autocrat" of the double-talk later invented by the *real* power group who inherited control over the greater mass of his spiritual children. He states: "...such factors may have been very much entangled with Jeffreys' distrust of the centralised organisation which had come into being, *not at his instigation, but rather by force of circumstances*" (p. 43 — reviewer's italics).

Certainly the "force of circumstances" was not unknown to the rather more earthbound personalities who watched developments, not without intelligent interest and calculation, both in their trend and in the simple—hearted and unseeing enthusiasm of the servant of God.

Dr. Wilson continues: "As new contingencies occurred, so administrative machinery developed. Administration was refined and regularised until Elim had evolved a powerful central bureaucracy hidden behind its evangelist-leader, who appears, from his later statements, *to have been wholly unaware of the process*" (p. 43 — reviewer's italics).

If the servant of God (for so an illuminated address from his associates at this time designates him) is to blame for being so trustful, naive, and unobservant, and I think he would admit this, what of those who were the *real* "managers" who failed loyally to inform him of this situation and later, in 1941, presented him to his flock as the "autocrat" from which *they* had delivered Christ's people? There is still time for repentance on their part before the Appearance of the Judge Who will render unto every man *according to his works*.

Dr. Wilson is not deceived by such transparent pretexts designed to cover up a power pattern working feverishly.

Yet the servant of God, quite unaware of the drift of events, remained: "Tall, suncrowned, standing above the fog", wielding the Sword of the Spirit with idealistic Celtic fire, finely disregarding the mounting number of his converts and the flood of moneys and properties cascading into a Movement that with all his honest soul he did not desire to see transformed into an ingrowing dreary sect that would develop ultimately into an organisation of the "chain-store" variety, where branch managers served the will of the managing director and his committee caucus at headquarters.

The author continues his theme in these words: "Yet even from an early date, it seems likely that he (Jeffreys) had ceased to be in day-to-day, or week-to-week, *or perhaps even month-to-month* (reviewer's italics) control of the movement. Quite early he had developed a system of overseers appointed at his own discretion, with himself as Principal Overseer" (p. 44). Obviously this was a process of delegation to others to "serve tables", but it was also a trust assuming loyalty to his apostolic leadership as the responsible servant of God in winning souls.

A struggle of opposing ideals, strangely similar to that depicted in St. Paul's Epistle to the Galatians, was obviously in progress, but even in this it must *at the last transpire* that "the son of the bondwoman shall not be heir with the son of the freewoman" (Gal. 4:30) when spiritual and historical judgments catch up with human "wisdom and prudence" legally expressed in Christ's Body — His Church!

Of the servant of God — the charismatic leader — "the shackles of denominationalism always appear to have chafed Jeffreys himself" (p. 44) — and this marks him as a gift to the Church Universal, whilst the lesser personalities around him, "sons of the bondwoman", could not see beyond the horizons of legalism that invariably lead to the graves of sectarian skeletons unless, and until, nobler visions are reborn in Christian love and repentance — *a door not yet closed.*

Continuing we read: "The familiar pattern of the charismatic leader's coming increasingly to rely on the technical, legal and administrative knowledge of the bureaucrat is apparent: routine administrative devices, written instructions and defined spheres of competence replace the spontaneity of charismatic impulse" (p. 45). We read again: "Jeffreys now relied increasingly on the technical knowledge of Phillips; he later declared that when he signed the 1934 Deed Poll he did so only after seeking reassurance about the effect of the instrument from the Secretary—General"* (p. 46).

When the "son of the freewoman", the servant of God, was at last awakened to the real situation he found himself a mere figurehead within a net of cleverly contrived legal and procedural fibres, whose only function was to provide a "Father—image" as a useful device to inspire and maintain the morale of an undoubted Movement of the Holy Spirit that was now being compressed into the usual mould of sectarianism, and requiring

* N. Brooks, *Fight for The Faith and Freedom*, 1948, p.69.

the familiar ecclesiastical manoeuvres and ultimately "stunts" to maintain its identity, vitality and numbers.

Dr. Wilson sums up this intolerable situation as follows: "The struggle is thus virtually typified in these remarks as a struggle between the administrator with his specialised legal knowledge and bureaucratic machine, and the charismatic leader whose only weapon is the source of his inspiration — the Word of God. The struggle was between the two dominant figures of the movement, the titular leader and the expert administrator. Their contention became more and more pronounced, but the concentration of power in the hands of the Secretary—General, who had the normal channels of distribution and transmission of information at his disposal, made it increasingly apparent that the leader had little chance of carrying through the reformist ideals which now inspired him" (pp. 48—49).

Again: "Elim was no longer a community of converted souls under inspired leadership: it had become a complex organisation with involved administrative and financial systems supporting it" (p. 49). Further: "It was no longer a free revival force operating in the national life...Elim was rather a sect..." (p. 49). The loss to our Nation during the war and post—war years is indeed incalculable in this tendency to quench the Holy Spirit.

Regarding the British—Israel controversy, which is dealt with in detail by Dr. Wilson, George Jeffreys' view and the later history in the Bible—Pattern Church Fellowship Movement abundantly demonstrates that it is regarded as a *non—fundamental*, left open to the individual exegete and entirely subservient to the Evangel for soul—winning and sanctification. It may here be noted that the real arguments for the British—Israel thesis are much more profound and scholarly than those mentioned by Dr. Wilson.

The various attempts of the "sons of the bondwoman" to give the servant of God the sop of a fictitious leadership for the exploiting of his spiritual prestige, and the devices employed to avoid letting his converts under God *know* the full facts about his resignation and its causes, as described on pages 52—54, are nauseatingly familiar to all who are acquainted with the "take—over" mechanisms achieved by committee caucuses and voting majorities in ecclesiastical, business and worldly affairs.

The enforcement where necessary of legal proceedings against George Jeffreys, and certain of the Churches themselves, as formerly resolved by the Elim Conference over the question of the Church properties, is also dealt with on page 54. *Surely this, to say the least, was shameful expediency when one considers that the servant of God was not contending for his own self—interests but for the just rights of his converts in the Churches he had founded!*

Dr. Wilson continues on page 54: "At the same conference in 1941...the conference deprecated Jeffreys' 'deliberate attempt to split the Elim Churches after his solemn pledge to the Ministerial Conference of 1939 not to disturb these churches. It therefore has no choice but to disassociate itself entirely from him according to the teaching of the Word of God'". *

We have already seen that George Jeffreys' converts were deliberately prevented by certain anti-publicity devices from having any clear picture of the several causes that made his resignation inevitable from the entire Elim work he had so assiduously founded and built up. As he was also prevented from entering any Elim Church it was most natural that his converts should anxiously engage public halls on their own initiative (as in Dundee, York and Bournemouth), to hear first-hand the account of this serious event from their charismatic leader under whose ministry they had learnt to know Christ. Even on these occasions members of the Elim Executive Council and local Elim Ministers were not above attending such proceedings and interrupting them of set purpose, to muzzle the truth, amid scenes of indescribable confusion.

It is therefore abundantly clear that the with-holding of the full facts surrounding his resignation, coupled with such unfair tactics, fully released George Jeffreys from any undertaking he may have made in good faith in the 1939 Conference. Accordingly the reason given by the 1941 Conference for casting off the undoubted leader of Elim and finally separating him from his own spiritual community can now be assessed for what it is worth.

On page 64, Dr. Wilson writes: "Of the three large Pentecostal bodies in Britain Elim has the most centalised form of government. Each movement seeks to justify its own particular polity, and Elim executives have at times found reason to defend the extent to which they prevent church members from deliberating on disciplinary matters". He then goes on to quote

* *Elim Evangel* XXII, 1941, p.566ft. This amounts to a form of excommunication or 'disfellowshipping'.

111

from an article by J. Smith, then an Executive Council member, in which he wrote:

"'In every country men have found it necessary to set aside certain people, trained and qualified to deal with offenders. Mob law is disastrous, either in church or state...Before I came into Elim I was a member of a pentecostal church where doctrinal matters were judged by the local assembly, and I know how the church was rent asunder because of that very thing...For God's sake let us keep these things out of our local churches. A Conference is the place to settle disputes — a church is a place to worship God.'"*

Regarding this specious plea for a rigid totalitarian and legal control of local Churches, it should be made clear that the fundamental Christian doctrines, as derived from Holy Scripture, are unanimously agreed to by all the Christian assemblies concerned. In the Bible-Pattern Movement, which has dissented from the principle of Central Bureaucracy, every local assembly is obliged to make these doctrines fundamental to their Model Trust Deed. Here there is no dispute.

It is the realm of buildings, properties and moneys that provokes the Central Bureaucracy in its desire for control!

It is certain that our Lord's words in Matthew 18:15-20 authorises the whole local assembly of born-again members to be the arbiters in such matters, as well as in discipline, whereas the Constitution of the Elim Foursquare Gospel Alliance, under "Discipline", makes the local minister answerable to the Executive Council (p. 59) and the Church member answerable to the local Diaconate known as "The Church Session" (p. 42). *Thus the local Church in Elim, with its minister, is bound in the very matters in which our Lord intends it to have full freedom and discretion.*

J. Smith's last two sentences, as quoted, come strangely from one who, with others from Elim headquarters, in company with a detective, interrupted a Communion Service in a local Church (Portsmouth) on a Sunday in war time that same year (1941) and forced its minister and congregation to leave the building — which they did! — under legal threats. If, as he has written, "a church is a place to worship God", it is surely a piece of consummate hypocrisy to cause its public celebration of Holy Communion to cease by these shocking methods. Those

* J. Smith in *Elim Evangel* XXII, 1941, p.p. 267-8.

responsible for such actions in the Visible Church will surely be accountable to God at the last, unless they make reparation before departing from this earthly sphere.

From pages 65 to 69 Dr. Wilson continues his penetrating analysis of where the real power in Elim is to be found, adding on page 66: "In particular these staff and council members held all the places on the Elim Trust Corporation and the building committee, four of five places on the Elim Pentecostal Alliance Council, and eight of ten places on the Elim Bible College Synod. In 1954 the Secretary-General of the movement was serving on ten of the thirteen committees listed.* Thus in spite of the theoretical control by the representative conference, there can be little doubt that most of the activity of the movement is controlled and regulated by a relatively small number of administrators at the central headquarters. Information, administrative capacity, experience, prestige, familiarity with the work, and various other advantages concentrate on the relatively small number of men who occupy the central positions, and who, as a consequence, have a strong informal pre–emption upon them...*and inevitably power tends to concentrate in the hands of these permanent administrators"* (reviewer's italics).

After showing the powerlessness of the district presbyteries in Elim, the author continues:

"At the local level the Elim church has a diaconate system and an optional quorum of elders. Deacons alone are more usual. Deacons and elders (if any) form together with, and under the presidency of, the minister *what is somewhat misleadingly called the church session"* (p. 67 — reviewer's italics).

"The details of administration of the local church are governed by a body of general rules and regulations which are published with the movement's constitution, and which, together, comprise a closely printed volume of eighty pages. It is a far larger and more systematic document than the *Manual of The Mother Church* in Christian Science, although it is by no means so widely circulated among Elimites as is the *Manual* among Christian Scientists. The regulations cover a multitude of operations and contingencies, but in all provide for the systematic relationship of the local church with headquarters. All major issues in church life must be referred to Clapham, and even ministerial discretion is narrowly circumscribed...There is, then, an extraordinary

* Information derived from the *Elim Year Book*, 1954.

degree of control exercised by a small group of leaders over the movement's ministry, *certainly greater than in most nonconformist organisations*...(reviewer's italics).

"All financial matters in Elim are subject to precise and detailed written instructions, which list permitted expenditure by the minister and treasurer of the local church, stipulate that ten per cent of all offerings shall go to headquarters, and require monthly, quarterly and annual returns of church finances to be sent to Clapham. Local churches have little autonomy; they are controlled by the senior officers whose duties require them to be constantly available at headquarters.

"Despite this close supervision, evident in the constitutional provisions, the local Elim church operates without obvious intrusion into its affairs of the organisational requirements of headquarters. These demands are made on the minister, and are communicated by him to his church officers, but to all appearances he regulates the life of the local church. The congregation have little voice in either organisation or doctrine: they are a flock to be ministered unto. The individual has little opportunity to become a leader in his own assembly, at best he may become a deacon or elder, and will remain under the control of the minister. *The minister is sent from headquarters, which may well add to his prestige with the congregation, to whom he is a man of authority with a vocation. The circumscription of his office, his allegiance to headquarters, his operation as their agent, and his susceptibility to their close supervision — all this is unseen"* (pp. 67-69 — reviewer's italics).

This is the sorry diagnosis of an outside onlooker, a student of social science, who has made a study of the development of a Christian Revival which is not only written into modern Church History but is noted in Heaven as a response to the Holy Spirit through the dedicated work of a servant of God.

As Dr. Wilson has taken pains to document his subject from official records to an astonishing degree, his readers ought undoubtedly to be convinced of the true position, especially those who have falsely believed that the Founder resigned from the Elim Movement on unimportant issues.

At the same time neither side of this crucifying schism are in any conflict over their fundamental beliefs which define them as members of the Universal Christian Church, holding the Apostolic doctrines of the Word of God and the definitions of the

Primitive Church up to the Councils of Nicea and Chalcedon. Such doctrines were reaffirmed by George Jeffreys, the servant of God who founded this revival, *not for the purpose of adding a sect to Christendom,* as we have seen, but to bless the whole Church with the charismatic gifts of the Holy Ghost, and to prepare Her for our Lord's Appearing.

But this purpose has been sadly aborted and the cross of division has fallen on the children of this revival through a conflict of power patterns, one after the Spirit and the other after the flesh.

We agree with Dr. Wilson when he writes that George Jeffreys did not "claim authority by asserting his own possession of the gifts of the Spirit" (p. 61), but we emphatically state that he has faithfully preached "pentecostal teaching in his revivals". The Campaign Hymnsheet, with its message on the front cover — "We preach Christ Jesus Our Lord: SAVIOUR (Matt. 1:21), HEALER (Matt. 8:17), BAPTISER (John 1:33), COMING KING (1 Thess. 4:16) confirms the Foursquare aspect of the Gospel which he has declared in all his campaigns. He also encourages believers to come forward for the laying-on of hands, that they might receive the Holy Spirit, with signs following, as an enduement of power for service.

Dr. Wilson continues: "His (Jeffreys) agents (in Elim) took control, and later became the agents of the bureaucratic organisation which grew up under the shadow of his charismatic prestige" (p. 63).

If Principal George Jeffreys is to blame for failing at an earlier stage to observe many damaging developments in the Movement he had brought into being, in mitigation it should be borne in mind that his time was mainly taken up on the field with the great work of Bible-teaching, soul-saving and healing, with such tremendous results. He has in any case sought, in great agony, to rectify the position since becoming aware of it.

He is well acquainted with the fact that infant Churches, as in the British Commonwealth States, need training and guidance in self-government, and that these should be provided by those of experience. But he is right in holding that the "Candlestick" Churches of the New Testament should, under the advice of experienced elders loyally accepted, achieve Christ's desire for them as free and self-governing Scriptural Assemblies under the

115

Cross and in the power of the Holy Spirit — for this is their veritable New Testament birthright.

This is the doctrine of the sons of the freewoman — "the Jerusalem that is above and is the mother of us all" — and She has always in history burst the bonds of spiritually blind legalism, whether of the Jewish or Roman varieties.

Let there be no mistake about it: the Elim Movement will in the end be no exception as the mills of God grind on inexorably.

I earnestly appeal to those who have been betrayed into using their administrative gifts shamefully to ill-use George Jeffreys, the servant of God who brought Elim to spiritual birth, to consider means for bringing unity between Elim and the Bible-Pattern Church Fellowship on the basis of providing for the Scriptural sovereignty of each local Church, as taught by Christ in Matthew 18: 15-20 and God's Word elsewhere in the New Testament.

This means that the local assembly adjusts matters of local Church order and government, and owns and administers its property absolutely at its own discretion, in obedience to the Spirit and the Written Word; nor is it beyond the advice of godly elders. In this sense local Churches are governed, under God, by the members and for the members, remembering that they must account to God for their decisions.

If this is achieved, all Elim and Bible-Pattern Churches, trained by those of experience in the skills of dignified self-government, would become self-propagating Assemblies in the Mystical Body of Christ, thus presenting a united front to the world in the unprecedented time of crisis now dawning.

The leading personalities involved in this grievous schism are, by the mercy of God, still with us, and in response to the moving of the Spirit we should remedy the situation and seek reconciliation on this side of eternity on these righteous grounds, with the blotting out of past mistakes, when the destinies of so many souls under our oversight are at stake.

The God of the impossible Whom we preach is able to do this if we are faithful and humble enough to let Him!

I am persuaded that such a disposition to seek unity in Truth would *at once* redeem our people from the yawning grave of sectarianism and create a great company of Christians, conquered by the Word, and filled, by such a reconciliation, with unspeakable joy in the Spirit.

116

Furthermore it would mean a mighty Revival in our Nation through us as Pentecostal people in these times of declension and apostasy. In our mutual reconciliation streams of blessing would follow the removal of division in the Body of Christ, and Rome would be stopped in her subtle ambitions for control as the Spirit takes toll amongst our spiritually-starved multitudes. They are looking for a truly Ecumenical body of Christians endued with spiritual unity and power.

Time is running out!

The Judge is at the door and His eyes are as a flame of fire and miss nothing!

Brethren, if we judge ourselves now we shall not at the last be judged by Him, for He has promised to forgive our trespasses if we forgive those who trespass against us. Then why not make constructive reparation for the sake of the sheep of His pasture?

As we humble ourselves in obedience to His Word, the Spirit in cleansing majesty and unprecedented beauty will fall upon the sacrifice. And none shall be ashamed before Him at His Appearing!

Maranatha!

Amen!

So wrote Dr. Bryan Wilson, as reviewed by Commander Macmillan, before Elim Headquarters moved from Clapham, London, to Cheltenham, Gloucestershire. Commander Macmillan was called to higher service 10 years later, and the leading personalities he refers to as being "still with us," viz. Principal George Jeffreys and Pastor E.J. Phillips having also gone on.

The Bible-Pattern Church Fellowship faced exceptionally difficult circumstances at its formation, with the Second World War on and the population of our country either away serving in the Forces or at least concerned with their own preservation and that of the nation. As one intimately involved with the Fellowship from the beginning, and in answer to critics who decry it and its lack of progress in these later years, I give the facts as they relate to the present time, grievous as these are. Should they be given? Readers can form their own judgment, but for my part this biography would be incomplete without them.

The earnest appeal for unity between Elim and the Bible-Pattern Church Fellowship in Commander Macmillan's scholarly review "on the basis of providing for the Scriptural

117

sovereignty of each local church, as taught by Christ in Matthew 18:15-20 and God's Word elsewhere in the New Testament," and which was the desire of Principal Jeffreys' own heart, went, as we have said, unheeded. Instead, there has come into being a spurious unity-cum-reconciliation through the Advisory Committee of the Fellowship working in close co-operation with the Elim Alliance Executive Council, the opponents of such sovereignty.

Reconciliation on righteous grounds is commendable at all times, but how has this sorry state of affairs come about in view of the rejection by Elim of our godly leader and the message, "Set your house in order," once having had the support of the Advisory Committee? The December, 1983, issue of *The Pattern* magazine provides the answer under the heading:

"Good and Pleasant"

"With great gratitude to God for the evident guidance of the Holy Spirit and for the precious spirit of unity prevailing, especially upon the times of prayer and seeking the face of God, the Advisory Committee of the Bible-Pattern Church Fellowship and the Executive of The Elim Church Incorporated issue the following joint Statement and Declaration of Intent:

"Believing we have been signally led of God in our consultations and discussions, we avow in our official magazines that it is our decision and determination, mutually agreed in the oneness of the Spirit, to seek to work ever more closely together at local, regional, national and international levels. We call on the members of our Fellowships to pray with us that we may be led step by step to those avenues of mutual service, ministry and fellowship that will bring about what we feel to be the fulfilment of God's will."

This, with its several references to God and the Holy Spirit, was accompanied by a photograph of 17 persons, as named, with a drawing of clasped hands, a symbolism depicting "Psalm 133." These consisted of eight Elim Alliance Executive Council ministers, part of the majority of the Executive Presbytery of the Elim Church Incorporated, four of the seven members of the Advisory Committee of the Bible-Pattern Church Fellowship, three Elim District Superintendents, and two other Elim ministers.

118

Such a declaration as this to those of us who have never wavered from the reason for the division in the Elim Movement poses the question: what has the Advisory Committee of the Bible-Pattern Church Fellowship accomplished in committing the Fellowship to the Elim Church Incorporated in this way, these who have had the advantage of reading and supporting the numerous writings of George Jeffreys and others, as well as of hearing him speak, of seeing the book *Fight for the Faith and Freedom,* and the Review as given in this chapter? Have they achieved the desired unity, as is implicit in the joint Statement and Declaration of Intent, and as they claimed by way of justification, in writing the Churches of the Fellowship on March 1st, 1984, under "DIALOGUE WITH ELIM"?:

"Our aim is to remove the bitterness and malice of bygone days as we seek a righteous solution and reconciliation before the return of our Lord Jesus Christ, and thus realise the cherished wish and desire of our beloved Principal."

This is almost unbelievable — "to remove the bitterness and malice of bygone days,"! on whose part? with the 'disfellowshipping' of the Founder still, presumably, in Elim's records and without a public word of regret having been expressed since for such a shocking action. And to "realise" what he desired, with him outside of Elim until the end of his life, with what he stood for rejected over and over again! Are we to accept that "a reconciliation (which was) not possible during the lifetime of the Principal" (Desmond Cartwright's book, page 156) has now come to pass through this move of theirs? Surely they cannot be so naive as to think this, when all they have done is to effectively gag themselves as regards protesting against Elim's central government system of control, as George Jeffreys protested, have weakened the witness of the Bible-Pattern Church Fellowship, and given moral support to Elim's contention against the Scriptural sovereignty being established in its own *Elim Foursquare Gospel Alliance Churches* throughout the country. They have therefore accomplished nothing in furthering George Jeffreys' vision *for the Elim Movement and these churches he founded,* and for which he paid so great a price. He came out and was free to speak — they have gone in and are bound!

The steps leading up to this state of affairs in the history of the Bible-Pattern Church Fellowship have been over a period of years, resulting in two former members of the Advisory Committee becoming Elim Foursquare Gospel Alliance ministers in Elim Alliance Churches; the seven members of the Advisory Committee of the Fellowship being received into the Elim Church Incorporated, finally renounced by Principal George Jeffreys in November, 1940, on the formation of the Bible-Pattern Church Fellowship! The seven members being Pastors R.G. Tweed, G.I. Francis, D.Th., D.D., E. Marsh, R.W. Chewter, J.S. Reid, Una Macmillan and G. Girvan, with one of them elected in Elim to serve on the Executive Presbytery of the Elim Church Incorporated, a minority of one with the remaining nine being ministers of the Elim Foursquare Gospel Alliance.

Furthermore, the Nottingham Bible-Pattern Church which, like others, is now affiliated to the Elim Movement in the Elim Church Incorporated, had an Elim minister inducted as pastor in 1986, proclaimed by both Elim and the Fellowship as "a unique occasion." This is the church associated with the birth of the Bible-Pattern Church Fellowship and which saw the aforementioned renunciation of the Elim Church Incorporated.

Co-operation? Yes, but entirely in the interests of the Elim Movement, bringing about what we said would happen, a division in the Fellowship. This is obliquely referred to in Mr. Cartwright's book (page 157), where he writes: "A number of their churches have joined the Elim Church Incorporated in recent years. It is to be hoped that one day there may be a full reconciliation."

All of them in, no matter on what grounds?

This close contact with Elim in this way has had other repercussions:

The Advisory Committee has (a) committed the Bible-Pattern Church Fellowship in support of the Pentecostal World Conference, together with Elim and others, despite Principal Jeffreys' reasoned contention and warning note relative to the Conference, as constituted (chapter 5) and (b) although the Bible-Pattern Church Fellowship as such is legally bound to subscribe to and maintain the seven Fundamentals (chapter 6) — *the seventh being of vital importance to each local Bible-Pattern Church as to its government* — they were prepared as a Committee in 1984 to have the Fundamentals of the Elim Foursquare Gospel Alliance and the Elim Church Incorporated

120

substituted for these, with other changes in the Constitutions of the Fellowship. As these twelve Fundamentals are doctrinal and non-governmental, what did they think they were gaining by adopting them in the place of the seven? Certainly this again was in the interests of Elim, with the Fellowship churches the losers. This endeavour was vigorously opposed by some of us and it was quietly dropped.

It can be said that the World Revival Crusade has the same Fundamentals as Elim. This is because we were in the Elim Movement when the Crusade was founded, but these give it no authority of control constitutionally over any local church such as the Elim Alliance has under its Constitution, Deed Poll and Property Trust Corporation. Our aim since the Crusade's inception in 1935 has been to pioneer, to win souls, to be a help and blessing to churches, and to give valuable support to the work of God overseas.

These actions of the Advisory Committee have led to the Church of which I am Pastor becoming an independent Bible-Pattern Pentecostal Church after many years in the Fellowship, the irony of the situation being that Principal George Jeffreys died in the Fellowship, not having achieved what he strove after for the Elim Movement, and with ourselves now outside the official Fellowship without having deviated from his fight for the Faith and Freedom. There is this redeeming feature: we are still free to speak and write as he was.

We can be sure of this: *the fault does not lie with the Truth* but with those who are prepared to gloss over the past in order to entertain such misguided co-operation. One may well ask: how can the Bible-Pattern Church Fellowship be expected to make progress in the face of such actions by its present leaders? Furthermore, the sovereignty issue having been rejected by Elim, *it was clearly intended that the Fellowship as such should go forward as a separate entity without compromise and free to protest as necessary, as was the Founder, yet without enmity towards the Elim Movement.*

George Jeffreys was "not disobedient to the heavenly vision." This is why, when looking back to that extraordinary experience of 1937 (chapter 6), he could write:

"God bestowed the greater honour upon me, not when He called me to preach to crowded congregations in the Royal Albert Hall, London, and in other large halls at home and

121

abroad, and before Royalty at Stockholm, but when He called me to renounce and denounce Babylonianism in organised religion and suffer for the sake of free, self-governing churches according to the New Testament.

"Notwithstanding the half-truths that have been circulated against me, and all I have suffered, not one day has passed since December 1st, 1939, without thanksgiving rising from my full heart to God for the courage He gave me to renounce the wrong that day, and for the abiding peace that has settled in my soul."

As one so close to him for so many years I can say his whole demeanour was a constant witness to the truth of this.

He has been spared seeing the present situation which has foolishly been brought about by these leaders in the Fellowship, one of whom wrote at his death: "We must, by the grace of God, endeavour to follow the example he has left us, *and the full vision he had must still be ours also,* if we are to be instrumental in bringing other souls to Christ," (Author's italics.)

I close this chapter with the tribute of the Rev. Raymond H. Belton:

"George Jeffreys, whose sanctified personality and Spirit-filled life moved thousands, was never more truly noble than when he sacrificed himself for the cause he had at heart. The conviction came to him that there was something wrong with the organisation he had built up. It was not sufficiently democratic, central control being in the hands of a small Executive Council, of which he was President. The annual Conference was for Ministers only; there was no lay representation...and, whatever may be the reader's view on the vexed question of Church government, he will be stirred to admiration of a man who, at great personal cost, was true to his conception of Truth..." (from a review of *Fight for the Faith and Freedom* by Noel Brooks).

Chapter 9
A Spirited Defence

NOTHING could be more conclusive than the following article, to turn back the falsehood that George Jeffreys left the Elim Movement on the "British-Israel" issue. It was written and published by Dr. LEWI PETHRUS in the Swedish magazine he edited called *Herald of Faith* dated June, 1941. He himself held no brief for British Israel teaching as such. I have quoted from this in my *Open Letter*. I now give it in full:

"It was my privilege to be the guest of George Jeffreys at Blackpool, as well as London in the Spring of 1939, and during that time I had many opportunities to hear Principal Jeffreys explain his viewpoint on this question; and also during his visit to the European Conference in Stockholm in June of the same year, when he was my guest for a week after the conference, he and I often discussed these questions.

"We have learned that the opponents of George Jeffreys within the Elim Foursquare Movement have tried to assert the opinion in private letters to others in America that the reason for his resignation was based on a theological question, namely that of 'British Israel.' This is absolutely wrong, even if such a reason is given. The question as to whether the British (Anglo-Saxons) are the descendants of the ten lost tribes of Israel or not, is of little importance to George Jeffreys, as far as I understand. What is far more important to me in this matter, are the reasons which George Jeffreys himself says are the cause for his resignation. For my part, I have so much faith in George Jeffreys that if the question concerning 'British Israel' had been the reason, then he would have so stated in his own letter of resignation. Instead he writes that the real reason for his resignation is the unscriptural form of government exercised over the various churches, and that these same churches have lost their spiritual freedom through this; and when George Jeffreys says this — I believe him!

"I have also had the opportunity of reading the statement given out by the leaders of the Elim Foursquare Movement against

Brother George Jeffreys' resignation, and in this statement they have not mentioned the question of 'British Israel.' If this question of 'British Israel' was their reason, or any part of it, then they should have mentioned it in this statement in which they try to explain the real cause for the resignation of their former leader. Their failure to do this proves that 'British Israelism' is not the reason at all for the new attitude on the part of George Jeffreys towards the Elim Foursquare Gospel Movement.

"It is hard to understand how Christian brethren can broadcast such an accusation which they do not dare to mention in their public declaration. These facts which George Jeffreys gives in his statement as the reason for his resignation, and when his opponents do not even mention the doctrine of 'British-Israel' in their declaration concerning the same, clearly show and prove that this teaching has nothing to do with the new step taken by our dear Brother George Jeffreys.

"George Jeffreys has been one of England's most prominent spiritual leaders during recent years. There have been very few who could gather such crowds around their pulpits as he has. Therefore an extremely serious condition must exist in which the Elim Foursquare Movement has been led astray through its government, a government that has not been willing to yield to the demands of their leader for greater freedom in its assemblies.

"But even this is a promising sign for the wonderful outpouring of the Spirit which is generally given the name of the Pentecostal Revival. This wonderful revival has been greatly harmed in many lands, simply because it has been subjected to an administration which is not biblical. The work of the Spirit has in many places been hindered because of this and in some instances come to a complete standstill. But there is hope that these mistakes can be corrected when there are such mighty instruments of God as George Jeffreys, who are willing to break with that which is not biblical and harmful to the work of God.

"To leave a movement for which one has been the leader for twenty-five years, and for which one has laid down the best part of one's life, is not an easy matter. There must be a weighty motive back of such a step and that motive is an irresistible desire to live and work in accordance with the Word of God."

Having given this spirited defence by this great Pentecostal leader, it is appropriate that I follow on with an article by Principal Jeffreys. First, let me say that false views continue to be propagated in books, not only about basic British-Israel belief, but as to the attitude of George Jeffreys regarding this teaching and Bible prophecy in general. If the propagation of British-Israel belief is denied to any Movement, Pentecostal or otherwise, is it not logical for the propagation of Futurist and Historicist beliefs to be similarly denied? It seems to me there is a dogmatism abroad in Protestantism in the prophetic field which closes the Bible to seekers after truth as effectively as does the inflexible attitude of the Church of Rome, with its false claims and pretensions.

Under the heading MY ATTITUDE TOWARDS THE PROPHETIC SCHOOLS, George Jeffreys wrote an article which was first published in the January, 1940, issue of *The Pattern*. By way of Introduction he stated: "The following article was written some years ago, but it is only now that the opportunity has come to publish it. I am leaving the article as I wrote it *before* my resignation from Elim (on December 1st, 1939).

"As the acknowledged leader of an extensive work like the Elim Movement, I had always thought that I should be free to express my views on the topical subjects of the day, including doctrine, prophecy, church government, reforms, etc., even though they did not exactly agree with the official side of the Movement.

"This particular article deals with MY ATTITUDE towards the various schools of prophetic thought and seeks to emphasise Christian toleration, on the part of all lovers of the Bible, especially when dealing with prophecy, owing to its paramount importance in these last days.

"This article," he concluded, "has been submitted to able students of the Word, who are not in agreement with my particular view concerning Israel, but who have definitely stated that in the Elim Movement my attitude, as expressed in this article, was the only possible one for its leaders to adopt."

During latter years I have been inundated with inquiries concerning my views on prophecy, especially that phase which has to do with the restoration of God's Chosen People, Israel. These inquiries have come chiefly from our own Elim people, some of whom have been converted and led into the glorious truths of the Foursquare Gospel under my ministry. A casual reading of some of the letters of inquiry reveal glaring misrepresentations of my personal views on Israel, and these call for a clear declaration of the true position. This can only be done in print, for it is impossible to deal with them by correspondence. There are three reasons why I should clarify my position by making a positive statement:

Firstly, there is the fact that the identity of Israel is becoming a burning question, especially amongst baptised believers.

A. Some confine the whole of Israel to the Jews.
B. Some to Jews and the ten tribes which are still lost.
C. Others identify Israel with the Jews and the Celto-Anglo-Saxon peoples of to-day.

The attitude of God's people towards the restoration of Israel very much resembles that with which the Pentecostal outpouring was received in the early days. Then, as now, there were some for Pentecost, some against, and many were the misrepresentations and exaggerations with which both sides had to contend. Sometimes real issues were so clouded that some people became extreme in their views on both sides. Well do I remember the many times I had to dispose of the distorted view that "George Jeffreys believes that a person had to speak in tongues before he or she could enter the Kingdom of God," just as I have now to deal with the frequent misrepresentation that, "George Jeffreys believes that every Britisher, being an Israelite, is in the Kingdom of God."

Secondly, it is well known throughout our land that I hold views concerning the restoration of Israel that are not the declared official views of our Elim Movement, and it is only fair, at least to our own people, that I should openly contradict the exaggerated and distorted views that are being linked with my name. I love my people and I know they love me, and for their sakes I am honour-bound as leader to give a brief but positive statement concerning the fundamental features of my prophetic viewpoint.

Thirdly, and this is most important — My attitude towards others who do not see eye to eye with me on the question of a restored Israel. Nothing could serve the purposes of the Enemy better than to represent one as being a dictator who insists that all in Elim must believe what he believes concerning things that are not fundamental.

Let me now try to define as clearly as possible my attitude

126

ELIM EVANGELISTIC BAND IN 1915

to right (seated): Principal George Jeffreys, Founder of Elim, and Pastor R.E. ragh, his first Evangelist in the Elim work in 1915. Standing: Pastor Frederick ow, Miss Margaret Streight (later Mrs R. Mercer) and Pastor William Hender-

Revival Party, taken in Manchester in 1934. Left to right: A.W. Edsor, George ys, R.E. Darragh and James McWhirter.

The Westminster Central Hall, London, taken by George Jeffreys for Bible-P... Church Fellowship demonstrations each Easter Monday, morning, afternoo... evening, from 1942-1961. It was again booked for Easter, 1962, before the ... call came in January.

George Jeffreys (left) and ... Pethrus, Pentecostal pioneer, of ... holm, Sweden, outside the for... home in Clarence Avenue, Cla... Park, London, SW4 in 1952.

(above): George Jeffreys at the ... Norway in 1947 of T.B. Barrat... ecostal pioneer, of Oslo.

*al Palace, London, reported as the largest Exhibition Building in the world,
e the Revivalist preached at seven annual Elim demonstrations in succession,
1930-1936, and in which he conducted Divine healing and baptismal services.
ast, held two months before the Crystal Palace was destroyed by fire, was the
ng of Age of the Elim Movement.*

Principal George Jeffreys ministered to almost 50 such gatherings in the Royal Albert Hall, London between the years 1926-1939 at the annual Elim demonstrations on Easter Monday, and other Elim occasions notably on Good Friday, 1928 when he baptised over 1,000 believers by immersion in water before a congregation of 10,000 which was the official capacity of this world-famous Hall up until the Second World War years.

ROM THE DEAD 'HOU HALT BE SAVED ROMANS X 9

It is noteworthy that these demonstrations consisted chiefly of the converts won to Christ through his phenomenal revival and healing campaigns. Here is seen one of the impressive Easter Monday Communion Services. Before these crowded gatherings hundreds of people testified that they had been miraculously healed. Extensive newspaper reports and pictures carried the news to the British Isles and abroad.

Following in the trail of D.L Moody in 1875 and Dr. Torrey in 1904, Principal George Jeffreys has in 1930 preached to crowded gatherings in the great Bingley Exhibition Hall that can only find parallel in the two former campaigns. Only on these three occasions has this vast hall ever been used for revival services. During the last two weeks of the Principal's campaign monster congregations have been held in the grip of Foursquare Gospel revival. Over 10,000 converts have been registered in the Birmingham Campaign, over 1,000 cases of miraculous healing, nearly 1,100 candidates have been immersed in water, and this same vast auditorium has been filled for a communion service. The above is a picture of the mid-week service. "Imagine Bingley Hall

...rge Jeffreys outside the Big Tent, one of a number used for his summer revival healing campaigns and conventions right up until 1955. He is seen with his ...h "Corgi" dog when the Tent was erected on the sea-front at Kingsway, Hove, ...ex, in 1949.

The famous Salle Pleyel, Paris, crowded to capacity during the Revivalist's furth memorable campaigns in France and Switzerland in 1950.

The author standing beside the Revival Party car, a Chrysler, DLP 963, whic drove for 32 years at home and abroad, from 1937 to 1969.

towards all schools of prophetic thought. There are at least six schools, namely, the Idealist, Præterist, Futurist, Historicist, Harmonist and National-Historicist. In all six, there are scholarly saints and saintly scholars, men whose spirituality is an example to others in the Christian Church, and whose judgment on Doctrinal matters have proved to be absolutely sound. These faithful men of God, while standing Foursquare on the fundamentals of the Christian Faith, find themselves in different schools when it comes to the question of prophecy.

In our beloved Elim the number of schools can be reduced to four. Personally, I have not come across the Idealist, who holds that the prophetic Word simply contains ideal moral teaching, from which the Church can derive spiritual lessons; neither do I know of one Præterist, who believes that nearly all prophecy became history within some fifty years after Apostolic days.

1. We have Futurists who postpone the fulfilment of most prophecy to future ages.
2. Historicists who see the gradual translation of prophecy into history right from the days of the Apostles up to our day and on until the Consummation.
3. Harmonists who try to find a note of harmony between Futurist and Historicist by introducing minor and major fulfilments, although a very large percentage of the Futurists, and nearly all the Historicists, consider such an impossibility.
4. Then we have the National-Historicists who practically agree point by point with the Historicists until they come to identify Israel to-day.

Historicists, to my mind, are rather vague on this particular point, while the National-Historicists firmly declare that God is restoring Israel as a servant-nation in the Celto-Anglo-Saxon peoples as the descendants of the ten-tribed Kingdom of Israel, just as the Jews are the descendants of the Kingdom of Judah.

Soon after the commencement of the Elim work in 1915 I was introduced to what is now known as the National-Historicist School, when many of the perplexing questions concerning the Covenant promises of God were answered to my intense satisfaction; but the fact that I became a believer in the restoration of Israel as a servant-nation in this dispensation, did not alter my attitude towards the other schools of prophecy. I did not take the stand that I was absolutely right and that everybody who differed with me was absolutely wrong. I kept reminding myself of the possible element of uncertainty in all schools of prophetic thought; at the same time I was fully satisfied, and have been satisfied ever since, that the National-Historicists hold the most accurate interpretation of the prophecies concerning Israel.

From the day I was born-again I have held tenaciously to the right of every man to interpret the Scriptures as he believes God would have him do so, and I have maintained the stand that the highest Court of Appeal on all Doctrinal questions is the Word of God. There are, I believe, quite a few reasons why God allows His children to differ on points that are not fundamental; one is, to prevent any person boasting in his or her monopoly of truth; another, that students of the Word might ever be kept searching the Scriptures in quest of further light and truth.

Now concerning my attitude towards the prophetic schools in Elim. Let me appeal to the reader to place himself in my position as leader of this glorious work, to look at things from my standpoint and to ask himself the question: What would I do if I were leader of the work? In Elim to-day we have a splendid band of Ministers, absolutely united on the fundamentals, yet belonging to different schools of prophetic thought. When I come to determine my attitude towards these different prophetic schools, I find myself reasonably compelled to adopt one course out of a possible three, as follows:—

(a) Allow ALL the schools to give their interpretation of the prophetic Word.

(b) Allow SOME of the schools to give their interpretation of the prophetic Word.

(c) Allow NONE of the schools to give their interpretation of the prophetic Word.

Let me show you the position as it appears to me:

If I adopt (c) it will mean forbidding preachers to preach from a very large portion of God's Word.

If I adopt (b) I might favour those who are not as capable of judging prophecy as others who would be forbidden.

The only attitude left is (a), and this to my mind is the only reasonable one, for it gives a square deal to all; it affords an opportunity of exercising loving Christian toleration amongst the students of all prophetic schools.

It might be well at this juncture to state briefly my personal views on the subject of the Israel identity. Let it be understood, however, that my purpose in this article is not to prove, but to simply state what I believe.

(1) I believe that all Jews are Israelites, but not all Israelites are Jews; just as all Welshmen are Britishers, but not all Britishers are Welshmen. In fact, just as the Welsh people are only a small section of the British people, so are the Jews a small section of the great Israel people.

(2) I believe that the greater section of the Israel people, viz: the ten-tribed Israel, was lost for a time, but is now identified in the Celto-Anglo-Saxon races of to-day.

(3) I believe that the only door into the Kingdom of God is the New Birth, through which every Jew, every Celt, every Anglo-Saxon, every person in the world must pass before he can enter the Kingdom of God.

(4) I believe that if the people of the Celto-Anglo-Saxon races reject Christ as Saviour and turn a deaf ear to the warnings and commandments of God, they will come under greater condemnation than other people who have not had their privileges; thus there is no room for national pride but rather for humiliation of heart.

(5) I believe that in view of God's goodness to mankind, all men everywhere should repent, more especially the Celto-Anglo-Saxon peoples who have undoubtedly been blessed of God more than others; that they should be reminded of God's far-reaching promises to a repentant Israel even to the extent of miraculously saving them in the day of battle; that our land should not depend solely upon the arm of flesh for protection against the aggressor, but upon the supernatural power of God; that they should humble themselves before God, receive Christ as Saviour, cast out all idols, obey the commandments of God and conform to the Scriptural pattern of the Christian Church.

Concerning the identity of Israel of the Bible, there are three different viewpoints in Elim.

(1) Some identify the Jews only with the Israel of the Bible.

(2) Some identify the Jews with a section of Israel; other sections, they say, may be in Japan, on the North-West Frontier of India, or are still lost.

(3) Others identify the Jews with a small section of Israel, the larger section being the Celto-Anglo-Saxon peoples.

In this article I am not clarifying the pros and cons of each viewpoint in order to decide which is correct, I am merely considering the question of attitude towards Israel as a whole. There are only three possible courses to adopt:

(a) Allow ALL Ministers to give their interpretation of Israel.

(b) Allow SOME Ministers to give their interpretation of Israel.

(c) Allow NONE to give their interpretation of Israel.

The question as it appears to me is this:

If I adopt attitude (c) I will have to ask each Elim preacher to ignore the word "Israel" every time he comes across it in the Bible, in case he be found guilty of identifying Israelites. This, of course, is impossible without becoming a mutilator of God's precious Word.

If I adopt attitude (b) I will be setting myself up as a judge over men's minds and consciences, and might prohibit the presentation of the most accurate view of Israel with all the loss such would entail.

The only other possible attitude is (a); it is not only fair to all concerned, but it is also gracious enough to allow God's servants freedom and liberty of conscience to preach what they believe without fear or favour as long as they stand Foursquare on the fundamentals.

Thank God, it is gloriously possible to keep the unity of the Spirit amongst followers even though they hold divergent views on prophecy, and at the same time maintain a right attitude towards the inspired prophetic Word. Christian tolerance and charity in all things succeeds every time. This to my mind is the only way to maintain the unity of the Spirit in any Church or Community; it has done so now in Elim for 23 years. I am persuaded that the average intelligence of our Ministers and people is such that we can feel quite happy in trusting them to judge these matters for themselves.

In the early days of my ministry I was deeply impressed by the loving tolerance of two Spirit-baptised believers who were great friends. Both were amongst the leading scholars of the country, one was a barrister-at-law and the other a Church of Ireland clergyman. Having struck a friendship with both, which, thank God, has lasted ever since, I frequently heard them debate on prophecy; one was a Futurist and the other a National-Historicist, and, of course, poles apart on some points. I must confess that I often started the discussion between them in order to listen, weigh up the opposite sides, and receive instruction myself. Time and time again I was present at the clash of those well-trained minds, but never once did I detect any sign of bitterness, both always revealing a spirit of loving toleration towards each other, an example I have ever since endeavoured to follow. One day I perceived that one was being heavily pressed by the weightier arguments of the other, and I fully expected at least some mark of resentment on the part of the former, but again there was the usual manifestation of liberal Christ-like charity; all he said was: "Ah! well, we can agree to stand together on the old Latin proverb which is ever practical —

"In things essential — UNITY.
In things doubtful — LIBERTY.
In all things — CHARITY."

I have always remembered this old proverb, for it sounded so much like the peal of charity bells which keeps ringing in the 13th Chapter of Paul's 1st Epistle to the Corinthians.

Chapter 10
Tributes to the Man and
His Ministry

AT the Coming of Age Celebrations of the Elim Movement in 1936 George Jeffreys was presented with the following Illuminated Addresses, with their tributes to him and his God-given ministry: one on behalf of the Headquarters' Staff and Ministers of the Elim Foursquare Gospel Alliance, given on his 47th birthday, and the other on behalf of the Elim Foursquare Gospel Churches in the British Isles:

PRINCIPAL GEORGE JEFFREYS

Beloved Principal,

WE, the undersigned, on behalf of the Headquarters' Staff and Ministers of the Elim Foursquare Gospel Alliance, wish to place on record our deep appreciation and heartfelt gratitude to God for the great work He has enabled you to accomplish in the Foundation and Leadership of this Movement from its inception unto this, its Coming-of-Age year.

WE have attended with joy the great demonstrations He has privileged you to conduct in the Royal Albert Hall, London, and other of the largest auditoriums throughout the British Isles, and have viewed with praiseful hearts the ever-growing streams of converts to Christ and the mighty miracles performed through your ministry.

WE pray that you may be spared for many years still to continue as Leader of this God-blessed work, should the Lord tarry, and be yet more mightily used in the extension of God's Kingdom.

Great grace and peace be upon you.

(Signed)   Ernest J. Phillips, Secretary-General
W.G. Hathaway, Field Superintendent
Ernest C.W. Boulton, Editor of Elim Evangel
Percy N. Corry, Dean of Elim Bible College

Joseph Smith, Member of the Executive
Council
28th February, 1936

To
PRINCIPAL GEORGE JEFFREYS,
WE, beloved Principal, the undersigned,
on behalf of the
ELIM FOURSQUARE CHURCHES
IN THE BRITISH ISLES,

wish to place on record our deep appreciation and heartfelt gratitude to God for the great service you have, through His grace, rendered to the people of these lands. Twenty-one years ago you were led to the shores of Ireland, and gave that island the honour of being the cradle of what is to-day one of the greatest religious awakenings of modern times. We have viewed with thankfulness the establishment of the Elim Bible College and the great company of preachers you have ordained to the ministry of Christ. We have watched with joy the extension and progress of the work in our own and in other lands, and have seen the answer to our prayers in the multitudes of lives and homes which have been transformed under your ministry.

AS an apostle, you have pioneered the Full Gospel message and established churches in the largest cities and towns in the British Isles.

AS an evangelist, your ministry has been signally owned and blessed of God. Through your faithful proclamation of the old-fashioned Gospel you have led countless thousands to Christ.

AS a preacher and teacher, you have stood uncompromisingly for the Word of God, your expositions of the Sacred Scriptures have enriched our minds and hearts.

AS a leader, you have stood like a bulwark in the midst of backsliding and departure from the faith.

Kindly receive this Address at the Coming-of-Age Celebrations in the Royal Albert Hall, London, as a token of our sincere regard for your past and as an assurance of our prayerful interest and loyal support for the future, as you continue to follow our Lord and Saviour Jesus Christ.

The Lord bless thee, and keep thee,
The Lord make His face shine upon thee,

133

and be gracious unto thee;
The Lord lift up His countenance upon thee,
and give thee peace.

Numbers 6:24-26

(Signed)   John Leech, M.A., K.C.,
              President of First Elim Council
              Geo. W. Gillespie, James Hetherington,
              Edward Ridge, Matthew McGibney,
              Elders of First Elim Church (in Ireland)
              Geo. E. Cooper, Elim Tabernacle, Clapham
              E.J. Osman, Elim Tabernacle, Swansea
              H.F. Mackenzie, Elim Tabernacle,
              Birmingham
              Robt. Waugh, Elim Tabernacle, Edinburgh
              E.R. Redwood, City Temple, Cardiff
              Representatives of English, Scottish and
              Welsh Elim Churches

Whit-Monday, June 1st, 1936

The *Elim Evangel* has a picture taken at the Royal Albert Hall with the caption: "The Principal is here seen receiving the illuminated address from Mr. John Leech, M.A., K.C., who on behalf of the thousands of Elim church members in the British Isles, made the presentation."

In view of these two Addresses, as well as the Resolutions of the Elim Conference of December 1st, 1939, extolling his ministry and requesting his continued leadership, it is incredible that George Jeffreys, who asked nothing for himself and who never failed to preach the same Full Gospel message described here, should be right outside the Movement so shortly after to the end of his days for the reason given in this biography!

Redemption Tidings, official organ of Assemblies of God in Gt. Britain and Ireland, published an article under the title "GEORGE JEFFREYS — APOSTLE OF GOD" by **John Carter,** General Secretary of Assemblies of God. Mr. Carter was first associated with him at the Sunderland International Christian Convention in 1913, two years before the beginning of the Elim work. He writes eloquently, with testimony to the division in the Elim Movement being based on local autonomy of the churches, and concludes with an account of George Jeffreys' funeral service in 1962, given here by way of tribute to him:

"Thursday, February 1st, was a cold, blustery day, but this did not prevent hundreds of people from all over Britain gathering at Kensington Temple, West London, to pay tribute to a beloved leader and outstanding Pentecostal figure.

"In they came, until they packed the body of the church and overflowed into the gallery. Many ministers and leaders from every section of the Pentecostal Movement could be seen in the congregation. What a company! He had drawn crowds in his lifetime, and in his death they gathered to do him honour. The sunshine streamed through the windows making bright the words over the rostrum, a motto made famous by the one we were honouring this day: 'OUR LORD JESUS CHRIST: SAVIOUR, HEALER, BAPTIZER, KING'

"The service was led by Pastor R.G. Tweed, his friend for many years, supported by Commander Macmillan, Pastors E. Marsh, G.I. Francis, D. Quy (representing Lewi Pethrus of Sweden) and A.W. Edsor, who presided at the piano, a service he had rendered the Principal on so many occasions through the years.

"Inspiring words of appreciation were expressed, both by the leader and other close fellow-workers of the Principal, who remarked on his passion for souls, his humility in service, his power with God, his pioneering successes in evangelism and divine healing, and the impact he made on his generation. Pastor Hunziker, who had flown from Switzerland to be present, spoke of the lasting good produced by the Principal's visits to the Continent, and the personal regard of many over there for his ministry and character.

"The interment took place at Streatham Cemetery where his mortal remains were laid with those of his beloved friend who preceeded him, R.E. Darragh.

"Only eternity will reveal the benefits conferred on the Pentecostal Movement and on our nation through His servant, George Jeffreys."

The great hymn, "Guide me, O Thou Great Jehovah!" set to "Cwm Rhondda", rang out, followed by the moving words of the chorus he had fervently sung, in Welsh and in English, less than three weeks before at that same church, in the key of F minor:

"Forgiveness, forgiveness, forgiveness is free,
No matter how sinful, how vile you may be;

135

O come to the Saviour, O come to the Saviour,
O come to Him now and be saved."

Then came the 23rd Psalm so often sung in his campaigns especially in Scotland.

As also reported: "The floral tributes which lined the path that led from the cars to the graveside were later laid on and around the grave. They included scores of the most beautiful wreaths from the relatives (sister, nieces and nephews), Churches, ministers and colleagues, together with a few simple sprays of flowers, all with their worthy tributes which served to express the high esteem in which the Principal was held by men and women in all stations of life."

Dr. Emmanuel Minos, of Norway, greatly used as an evangelist and studying then at Oxford University, who was present at the funeral service, wrote:

"What a deep loss he has left in our hearts! He was a shining light and an upright character, and is now receiving his well-earned reward…It was an experience to be present at our dear brother's funeral service. He has been a great man for the Lord."

From different parts of the world came testimonies such as that from Solveig Barratt Lange, daughter of the late Pastor and Mrs. T.B. Barratt, of Norway, named after Grieg's famous composition *Solveig Song,* who wrote:

"…A wonderful servant of God. I had the privilege to hear him preach once at the World Conference in Switzerland (1947), a very powerful sermon which I will never forget. My late father, Mr. T.B. Barratt, appreciated him very much. I think they more or less were very much alike in their struggle to bring the message of full salvation through the cleansing Blood of Jesus Christ and their opinion of the independent Church. Never seeking their own but filled with one desire — Thy Will, O God!…On behalf of our family." **Solveig Barratt Lange (Mrs.),** Oslo, Norway.

The next three are representative of those early days of the Elim Movement in Ireland 47 years before:

"Always I remember with gratitude and affection the great debt I owed him, that under God he was the means of my conversion 47 years ago. Today he has received the reward for the faithfulness and for the hardships, and often ridicule, he so faithfully endured in pioneering Pentecostal truths and establishing Pentecostal evangelism in those very early days in Ireland and also later in the British Isles and lands afar." — **Miss Adelaide Henderson,** a sister of Pastor William Henderson, one of the first members to join the Elim Evangelistic Band in Ireland.

"We cannot help looking back to the days when he started out first in Hunter Street, Belfast, 1915; the sweet fellowship we had there is something we will always remember and treasure..." **Mrs. M. Wallace,** Belfast 1.

"Deeply regret the passing of our dear friend and my spiritual father" — in telegraph form, from **Mrs. Ann Ralston,** Ballyholme, Bangor, Co. Down, another convert who stood from 1917 on.

This came from **Miss May Polhill,** daughter and niece respectively of Arthur and Cecil Polhill, of the 'Cambridge Seven' so used of God in China: "I thank God for the privilege of meeting the Principal...He was 'a burning and a shining light.'" Cecil Polhill played a responsible part in the early years of the Pentecostal Movement in our country, financially helping George Jeffreys undergo a course of Bible training with the Pentecostal Missionary Union of Great Britain, headed by Mr. Thomas Myerscough, at Preston, Lancashire.

"I shall never forget my first meeting with dear George Jeffreys. I believe it was in the latter part of 1909 in Bristol," wrote **Rev. Stanley Frodsham,** of San Diego, California, U.S.A., collaborator with Smith Wigglesworth in his book *'With Signs Following'* and one-time Editor of the *Pentecostal Evangel,* official organ of Assemblies of God, U.S.A. He went on: "I am glad Brother Jeffreys caught the vision of the pattern set forth in the Early Church, where every local assembly was sovereign. It was costly to follow, to walk in that light, but he paid the price. A goodly number of us in this country have been likewise led to sever connections with the various Pentecostal denominations in order to follow the light which God has shed upon our pathway." Both Stanley and his brother Arthur Frodsham were British.

The Christian head of the firm of Solicitors who dealt with Principal George Jeffreys' personal affairs and those of his revival work, including the legal side of his severance from the Elim Movement, wrote:

"I had an affectionate regard for Principal Jeffreys and, as having known him now for many years, I can understand, though I cannot measure, the loss he will be to your movement and to you personally. It is a comfort to think that, like so many of those dear to us, he is 'with Christ; which is very much better.'" — **Mr. J.T. Davidson,** of Messrs. W.A.G. Davidson, & Co., London, W3.

And this from a member of the staff:

"Although I have actually met him only comparatively infrequently I have felt drawn to him by the goodness and strength of his personality. To say that he will be sadly missed is to be guilty of a gross understatement. He rightly held his own exclusive place in the hearts of the people which cannot be filled by anyone else. I feel his loss as a personal one." — **Mr. E.F.M. Souch,** of Messrs. W.A.G. Davidson & Co., Solicitors.

Letters of sympathy came from Mr. and Mrs. Edwin Shepherd, of the London Emmanuel Choir, Rev. Eric Hutchings and relatively unknown friends blessed through his ministry, with tributes being published in *The Christian Herald, The Christian, The Life of Faith, Elim Evangel, Redemption Tidings, Pentecost Magazine, The National Message* etc., and in periodicals and papers overseas. The *Clapham Observer,* our local newspaper, published an account on its centre pages under the heading "THE LAST OF THE GREAT REVIVALISTS," illustrated with a large photograph of Principal Jeffreys. Attention was drawn to his three great annual meetings at Westminster Central Hall arranged for the coming Easter Monday which would now be services held in his memory. Incidentally, he saw the posters advertising these the night before he was called Home in January, having come in the car to Victoria Station, London, where I collected them through rail delivery from the printers at Brighton.

Appropriate obituary notices and reports were given in such leading papers as *The Times, The Daily Telegraph, The Guardian,* and many provincial newspapers. More sensational and not always accurate reports in other newspapers were not allowed to pass unchallenged. Through correspondence and at least one personal interview with a leading news representative, misstatements were justly retracted.

Having informed the *British Broadcasting Corporation* of the Homecall on January 26th, the following was included in the

News Bulletin that evening at 6.15 in English, in the BBC's Welsh Home Service:

"Principal George Jeffreys, the Revivalist, whose meetings drew congregations of thousands to the Albert Hall, Crystal Palace and other big halls in Britain died suddenly at his home in Clapham, London, today, aged 72 years. Born in Maesteg, he was himself converted in a revival campaign which swept Wales. He founded the Elim Church in 1915, was its leader for 25 years and was given the title of Principal. From 1926 to 1939, Principal Jeffreys held his great series of Easter Monday meetings at the Albert Hall. In 1928, at the Albert Hall he mass-baptised a thousand people in a canvas water tank. And at one of his meetings at the Crystal Palace there were said to be 20,000 people present. He last preached 12 days ago at the Kensington Temple, London."

Three years after these funeral tributes (1965), an evangelist who felt restrained from writing earlier, now paid his own tribute in these words:

"His ministry reminds me of Joseph, who was a fruitful bough, whose branches ran over the wall. The record of his labours more abundant speaks for itself. As he bore the seal of the Lord, so he did the marks of the Lord, until his work on earth was finished — although we might add, his works still follow him.

"Never can we forget the meetings at Clapham, the Royal Albert Hall, the Crystal Palace, etc. etc. Year after year God's seal was upon his efforts.

"How grateful we small evangelists and pastors felt in the success of this outstanding leader, who reminded us of D.L. Moody, Finney, and the like. Converts in thousands will ever remember him; they came from every walk of life and various countries.

"He embodied so many talents in one person; Evangelist, Pastor, Teacher, Warrior, able to minister to ones and twos as to the crowds (his own brother Stephen told me once that he found it most difficult to minister to individuals, even though great liberty was his when speaking to crowds).

"What can we say more? He, Brother George Jeffreys, has now joined the cloud of witnesses gone before, who through faith triumphed gloriously. (Hebrews 12:1)." — **Evangelist W.W. Rogers,** Croydon, Surrey.

Certainly the memories of him and his ministry still live, even after the passing of the years since 1962. My *Open Letter* of July 25th, 1986, has brought forth letters from this and other lands, such as Australia, America, South Africa, and the Continent, some known and others unknown to me personally. Here is one from a Christian lady who neither knew George Jeffreys nor myself, dated 27th May, 1987:

"Thank you, brother, in the Lord Jesus, for sending the book (the *Open Letter*) concerning Pastor Jeffreys, that true man of God. I never had the privilege of listening to the ministry of God from Pastor Jeffreys, but was taught to respect his memory.

"I came to know the Lord in 1961 when I was sixteen years of age, and our pastor was a Welshman, Pastor A.W. — who was then at the W. — Elim Church in London. As I listened to him talk of Pastor Jeffreys, I often thought 'How I would have loved to have heard that man preach the Word of God'!

"It is only Almighty God — the God of all Eternity, Who is the beginning and the end, Who has the eternal vision to know how a matter will fall out..."

After referring to certain happenings in church life which have disturbed her, and of "the complete inability of central government to sort it out," it would appear to her, she writes, "that Principal Jeffreys was absolutely right," adding, "That is only my humble opinion, and I do acknowledge it."

She goes on: "I am glad you wrote the book — 'A good name is rather to be chosen than great riches'...May the Lord help us to get back to the kind of standards that Principal Jeffreys would have lived in private, and preached in public..." (Name and address supplied).

Chapter 11
Members of the Jeffreys' Family
As I have known them

BECAUSE of my intimate association with Principal George Jeffreys I came to know other members of this remarkable family. I begin by referring to his eldest brother, Pastor Stephen Jeffreys, some 12 years his senior, so greatly used as Pastor and Evangelist in South Wales and in other parts of our country, as well as in America, Canada, New Zealand, Australia and South Africa, and whom I first met in 1933. Stephen had ministered with his brother George in South Wales with great effect before the formation of the Elim Movement by the latter in 1915. They were together in Elim for a few years in the early 1920s, either working together or separately in revival and healing campaigns and conventions.

Among other activities, there were the outstanding campaigns in Grimsby and Hull in 1922, conducted by the brothers, followed by visits that year to Goldiswil, Switzerland, with a great baptismal service being held at Berne, in the River Aare, then to Italy with others which included seeing the Colosseum, Catacombs and Vatican in Rome, and passing along the 'Appian Way.' 1923 saw visits to Sweden, Germany and Holland, with joint-ministry at times, of which foreign tour George Jeffreys wrote, "(It) cannot help deepen our lives, broaden our minds, and inspire us to attain greater things for our Lord in the homeland." In 1924 Stephen and George Jeffreys shared in the ministry in an extensive four months' tour of Canada and America, being enthusiastically received and greatly used.

After Stephen had been with his brother as aforesaid, which also meant joint-ministry in Conventions in N. Ireland and with him becoming a "Member of the Council of the Elim Pentecostal Alliance, with which is incorporated The Elim Evangelistic Band," already formed in Ireland, this announcement appeared in the *Elim Evangel*, Vol. 5, December, 1924: "Our readers are specially requested to pray for a Campaign that is to be held in the Public Hall, Barking, London, commencing January 18th (1925). The Missioner will be Pastor Stephen Jeffreys, who is now entirely in Evangelistic work for the Elim Alliance. He resigned his charge as Pastor of Dowlais Church (S. Wales) on Sunday, November 2nd, when crowded congregations attended the closing services of his pastorate." This campaign commenced as stated, being the forerunner of the revival and healing campaign meetings of 1925-26 conducted by the brothers in the East End of London and elsewhere in the capital, and which went on for months. There were great initial results at Barking, the campaign being followed on there by George Jeffreys with reported increasing power and spiritual momentum, and with him then carrying the revival fire to East Ham which speedily took a firm hold, we are told, of the whole district.

The brothers ministered together in the Surrey Tabernacle in Wansey Street, near the Elephant and Castle, a building comparable in size to C.H. Spurgeon's original Tabernacle in the same area. The Surrey Tabernacle saw further scenes of revival power and blessing, with great crowds in attendance daily. Hundreds of converts were baptised by immersion in water and there were mighty miracles of healing in these meetings, which are still talked about by people I know today who were there.

Other notable campaigns were held individually by them at this time at such places as Hendon, North London, Forest Hill in London's South-East, Canning Town, Ilford and Plaistow in the East End. Even during the General Strike of 1926, God was moving in mighty fashion in that vast area despite the adverse conditions, with conversions and healings in evidence on every hand. There were ugly scenes too, as striking workers were on the streets overturning cars in their bitterness. Mr. Darragh told me that as George Jeffreys and Party were approaching Canning Town bridge en route to their revival meeting, men made forward with this intention, when a woman cried out, "Don't touch that car, that's the divine doctor"! They went through unharmed. As a result of these campaigns a number of Elim Tabernacles were opened by George Jeffreys in the East End of London.

The brothers were totally different in style and demeanour — Stephen, by all accounts, having a flamboyancy that was exhilarating, and George with a dignified seriousness which had no need to admit of any change of style. Stephen was essentially a preacher of the Gospel, an Evangelist, whereas George's evangelistic ability was coupled with that of Bible teacher and expositor. God, in His infinite wisdom, chose both, with their own particular personalities and avenues of service, and made them channels, not only of His supernatural power in the salvation of thousands of souls, but in the propagating of fundamental Pentecostal truths leading to the establishing of churches which have stood to this day. In this we see God, Who is no respecter of persons, using these two brothers in the 20th century, brought up in humble circumstances, the elder taken from his heavy work in the coal mine and the younger from his less arduous duties as a shop salesman, contrasted by His use of two brothers in the 18th century, John and Charles Wesley, raised in a completely different environment and Oxford educated as they were.

1926 saw the departure of Stephen Jeffreys from Elim and by 1933, when I first met him, he was well established with Assemblies of God in this country, his exceptional evangelistic gifts being at their disposal in memorable campaigns and conventions. When campaigning in the Skating Rink at Scarborough in 1933 we drove up to Sunderland to meet Stephen, then 57, who was holding forth there. Frankie Allen, known as 'the boy preacher,' whom Stephen knew, was with us. We arrived at the house, and I may say it was with much anticipation I had looked forward to this moment. After standing at a respectful distance in the room as Stephen welcomed his brother and Frankie, I was greatly amused to hear myself being nonchanantly introduced to him as, "This is Edsor. I 'picked him up' at Brighton about five years ago"!

Undoubtedly these two greatly-used brothers, as pioneers, created church congregations for other evangelists and preachers and their Gospel ministry.

In the next 10 years of Stephen Jeffreys' life, the last years of which saw him weak in body but as strong as ever in spirit, I accompanied George Jeffreys on numerous occasions to "Bryntelych," Stephen's home on the Neath Road, Maesteg, S. Wales, where we had fellowship with him, his wife Elizabeth Ann and daughter May, afterwards Mrs. Llewellyn. Stephen became a minister in the Bible-Pattern Church Fellowship after its formation in 1940. In November, 1943, owing to a severe cold, George Jeffreys did not travel from London to attend his brother's impressive funeral service at Maesteg, much as he desired to be there to pay his last earthly tribute to one who had been so signally used of God. It was my privilege to attend on his behalf.

After the service at the Church we sang our final farewell at the graveside in the old Llangynwyd cemetery near by as he was laid to rest with his wife who had predeceased him by almost three years. One of the many wreaths bore the words, "Looking for that blessed hope — loving sympathy from his fellow-ministers of the Bible-Pattern Church Fellowship."

Under the heading: "AN INSPIRING VISION" Principal George Jeffreys wrote and published in *The Pattern* at the time:

"IN our heart to heart talks during latter years, my beloved brother, Pastor Stephen Jeffreys, and I, often expressed mutual regret that we had not seen the full Scriptural vision of free, self-governing Churches right from the beginning of our God-given ministries. Had we, and others, who were called of God to serve as pioneers and leaders in the Pentecostal Movement, seen the vision of the one body, with its members gathered together in free, self-governing Churches as our dear Pastor Lewi Pethrus, of Sweden, had seen it, the history of the Pentecostal Movement in the British Isles would have been vastly different. There would have been one great Pentecostal Movement instead of the various sections.

"Pentecost has demonstrated that it is far too big for sectarian frontiers, and that its leaders, clothed with power and graced with gifts, are called to fields of service far beyond the narrow confines of any one particular sect.

"Desires expressed in those heart to heart talks were laid before our Lord in prayer. Had it been our Heavenly Father's will to miraculously restore my dear brother to health, how it would have rejoiced my heart to have had him at my side, boldly declaring this full Scriptural vision of freedom for God's people! But it has pleased God to take him, and we can say, 'Thy will be done.'

"It is the privilege of those who remain to go on winning souls for Christ, and after winning them, to teach them to conform to the Scriptural Pattern of Holy Ghost Churches, free from the bondage of organised religion.

"What should we not be willing to sacrifice to see the

144

sectarian walls disappear in Pentecost and the greater Pentecostal Revival come!"

Stephen's son, Edward Jeffreys, F.R.G.S., his wife, son and daughter naturally came into our orbit, as did another member of this gifted family of preachers, viz. William Jeffreys and his family. Edward was used for some years in Pentecostal revival and healing campaigns in our land and in the establishing of churches under the Bethel Evangelistic Society he founded. Both he and his Uncle William, brother of Stephen and George, were ministers with the Bible-Pattern Church Fellowship. Then, quite unknown to his Uncle George, and following the death of his father, Edward negotiated with Elim Headquarters for the sale of his Evangel Temple church building at Southport to Elim and gave them his own life-story of his father for publication by the Elim Publishing Company at Clapham, London. He wrote of this to his sister May while she was on a visit to their Uncle George and ministering for him in London, to her distress and his hurt, in the circumstances of the Elim disputation. Such resulted in a number of regrettable misleading inclusions and omissions of essential facts when the book appeared in 1946. As Noel Brooks has written amongst other things of this episode in his book, *Fight for the Faith and Freedom:*

"Why did Edward Jeffreys react so drastically from the Bible-Pattern Church Fellowship, of which he had been a minister, and sell the Evangel Temple, Southport, to Elim? And why did his book omit such significant facts and lend itself so conveniently to bolster up the centrally-controlled Elim Movement, the principles of which were poles apart from those held by his deceased father? It would be futile for one mortal to attempt to plumb the depths of another mortal's soul, or to assess the motives that govern his behaviour."

Edward was well aware of the article "AN INSPIRING VISION" as given in this chapter.

Ultimately Edward Jeffreys became a minister in the C of E in the Chelmsford diocese. The last time I saw him was at his Uncle's funeral service at Kensington Temple in London in 1962. George Jeffreys had borne no antagonism towards him. On the contrary, he had been kindly received with his family at his Uncle's home once the matter, although unredeemable, had been dealt with between them.

I knew three of George Jeffreys' sisters, Margaret, Emily and

Chrisley, their husbands and families in the Maesteg area of South Wales, especially Chrisley, the youngest, with whom we would stay in the little home on Neath Road, Maesteg. In 1987 I had an interesting correspondence with Mr. Glyn Thomas, a nephew, about Kezia Jeffreys, mother of the three Jeffreys brothers and their nine sisters and brothers, six of whom, like her first and second husbands, predeceased her between the years 1879 and 1916. In Glyn's warm appraisal of his Granny Jeffreys he pictured her as being one of a generation of good upright folk whose principles would not tolerate compromise. I saw in this something of the same strong character in George Jeffreys, the son I was most intimate with for so long.

Chapter 12
Other Personal Glimpses
and Contacts

THE minister who wrote from overseas, and to whom I refer in the Introduction also had this to say of George Jeffreys: "It is not in the triumph of a great Revival Campaign that I remember him best. Many men can rise to great heights in public service, but off the platform lose much of their greatness. No one who has been privileged as we have been, to have God's servant as a guest in their home, can ever forget the gentleness and humility of the man. It did not matter whether the home was a castle or a cottage, George Jeffreys endowed it with grace and refreshed the lives of those who lived there." It could be said of him as was said of a noted national personality who recently died, "A gentle courtesy marked his inner strength."

It is this more personal aspect of George Jeffreys' ministry I shall touch on in this chapter. He was a remarkable soul-winner in so many ways, to be seen on his knees at times, with open Bible in hand, and pointing out the way of salvation. I was with him when visiting his solicitor's offices one evening in his latter years. The 'business' concluded with the leading of a prominent member of the staff to Christ as they knelt together and he read the Scriptures to him.

On another occasion in later life, when with a professing Methodist business man in a London hospital ward who had flown to England from Ceylon (Sri Lanka) for an operation, he earnestly talked to him about his soul, how that he could have the assurance of salvation by taking God at His Word. He responded and accepted Christ as his Saviour as they prayed together. Sadly, he died on the operating table, yet for him it was "...with Christ; which is far better." His widow and family invited Principal Jeffreys to take part in his funeral service held at Wesley's Chapel in London's City Road, attended by young men and their friends from Cambridge University, after which the body was flown back to Sri Lanka for burial.

During a passing visit we made to John Wycliffe's Church at Lutterworth in Leicestershire, when I was taken up with reading inscriptions about our great reformer of the 14th century, George Jeffreys was seated with the grave-digger in a pew showing him the plan of salvation from the Scriptures. On reaching London he saw to it that Christian literature was sent to him as a follow-up.

Other phases of his more personal ministry include the time I travelled with him by ship from Ardrossan, Scotland, to Brodick, Isle of Arran, in response to an urgent call to visit and pray for a needy sick person on the Island; that of his introduction to the Royal house where he witnessed to members of the staff at the invitation of a Christian member in charge of all the linens at Buckingham Palace. A few years later, in 1955, he accompanied Commander D.H. Macmillan, RNR., FRICS., FIN to the Palace, in which I shared as chauffeur, when at an impressive Investiture, Commander Macmillan was decorated by the Queen in the New Year Honours with the MBE for his services as Hydrographic Surveyor to the Southampton Harbour Board.

His prison ministry with the London Crusader Choir and its conductor Douglas B. Gray, together with that of the Revival Party, was greatly owned in various ways. In 1964 an ex-prisoner I still know today as an earnest Christian worker and witness wrote me that I had omitted to mention in my former book as part of George Jeffreys' ministry the following:

"After the campaigns in many towns there was always a prison officer who had been saved and who went back to help the work in jails.

"I well remember the day in 1936, in Wandsworth, when George Jeffreys spoke, and the singing after in the prison. You may remember that Sunday. A young lad was to die the next day. I was five cells away from him. I could have been that lad, but by the grace of God George Jeffreys came.

"George Jeffreys did a great work for men in jail and after they left it. I myself gave him a promise that I would never go back. By the grace of God, and help of George Jeffreys, I have never been in jail since May, 1937.

"In your book you talk of the money he left; you say nothing of the money he gave at his door to discharged prisoners or of the many jobs he found for men who had left jails."

This letter has helped me to make amends for what was

overlooked. It was signed, "One of many helped by G. Jeffreys."

I recall household names of some in prison in the 1930s, such as Clarence Hatry, the financier, Lieutenant Baillie-Stewart, known as 'The Officer in the Tower,' and Leopold Harris, the 'fire-raiser,' coming under the sound of the Gospel as the Choir and Party sang, and Principal Jeffreys preached the Word at Maidstone Prison in Kent. Brixton, Wormwood Scrubs and Holloway Women's Prison were also visted for ministry, besides those of Wandsworth and Maidstone. When Pastor Darragh and I would sing a duet at the piano entitled "Leave it there, Take your burden to the Lord and leave it there," with the words of the chorus being, "If you trust and never doubt, *He will surely bring you out,*" this invariably caused a ripple of laughter amongst the hearers in the prison chapel.

Just as there were outstanding healings (chapter 4), there were some outstanding conversions I can attest to in the campaigns. Lord Belhaven and Stenton, a representative peer for Scotland in the House of Lords, came with Lady Belhaven to the Tent campaign at Lincoln in 1935 through a handbill given to them on the street by a Christian worker from the city of York. He accepted Christ as his Saviour in the first meeting of the campaign that afternoon, and afterwards Principal Jeffreys stayed with him and his wife for a few days at Udney Castle, Aberdeenshire. On his return to London a kindly worded card signed "Belhaven," with a view of the castle, was received. Two years later, as reported in the *Elim Evangel,* this distinguished gentleman spoke at a Crusader Rally held at the City Temple, Bath Street, Glasgow, testifying that both he and Lady Belhaven had been "saved" through the Principal's ministry.

Mrs. Marjorie Lancaster, a society girl and cousin of Lord Glanusk, another British peer, had strayed both spiritually and materially into the 'far country,' leading a life of 'riotous living' (Luke 15:13) in South America. She became manager of the England Polo Club in Uruguay, playing in polo matches there and in other South American countries. In 1936 she returned to England and was invited to play in a polo match at the Olympia in London, although it was not permitted for a woman to participate in 'indoor' polo. She did so in the guise of a man, by tucking her hair up under the helmet, and was billed as such! In the rough and tumble of the game down came the hair…Her godly mother and sister persuaded her to attend one of George Jeffreys' revival meetings at that time in Kensington Temple, Notting Hill Gate, and such was the power of God in that crowded gathering, that there, away in the gallery, she came under conviction of sin. To use her own picturesque words: "Never shall I forget that night," she wrote, "shaken myself by the power of God, from head to foot, I witnessed others around me smitten to the ground. I was stirred to the very depths of my heart by the power of the Holy Spirit and cried unto God, 'I have sinned against heaven and before Thee — and as the appeal rang out to sinner and backslider I fell at the feet of Jesus, and from that hour I knew He had clothed me in the robe of His own righteousness and put the ring of the Covenant of His Blood on my finger."

Having yielded her life to Christ, after the passing of some eventful years during which she had an adventurous journey right round the world in war time (a remarkable story), she again went back to Uruguay in 1947 as a Bible-Pattern Church Fellowship missionary. There she is still serving as such, having founded a number of churches in Montevideo and district for the converts she in turn has led to Christ for salvation. Only once has she returned to Britain on furlough and that was in 1963, when she attended our wedding in London as a guest.

Mr. Lewis Byng, half-brother of the actor Douglas Byng, and proprietor of a guest-house and grounds known as "Strathmore" in the Sherwood district of Nottingham, where we stayed when campaigning as a Party in 1938, was led to Christ by George Jeffreys. He had paced up and down on the landing outside George Jeffreys' room under deep conviction of sin, before venturing to knock on the door. He became a good friend of ours and of the Nottingham Bible-Pattern Church, living until the 1980s to the grand old age of 103. Things do not always happen by chance: on driving up from London to fulfil these meetings at Nottingham, I had called at a newsagent's shop for the local paper in which we saw "Strathmore" advertised and this led to the conversion of the proprietor.

Mrs. Gordon, of the Caledonian Hotel, Aberdeen, and Dolphin Square, London, whose sons were Army Officers, one being aide-de-corps to Lord Gort, VC., Commander-in-Chief of the British Field Force in the Second World War, attended the Aberdeen campaign of 1933 in the Music Hall, Union Street. She was converted and purchased an empty church building in

Marishal Street, Aberdeen, and gave it to Principal Jeffreys as a mark of her gratitude, in which to house the converts of the campaign. It was crowded to capacity at its opening in 1934 as an Elim Church, and still functions as such.

As a Party we were entertained by Colonel Gordon, another of Mrs. Gordon's sons, of the Gordon Highlanders, at his home on the River Dee in the Granite City, when he recounted to us how that one morning he saw a large salmon on the door step with a note attached, "With the compliments of the poacher"! I recall Colonel Gordon in the revival meetings waving his hymnsheet and singing with the rest of the congregation, a monocle firmly fixed in place. When re-visiting Aberdeen in after years Principal Jeffreys again visited his home to pray for his sick wife.

I recall George Jeffreys' friendship with that staunch Protestant Christian scholar, Professor Sir Douglas Savory, M.A., of Queen's University, Belfast, and Member of Parliament in London. In 1947 Professor Savory wrote 'An Appreciation' for the third edition of George Jeffreys' book, *Healing Rays,* as follows:

"I heartily congratulate you on your book, which I found most fascinating; above all, from its profound knowledge and interpretation of scripture; and next, owing to the charming style and choice of the most perfect vocabulary.

D.L. Savory
House of Commons,
London, S.W.1.
21st October, 1947"

Another valued friendship was that with Dr. Thomas Cochrane, M.B., C.M., and his second wife whom he married in 1935. Dr. Cochrane was for long a prominent medical missionary in China and co-founder and president of the Mildmay Movement for World Evangelization. In 1953 he invited George Jeffreys to conduct the last revival campaign to be held in the Mildmay Hall in North London, before it was pulled down, of which he wrote: "Never in its long history could Mildmay have had a better example of Biblical Evangelism than that conducted by Principal George Jeffreys in a recent two weeks' campaign. As he stood with his open Bible in his hand he was never at a loss in citing it for confirmation of everything he said. It was quite evident that he had not only fallen in love with The Book, but that he accepted it simply and literally. The 120 who were saved during the campaign were a direct result of the Holy Spirit's application of the Word of God, and not by any form of high pressure evangelism..."

Dr. Cochrane wrote 'An Appreciation' of the book entitled *Pentecostal Rays,* in which he stated: "The loss of spiritual power down through the years is, with occasional exceptions, accounted for by the luke-warmness of the Churches, and now we have spiritual pioneers like Principal George Jeffreys bringing us back in *Pentecostal Rays* to a realisation of our failure and to the need for an infilling of the Holy Ghost with signs following.

"Thousands upon thousands are grateful to God (and none more grateful than the writer) for raising up Principal Jeffreys to meet the need for a New Testament Church in these latter days when we should be doing everything to hasten our Lord's return."

As long ago as 1929 we met the Rev. H. Gahan, the godly vicar of Thrussington in Leicestershire. He and his wife attended the Leicester Campaign of that year where he was anointed and prayed for by George Jeffreys, after which a colleague and I visited him at his rectory at Thrussington. *The Encyclopaedia Britannica* reports of the heroic Nurse Edith Cavell having faced the German firing squad in Belgium in 1915 "with a dignity which moved the world," adding: "To the British chaplain who administered a final sacrament, she made the remark, 'patriotism is not enough,' which at once became as historic as Nelson's utterance at Trafalgar." The British chaplain was the Rev. Horace Gahan whose death at Leicester on February 3rd, 1959, thirty years after we had been privileged to meet and talk with him, was reported in the *Daily Express* under the heading, "THE CAVELL VICAR DIES AT 88."

And what shall I say of that doughty warrior for Christ, Mr. Edwin Scrymgeour, the first and only Prohibitionist to enter our Parliament as Dundee's M.P? He won that Election in 1922, such was his standing in the city, and caused a major political sensation by defeating Winston Churchill at the polls. Churchill, ever magnanimous, wrote in his book, *Thoughts and Aventures,* "I was beaten by over ten thousand votes. And who was the victor? It was the same Mr. Scrymgeour who, at the sixth time, at last had increased his original poll of three hundred to a total of thirty-five thousand. I felt no bitterness towards him. I knew his movement represented after a fashion a strong current of moral and social revival...He lived a life of extreme self-denial; he represented the poverty and misery of the poorer parts of the city and the strong movement towards prohibition of all sorts of alcoholic liquor. When it came to his duty to move the customary vote of thanks to the returning officer, Mr. Scrymgeour moved it instead to Almighty God." He held the seat for nine years until 1931.

Mr. Scrymgeour was present in Dundee's Caird hall in 1932, stirred to the depths at the results attending the revival and healing campaign and, with tears in his eyes, he said to George Jeffreys as he saw the great crowds leaving at the end of a meeting, "To think that people can come into this magnificent hall freely to hear the Gospel as you have preached it tonight!" That was Principal Jeffreys' introduction to Edwin Scrymgeour, of Dundee, Scotland, and both he and his wife remained close friends.

Two other remarkable characters come into focus, Grandpa and Granny Walshaw, of Halifax, Yorkshire, although Granny, an American by birth, first came over to England as a child from USA in a sailing ship in 1853! They fully supported George Jeffreys throughout his ministry in Elim and after until they received the call to higher service; Grandpa at 94, having been one of England's oldest practicing solicitors, and very set in his ways as could be expected, and Granny after him in her 98th year. I represented George Jeffreys and Party at her funeral service at Halifax.

Granny Walshaw was a gifted Pentecostal speaker, with a great sense of fun despite her years, and Grandpa, if somewhat overshadowed by his vivacious wife, was delightful to see, complete with long flowing beard, as he held the anointing oil and joined with Principal Jeffreys and others in prayer for the sick. When their only son Saxon brought his bride-to-be to the home, his mother promptly said to her, "I've been pushing two wheel-barrows for years, now you can push one of them!" Having broken her leg when in her 80s the family doctor said to her, "Granny, you've got grit." "I don't spell it that way, doctor," she replied, "I spell it G-O-D." And walk normally again she did, as we saw for ourselves.

It was Granny who telegraphed Principal Jeffreys in 1941 in this simple form, naming the Scriptural reference only, when he was being sorely tried in the Elim division and facing up to the 'disfellowshipping' alluded to in chapter 8: "Luke, chapter 6, verses 22 and 23 — Lydia Walshaw." Such was the spiritual perception of this grand old Pentecostal lady at 88 years of age in sending a message that did as much as anything to lift the heart of God's servant: "Blessed are ye, when men shall hate you, and when they shall separate you from their company, and shall reproach you, and cast out your name as evil, for the Son of man's sake. Rejoice ye in that day, and leap for joy (or 'spin round for joy' as a version has it) for, behold, your reward is great in heaven: for in the like manner did their fathers unto the prophets."

Christianity is a record of triumph and tragedy. Helen Mary (Mollie) the granddaughter of the Walshaws, married Edmund (Teddy) Hodgson, a greatly-used missionary in the Congo (now Zaire) with the Congo Evangelistic Mission, founded by our Pentecostal brethren, W. Burton and J. Salter. George Jeffreys conducted the marriage service at the Elim Tabernacle, then in Bond Street, Halifax, on Saturday, January 7th, 1939. Prior to this we had driven under hazardous road conditions from London to Stranraer, Scotland, en route to Belfast via the sea crossing to Larne, for the annual Christmas Convention, 1938, with three meetings on Christmas Day and three on Boxing Day. We had actually been snowed up all night on the Pennines between Scotch Corner and Alston, a detour we tried in vain with the main road to Bowes, Brough and Penrith being blocked. With the exceptional wintry weather still obtaining, we left Belfast for Glasgow, for the New Year Convention at the City Temple and Regal Cinema. Then came the journey to Halifax.

After the wedding service in which two souls decided for Christ, one being the eldest sister of the bridegroom, we drove back to London through the night, taking passengers with us, with the Great North Road, the A1, like a ploughed field. It was necessary for us to return right away as Principal Jeffreys had been announced to preach at the Clapham Elim Church that Sunday, January 8th.

Unknown to us our brother-minister at Glasgow, Leslie Newsham, aged 33, coming to the wedding by car, had met with a serious accident on the icy road near Beattock, being taken into the Cottage Hospital in Moffat, Dumfriesshire — the news came through by 'phone that Sunday morning as we were about to leave for the Church. He died the following Thursday evening.

154

On the Friday morning George Jeffreys and I left on the 'Royal Scot' train from Euston to Glasgow for his funeral service at Moffat on Saturday, January 14th, where the text of his last sermon given at the Glasgow City Temple is to be seen on the gravestone, "I have a desire to depart, and to be with Christ; which is far better."

Ministers and friends came from various parts to join with the sorrowing family in the bitter cold, to walk behind the hearse from the Presbyterian Free Church of Scotland loaned for the service and conducted by Principal Jeffreys, to the cemetery outside the little town, the houses with drawn blinds as a mark of respect and sympathy. The sequel being that 20 years later, in 1959 Edmund (Teddy) Hodgson and a New Zealand missionary colleague, Elton Knauf, were brutally murdered in the Congo, the latter bravely offering his own life in an effort to save that of his friend. A remarkable factor in this record being: at the marriage service on that January day in 1939, we had sung something not usually associated with a wedding, viz. *The Te Deum,* with its poignant prophetic words, "The noble army of martyrs: praise Thee." At the impressive Memorial Service to these modern martyrs conducted by Donald Gee at the Bloomsbury Chapel in London, it was appropriate I was invited to make reference to the marriage service and the *Te Deum* and to read from Revelation, chapter 7, vv. 9-17.

Death in its various forms is near at hand at all times for the Christian and non-Christian alike. In the 1950s George Jeffreys, for the pleasure of a young lad of about 12 visiting him in London from Northern Ireland, accompanied us to the Farnborough Air Show, with its then advancing technology in the breaking of the sound barrier for the first time. This had been well publicised, with John Derry as the test pilot. As he and the navigator flew over us, and the thousands gathered closely together on the airfield, he did just that, then at a speed of some 600 miles an hour, tragedy suddenly struck. We saw the plane disintegrate high in the sky ahead of us as it was turning again to make a repeat run and two 'specks' coming from it and going away to the right of us behind a ridge which hid them from us and our section of the crowd. Not only were the pilot and navigator killed as the plane fell on an unoccupied part of the airfield, but the 'specks' were, I believe, the engines, red hot, which plunged into the crowd killing 32 onlookers. We did not know the full extent of the

155

tragedy until we heard the 6 o'clock news that evening. We grieved with the Nation for the mourning relatives, and the injured, realising that had the plane been positioned a fraction to the left on turning those 'specks' could have come our way with the three of us possibly being among the dead or injured. In such circumstances the Word of God comes home in all its stark reality when it declares, "My times are in Thy hand..." implying how essential it is to be ready for Eternity which faces all men everywhere.

In this account of personal glimpses and contacts must be mentioned certain other outstanding personalities George Jeffreys invited to minister from time to time at the Bible-Pattern Church at Kensington Temple, London, and elsewhere, such as Smith Wigglesworth, renowned as 'the apostle of faith' who, when I was about to drive him home after the meeting, suddenly placed a huge right hand firmly upon my hat and head from where he was sitting in the front passenger seat of the car and vehemently prayed, as he pressed the hat over my ears, "Lord, keep your hand upon this wheel!" There was also Gladys Aylward whom we took in the car, converted at Kensington Temple some years before when it was known as Horbury Chapel, that intrepid little missionary who, against all odds, got through to China with the Gospel and whose fame through her exploits for God and escape with the children in her care from before the advancing Japanese, is so well established in Christian circles world-wide.

I recall Hugh Redwood, famous author of *God in the Slums* and *God in the Shadows,* and Fleet Street journalist, who testified at one of Principal Jeffreys' Easter Monday meetings at the Westminster Central Hall.

Among those who became missionaries is John H. Dring who, in 1958, wrote to me as Editor of *The Pattern* from Formosa, Argentina: "I am from Nottingham and attended the Nottingham Campaign almost from its beginning, and was baptised (in water) on December 18th, 1930...I have been out here since 1935, working among Creoles and Indians. Praise God for the wonderful things that the Lord has done during these years. Looking back it is more wonderful than any novel could be; and, praise God, the seed was set right back there in the 1930 Nottingham Campaign. To Him be the glory!"

In 1957 George Jeffreys received a letter from Rev. F.O.

156

Bennett, M.A., of the Presbyterian Church of South Africa, Newcastle, Natal, in which he testified to his miraculous healing of 26 years before at Sheffield when he was Mr. Bennett. He could not stoop without pain and wore first a semi-rigid belt, then a plaster jacket with metal stays, for two years. He wrote: "I do praise the Lord for all the ways He has led me and I thank Him for using you in 1931...I have never once kept quiet about what I owe to you."

Albert E. Munday, founder in 1938 of the "Gospel to Brazil Faith Mission," wrote George Jeffreys from Brazil on Easter Monday, April 7th, 1958, to say he had heard his IBRA radio message, having turned on the radio at random without any idea of wave-length. He went on, "I came into the Pentecostal truth during your first campaign at the Central Hall, Southampton, 1927. From then on, by the grace of God, I continued seeking ever to make known the glorious message as a local worker. Then God called me for missionary work in Brazil." He referred to the great Easter Monday gatherings at the Royal Albert Hall, adding, "It seemed so fitting that tonight (Easter Monday) I should be sitting at home here in the vast hinter land of Brazil! Here too souls are coming into the wonderful liberty of salvation and healing in Christ Jesus. Be encouraged, Jesus will never fail, your message is reaching farther than you think." Some 13 years later the news came through that Albert Munday had died in a car accident in Brazil on February 28th, 1971, George Jeffreys' birth date, again demonstrating Christianity to be a record of triumph and tragedy.

A boy of some 12 years of age was baptised by immersion in water with hundreds of others in the 1930s at the Crystal Palace in London. In later life, now Rev. Philip Audemard, L.Th., Dip. R.E., Th.L., he became a Baptist minister serving churches in England, then in Australia until his homecall there in 1986. For many years he publicised of what he knew of Principal George Jeffreys' ministry and meetings in the Old Country, helped by my regular correspondence with him and fired by a Pentecostal fervour created early in his own heart and life.

Two brilliant musicians were in touch with George Jeffreys and had fellowship with him in meetings and in our home in London between 1958—1960, namely the celebrated Finnish concert violinist Heimo Haitto and the pianist Robert Harkness, from USA. Heimo Haitto in February, 1939, at the age of 13, made his debut with the Helsinki Philharmonic Orchestra and immediately won the musical attention of Finland. In May of that year he travelled to London to participate in the International Competition of the British Council of Music. Although the youngest competitor he won the 1939 award...In 1940 he appeared as soloist with the Stockholm Symphony and the Malmo and Oslo Philharmonic Orchestras. He went to the United States and made his American debut with Eugene Ormandy and the Philadelphia Orchestra.

This celebrated violinist played the violin and testified at Kensington Temple here in London on May 11th, 1958, telling of his conversion to Christ some 18 months before through the faithful witness of an artist who painted his portrait. It was my privilege to accompany him at the piano as he played several spiritual items after which George Jeffreys gave the message. Having played the Sibelius Violin Concerto with the London Philharmonic Orchestra (he had come specially from USA for this one performance), Heimo Haitto left for a series of evangelistic campaigns in Finland and Scandinavia.

Robert Harkness, as long ago as 1902 was with the Torrey-Alexander Mission Party as pianist, being musical composer of over 2000 hymns and gospel songs still sung by congregations and Christian soloists all over the world. In 1904 he played for Dr. R.A. Torrey's great campaign in the original Bingley Hall, Birmingham, a function I was to perform for George Jeffreys in that same hall 26 years later. Born in Bendigo, Australia, he lived for many years in USA. When asked why he had never taken American nationality, he would answer with a twinkle in his eyes, "I am British. If you can give me something better than being British I'll accept it."

Our first contact with Robert Harkness was on the occasion I drove George Jeffreys and some Swiss friends visiting us, to the Baptist Church, Lewin Road, Streatham, in April 1960, where we heard him minister at the piano. He invited those in the congregation to choose one of his solos on which he would improvise. I asked him to play his very tuneful composition entitled *"On Calvary,"* a copy of which I held in my hands as I stood up at the back of the church. To my surprise, on noticing the copy, and wishing to refresh his memory as to which solo it was, he asked me to come to him at the piano, whereupon he went further and requested me to sing it, which I did to his accompaniment. He ministered in Bible-Pattern Churches and had fellowship with us as a Party in our home on a number of occasions.

During George Jeffreys' meetings in Denmark in 1947 and again in 1949, when he preached to crowded congregations in the Concert-Palace Theatre and the famous 'Grundtvigs Hus' Hall in Copenhagen, where crowds began to queue outside some two hours before the announced time, with a meeting also in the Casino Theatre in the town of Slagelse, his interpreter was Mrs. Anna Larssen-Bjorner who is well worthy of mention. She was one of Denmark's greatest dramatic actresses, in Shakesperian and other roles until at the height of her powers and successes she renounced the stage for ever. She had found the Lord Jesus Christ as her Saviour and from that moment dedicated her life to evangelism. Those with her in the theatrical world thought she was out of her mind, such was the change wrought in her life, but like the Apostle Paul she could say, "I am not mad, most noble Festus; but speak forth the words of truth and soberness." (Acts 26:25).

We visited the Royal Court Theatre in Christiansborg Palace, Copenhagen, erected in 1766. It is preserved as an historic building only and is known as "The Danish Theatre Museum" containing many interesting relics used by stage personalities of the past. A room in the Theatre Museum was exclusively dedicated to Anna Larssen as a mark of her fame, then the only living legend so honoured. We stood with her and her husband, Pastor Sigurd Bjorner in that room and gazed upon various pictures of her in her stage roles as well as on objects used by her in her career as an actress, but one thing stood out above everything else — her own letter of resignation from the theatrical world in 1909, with its clear testimony of salvation, framed on the wall for all to see and read. The director's son, our escort, made a special point of drawing our attention to this document, and of playing Anna Larssen's own recording of the well-known hymn, "Oh, the peace my Saviour gives, Peace I never knew before; For my way has brighter grown, Since I learned to trust Him more."

Singularly, the Casino at Slagelse where George Jeffreys preached and Mrs. Larssen-Bjorner interpreted was the very theatre in which she had played her last stage role those 40 years before! No longer acting in the world but still witnessing for her Lord and Saviour.

George Jeffreys could sometimes do the most unexpected things, especially with his interpreters on these foreign tours. Although adept at speaking in this way he would take them by surprise in humorous fashion. For instance, in Copenhagen he began a message by reading Isaiah 41 and verse 1, "Keep silence before Me, O islands..." when Anna Larssen-Bjorner, who was a fervent believer like himself in the Israel identity, ejaculated, "That's it!" whereupon he spontaneously said to her, "You tell the people 'that's it!'" On another occasion in Finland, in 1947, accustomed as he was to male interpreters, he again had a lady by the name of Miss Sylvi Mommo in this capacity and splendid interpreter she was too. As we came to the last meeting of the tour he said how much he had enjoyed ministering in Finland, seeing the beautiful lakes and countryside, hearing the singing in minor keys, so like his own native Wales, then he suddenly added, "I have had one great blessing here," and as she interpreted this he paused, looked at her and said, "My interpreter!" much to the amusement of herself and the congregation.

Incidentally, when we left Pori following the great summer Pentecostal Convention there, for the capital Helsinki, many young people came out very early in the morning, to bid us farewell, playing and singing with their musical instruments.

Another celebrity who must have a place in this chapter is Mrs. Arthur Booth-Clibborn, better known by the title 'The Maréchale,' bestowed because of her great soul-winning work on the Continent. She was the eldest daughter of General William Booth, the Founder of the Salvation Army, and had contact with George Jeffreys at the long-established Keswick Christian Convention in the beautiful Lake District of England. Being at Keswick himself and hearing she was there also, he instructed me to call on her, to ask if she would like him to send the car to take her to a Tent meeting. I was invited into the house by her daughter Catherine, the wife of the Rev. Noel Palmer, who was caring for her mother. I came face to face with this formidable lady clad as she was at that hour of the morning in a dressing gown fastened together by a very large safety pin, which in no way detracted from that air of authority one associates with the Booth Family. I said I would call and 'collect' her at the agreed time, whereupon she laughingly said, "Am I then a Post Office parcel, to be 'collected and delivered?'"

Later, in the short time I was alone with her in the car, she took the opportunity to ask me, "Why did George Jeffreys resign from the Elim Movement?" a question I was in a position to answer to her satisfaction I felt. For a number of years until her death in 1955 she exchanged warm Christian greetings with George Jeffreys at Christmas from her home in Devonshire, hers being boldly signed 'The Marechale.'

I was with George Jeffreys in 1961 when he met Dr. Martyn Lloyd-Jones, having attended a Sunday evening service at the Westminster Chapel in London. At the close of the service he was invited to meet his famous contemporary in his vestry. As he entered Dr. Martyn came forward to warmly shake hands, saying as he did so, "This has just made my day," to which George Jeffreys responded by asking, "Where did we last meet, in one of my meetings?" "No," replied the doctor, "in one of mine." George Jeffreys sent him a copy of his book *Pentecostal Rays* and had a kind acknowledgment in reply.

At the end of February, 1952, Principal Jeffreys and Party held meetings in the Bedford Town Hall, with the hall crowded and people having to be turned away. During that two weeks' campaign we visited Mrs. Paske, widow of Colonel Henry Paske, then in her 96th year and resident in Bedford. She had been associated with the 1907 Pentecostal outpouring in Great Britain, recalling many names of that period, such as, Mr. Cecil Polhill, of the Cambridge Seven, Mr. Mundell, a London solicitor, Pastor T.B. Barratt, of Norway, Canon Alexander Boddy, of All Saints Church, Monkwearmouth, Sunderland, Mrs. Catherine Price, and others. She had attended the Royal Albert Hall meetings, particularly remembering the great occasion on Good Friday, 1928, when Principal Jeffreys had held that memorable initial baptismal service in that famous auditorium.

Because the late Colonel Paske, also an earnest Christian believer, was a Crimean and Indian Mutiny veteran, and in consideration of the family's services to the Sovereign, Mrs. Paske had occupied a grace and favour residence at Hampton Court Palace for nearly 40 years, holding Christian meetings in her rooms there.

During the 1914—18 war she received special permission from

the Army authorities to visit the main railway termini of London, to give out gospel tracts to the troops as they entrained for France and other battle fronts. Some 67,000 tracts were disposed of by Mrs. Paske in this way, to men of all ranks alike. Such devoted service will have brought its own reward.

We broke bread with her at the communion service prepared in her own room at Bedford.

I must mention Mrs. Eva Knott, of Kennington, London, who was 100 years of age on June 26th, 1987. She found Christ as her Saviour under the ministry of Stephen Jeffreys in the former Horbury Chapel, Notting Hill Gate, as a result of which she became associated with George Jeffreys and his revival work from the days of the first Elim Church at Clapham, London, in 1922. Recently, as clear brained as ever, although confined to the house, she was telling me she assisted at that initial 1000 baptismal service in the Royal Albert Hall on Good Friday, 1928. After the candidates were baptised by total immersion and came out of the water dripping wet, the women candidates were helped with the aid of towels being applied to their faces by Mrs. Knott and other lady helpers, as they made their way to the dressing rooms in the corridors behind the platform. She said with a chuckle that her beautiful new dress specially worn for this historic occasion was soaked through, something that had not been foreseen!

My wife and I were with her and relatives and friends on her 100th birthday, seeing her enjoyment at receiving many messages of congratulation including a telegram from HM The Queen, and baskets of lovely flowers. The day also saw the usual visit of the Mayor to offer his congratulations. A week before we took communion with her at her home during the prayer time of which she spoke in other tongues, in Pentecostal fashion. We also saw her in 1988 on the day after her 101st birthday, as alert as ever.

In such a full life over so many eventful years there are other contacts I could write about, such as when I drove Lewi Pethrus, of Sweden, and George Jeffreys from London to Cardiff in April, 1939, where they ministered to crowded congregations at the Cardiff City Temple (Elim), but space forbids. Yet I cannot close this chapter without referring to an exalted personage in connection with George Jeffreys' Easter ministry, from his Royal Albert Hall years until his last Easter Monday meetings in

London in 1961. I allude to the Monarch as the recipient of loyal greetings and assurance of prayers which he sent annually by telegram on behalf of himself and congregations, first to George V, then Edward VIII, George VI and our present Queen Elizabeth II. Usually an acknowledgment would be received signed by the Private Secretary on the Monarch's behalf, which would be read out followed by the people standing to sing the National Anthem, then "All hail the Pow'r of Jesu's Name!" The year 1956 proved to be an exception, the message as sent read:

GREAT ANNUAL BIBLE-PATTERN CHURCH FELLOWSHIP GATHERINGS AT THE WESTMINSTER CENTRAL HALL, LONDON, THROUGHOUT THIS EASTER MONDAY, SEND LOYAL GREETINGS TO YOUR MAJESTY, REMEMBERING YOU IN YOUR ONEROUS DUTIES OF STATE AND PRAYING THE BLESSING OF GOD UPON YOU AND THE ROYAL FAMILY ACCORDING TO NUMBERS, CHAPTER 6, VERSES 24 TO 26

GEORGE JEFFREYS

It brought this telegraphed reply from Windsor Castle, indavertently addressed to:

LORD JEFFREYS, GREAT ANNUAL BIBLE-PATTERN CHURCH FELLOWSHIP GATHERING, CENTRAL HALL, WESTMINSTER, SW1

reading as follows in the first person and signed by the Queen herself, as is customary to her Peers:

I THANK YOU AND ALL THOSE WITH YOU IN SENDING YOUR KIND AND LOYAL MESSAGE WHICH I SINCERELY APPRECIATE

ELIZABETH R.

I have called this chapter "Other Personal Glimpses and Contacts," but not forgetting those who were unknown to us apart from their letters. One vividly stands out who, when she sent her gifts from a small town in Scotland, requested that these be acknowledged under her initials only in the magazine. In 1950 Principal Jeffreys heard from the solicitor acting for her executor, that she had left the residue of her estate, i.e. £957.9.8d, to the work of the World Revival Crusade, having initially received so much blessing in one of his revival and healing campaigns.

163

Chapter 13
Six Messages Broadcast by Principal George Jeffreys over IBRA Radio —
The Swedish Pentecostal Radio Work

> Study to shew thyself approved unto God, a workman that needeth not to be ashamed, rightly dividing the word of truth — 2 Timothy 2:15.

> Earnestly contend for the faith which was once delivered unto the saints — Jude 3.

THESE radio messages are of necessity brief, yet to the point. Were his messages in general long? They might be at times, but between thirty and forty-five minutes was the usual order. Then would come an appeal for souls before ministering to those seeking Divine healing. Principal Jeffreys would emphasise the word 'Divine' as contrasted with 'Faith' healing which might merely mean the power of mind over matter, rather than the supernatural touch of God in answer to prayer and the laying on of hands. "There is nothing in my hands," he would say, "they are simply laid on those in need, according to the Scriptures." He would urge the Christian believers in the congregations to add to the exercise of faith for the healing of the sick, by their sympathy and prayers.

In dealing with Bible truths for the edification of God's people, George Jeffreys saw to it that he would bring in "enough Gospel to lead others to Christ for salvation."

His messages given at the Royal Albert Hall and elsewhere included such subjects as 'The Gospel of the Miraculous,' covering the miraculous in the Christian Religion — in the Virgin Birth and in the Life and Ministry of Christ; the miraculous at the Cross, the Resurrection, in the Outpouring of the Holy Spirit on the Day of Pentecost, and still to be at the Second Advent of

Christ; the miracle of conversion, of prayer, and of our Bible and its preservation.

He would draw practical lessons from such subjects as The Ass and the Lamb (Exodus 13:13) — representative respectively of the sinner and the redemptive work of Christ as the Lamb of God; Elijah and Elisha (1st and 2nd Kings); the Pharisee and the publican (Luke 18); the analogy between the birth of a baby in the natural and that of the spiritual 'New Birth' (John 3:3 and 7); the Apostle Paul before King Agrippa (Acts 26) — and other themes dealing with salvation, sanctification (a doctrine which can sometimes be confused in its propagation), water baptism by immersion, church order and discipline, healing, the baptism of the Holy Spirit and miraculous gifts, the fruit of the Spirit of Christ, the return of Christ, and Bible prophecies fulfilled and in the process of fulfilment.

He would 'paint' what he termed 'word pictures' which made the subject the more vivid to the mind's eye. A manager of a theatre said that he had never heard such a dramatic portrayal as that given from the stage of his theatre, i.e. Paul before Agrippa.

He would also deal with questions on particular subjects, those specially put to him in writing by enquirers seeking enlightenment on Bible truths.

FIRST MESSAGE — SALVATION

"What think ye of Christ?" The religious leaders of our Lord's day had to face up to this vital question and give their answer. The pharisees to whom it was addressed had been in close touch with our Lord and had known something of His manner of living. They had heard Him preach His powerful gospel and had witnessed His miracles. They had listened to Him as He opened up the Scriptures with great authority, but they never expected to be called to sit in judgment upon Him. Yet this question, "What think ye of Christ" placed them right on the judgment seat and demanded of them a verdict on the all-important matter: Was Jesus God or was He only a man?

Their verdict deprived Christ of His Deity, for they declared Him to be the son of David, not the Son of God. In their judgment He was not God's Lamb, destined to die an atoning death for the sin of the world. Our Lord then wielded the Old Testament Sword of the Spirit and proved beyond question that Christ was God manifested in human nature.

This great question put to every one within the sound of my voice tonight places you on a judgment seat, and you have to render your verdict. "What think ye of Christ?"

The Scriptures declare that there is to be a day when Christ shall take the judgment seat, to judge the quick and the dead at His appearing. A day when the world shall be judged in righteousness by Christ. Tonight the order is reversed. Instead of Christ judging you, you are judging Christ. In order to give righteous judgment you are asked to consider:

Firstly, a leading question, was Jesus of Nazareth a good man? Let me ask a few witnesses who lived in His day to step out of the New Testament to give evidence of His goodness. Pilate, who had closely examined Christ, publicly stated: *I find no fault in this man.* The governor's wife who sent a message to her husband said: *Have nothing to do with this just man: for I have suffered many things this day in a dream because of Him.* The inspired writer of the Acts of the Apostles tells *How God anointed Jesus of Nazareth with the Holy Ghost, and with power, who went about doing good and healing all that were oppressed of the devil.*

I don't suppose there is anyone listening to me who would say that Jesus was not a good man. The centurion who witnessed the crucifixion of Christ, as the rocks rent, the graves opened, the earth reeled, the sun hid its face, and as nature mourned, cried aloud: *Certainly this was a righteous man.*

I have ministered in revival and healing campaigns throughout the British Isles and elsewhere for over 40 years, and I have never come across one person out of the vast multitudes who has said Jesus was not a good man.

Secondly, was Jesus of Nazareth God? A young ruler once came to Jesus and addressed Him thus: *Good Master, what must I do to inherit eternal life.* You will remember our Lord's reply: *Why callest thou Me good, there is none good save God.* In other words, if you cannot believe I am God manifested in human nature, you cannot believe I am good.

Jesus was God veiled in human form. He claimed to be the only door into the Kingdom of God; the only Giver of eternal life to sinners; the only Bread of Life to satisfy spiritual hunger; the only Living Water to quench soul-thirst; the only Way, to follow; the only Truth, to lean upon; and the only Life in which to abide. He also claimed to be the only possessor of the keys of death and of hell.

I feel sure that all who are listening to me do believe Christ is the Good Samaritan. But it is through faith in God's definite plan of salvation we receive the forgiveness of sins and the gift of eternal life. Note the three steps to salvation and life given in John 5: 24. Our Lord is speaking: *Verily, verily I say unto you, He that heareth My word, and believeth on Him that sent Me, hath everlasting life, and shall not come into condemnation; but is passed from death unto life.* **Hearing-Believing-Taking** Eternal Life as a Gift!

SECOND MESSAGE — DIVINE HEALING

During the last 40 years the miracle of bodily healing has increasingly claimed the serious attention of the religious world. Today, in most denominations, church doors are wide open to the Truth.

It was not easy for its pioneers at the beginning of the generation, for they faced great opposition.

The subject has brought forth volumes from the pens of many writers — some relegating the miraculous to a past dispensation, others postponing it to a future Millennium. The pioneers, of course, maintained that God is unchanging. He is the same yesterday, and today, and for ever.

The one great reason why it is now dominating the mind of Christendom is the fact that thousands are bearing testimonies to bodily healings. They claim to have been miraculously healed in answer to prayer under the ministry of the laying-on of hands or the anointing with oil, as people were in Bible days. These manifestations of healing are not confined to the British Isles, they are being experienced over the whole world. Everywhere deliverances from deadly diseases are avowed, and miracles are being wrought, the replicas of which can only be found in the Bible. Neither are they exclusively experienced by any particular sect or community that holds Divine healing as one of its fundamental truths, but by spiritual ministers, evangelists and church workers of all denominations.

There is a big difference between Divine healing and what is known as faith-healing. We prefer the former term because it generally implies belief in bodily healing as it is exclusively taught in the Scriptures, whereas the latter might mean healing by faith along the many lines of psychology. The former denotes acceptance of the Bible as the Word of God in its entirety, and

167

healing through the Lord Jesus Christ. The latter can mean belief in some kind of faith-healing that might be decidedly anti-Christian.

God, in His love and mercy, has provided healing for the sons of men in two realms — the natural and the supernatural. There is a natural law of healing in the bodies of believers and unbelievers alike. Having studied this fundamental law, physicians are in a position to assist nature to heal itself. They minister to the needs of the sick and suffering in the natural realm. Doctors and nurses need our prayers as they seek to alleviate the sufferings of their needy patients. The natural law of healing in human nature, like sunshine and rain, is one of the many gifts bestowed upon humanity by the goodness of God, to lead all to repentance.

Bodily healing in the supernatural realm is clearly taught throughout the whole range of Scripture. The Christian Church right down through the centuries has emphasised the truth that the Bible is the Word of God, that its commandments should be implicitly obeyed, and its promises believingly appropriated. Why then should it be a cause for wonderment if thousands, having believed its teaching, can testify to miracles of healing, and cases that were incurable in the natural realm can testify to healing in the supernatural?

Let me now speak directly to those who are seeking bodily healing in the supernatural realm. God's Will concerning the salvation of the soul and the healing of the body is clearly revealed in the Bible. Listen to this Scripture, 1st Timothy, chapter 2, verses 3 and 4: *For this is good and acceptable in the sight of God our Saviour; Who will have all men to be saved, and to come unto the knowledge of the truth.* Are you thus in line with God's Will? If not, you can be by simply calling upon the Lord and accepting His Word as the answer. Listen to these Scriptures, Romans, chapter 10, verse 13: *Whosoever shall call upon the Name of the Lord shall be saved.* 1st John, chapter 5, verse 14: *And this is the confidence that we have in Him, that, if we ask anything according to His will, He heareth us.*

Have you been anointed with oil by the elders of your church, according to God's Will in this Scripture? James, chapter 5, verses 14 and 15: *Is any sick among you? let him call for the elders of the church; and let them pray over him, anointing him with oil in the Name of the Lord; And the prayer of faith shall save the sick, and the Lord shall raise him up; and if he have committed sins they shall be forgiven him.*

God bless you and keep you in His Will!

THIRD MESSAGE — BAPTISM OF THE HOLY GHOST

Have ye received the Holy Ghost since ye believed? The Scriptures make a difference between the gift of eternal life, which is offered to the unsaved, and the gift of the Holy Spirit, which is offered to the saved. Our Lord, speaking to saved disciples, said: *If ye love Me, keep My commandments, And I will pray the Father and He shall give you another Comforter, that He may abide with you for ever; Even the Spirit of Truth; Whom the world cannot receive, because it seeth Him not, neither knoweth Him; but ye know Him; for He dwelleth with you, and shall be in you.*

These disciples were living in the dispensation of the Son before the Holy Spirit had been poured forth. But they were in possession of eternal life which they had received when they accepted Christ as Saviour. They were therefore not of the world; they were ready for the Holy Spirit who was **with** them, soon to enter **into** them on the coming Day of Pentecost.

The twelve disciples in Acts 19, to whom Paul put the question *Have ye received the Holy Ghost since ye believed?* had received eternal life when they accepted Christ as Saviour under the ministry of John the Baptist. Now, some twenty years later, they received the gift of the Holy Spirit under the ministry of Paul at Ephesus.

John the Baptist, the forerunner of Christ, was ordained of God to go before our Lord to prepare His way, and to give knowledge of salvation unto His people by the remission of their sins. John ministered in the dispensation of the Son. Students of Scripture will know that the Bible divides the whole of time into three major dispensations: The dispensation of the Father, which commenced at the beginning of time, continued for almost four thousand years: the dispensation of the Son covered the period when God tabernacled in Jesus of Nazareth for about thirty-three years on this earth: the dispensation of the Holy Spirit, which commenced on the Day of Pentecost, continues to this, our day, and will continue until Christ comes in power and glory at His Second Advent.

The gift of eternal life has been received by penitent sinners from the beginning of time, and will be received by such right up to the end. Each individual in the numberless company of the redeemed in Heaven will only have one reason for being there, and that will be fully expessed in song: *Unto Him who hath loved us, and washed us from sin, unto Him be the glory for ever, Amen.*

The gift of the Holy Spirit was not poured forth during the dispensation of the Father, nor in the dispensation of the Son. The prophet Joel who lived in the first, foretold that the outpouring of the Spirit would take place in the third. Our Lord, in the second, made it plain that the Holy Spirit had not been given in His day, because Jesus was not yet glorified. The outpouring of the Holy Spirit was reserved for the third dispensation, which began on the Day of Pentecost over nineteen centuries ago and will continue until the return of Christ.

Peter's message on the Day of Pentecost gives the pattern for presenting the truth: *Repent, and be baptised every one of you in the Name of Jesus Christ for the remission of sins, and ye shall receive the gift of the Holy Ghost.* A sinner truly repents by turning to God and accepting Christ as his personal Saviour. Repentance is not a state of sorrow, fear or remorse; it is an act of obedience. Baptism by immersion in the Name of Jesus Christ is the outward witness that the penitent has found eternal life in the Death of Christ. Having obeyed the Divine commandments concerning repentance and baptism, each individual believer can claim the gift of the Holy Spirit, because the promise is made to all.

FOURTH MESSAGE — SECOND ADVENT OF CHRIST IN EVANGELISM

In our day attempts are being made to restrict evangelists to the preaching of Bible words about salvation to sinners. All the other words in the Bible are treated as not belonging to Evangelism.

Our answer is — The Evangel in Evangelism is the whole of the Written Word of God!

The teaching of the Second Advent of Christ is part of the evangelistic message, because it is in the inspired Word of God. The Second Advent of Christ is prophecy — history foretold — but if the world is to be saved from self-destruction it will soon need to be history — prophecy fulfilled.

Let us divide the subject under three headings: The Promise of

His Coming. The Manner of His Coming. The Effect of His Coming.

The Promise of His Coming was made by Christ Himself when He was on earth. I am reading from John, chapter 14:

Let not your heart be troubled: ye believe in God, believe also in Me. In My Father's house are many mansions: if it were not so, I would have told you. I go to prepare a place for you. And if I go and prepare a place for you, I will come again, and receive you unto Myself, that where I am, there ye may be also.

The Jesus who said. "*I go*", was the Jesus who said, "*I will come again*". True to His word He went along the road of suffering and shame, translating many Bible prophecies into history; passing through the death of the Cross, the triumph of His Resurrection, and the glory of His Ascension into His Father's house of many mansions, just as He had said. He will therefore come again as He said He would.

The Manner of His Coming was given by the two angelic witnesses of His Ascension from the Mount of Olives. I am reading from Acts 1, verses 9 to 12:

And when He had spoken these things, while they beheld, He was taken up; and a cloud received Him out of their sight. And while they looked stedfastly toward heaven as He went up, behold, two men stood by them in white apparel; Which also said, Ye men of Galilee, why stand ye gazing up into heaven? this same Jesus, which is taken up from you into heaven, shall so come in like manner as ye have seen Him go into heaven.

The Effect of His Coming is given in I Thessalonians. I am reading from chapter 4, verses 16 to 18:

For the Lord Himself shall descend from heaven with a shout, with the voice of the archangel, and with the trump of God: and the dead in Christ shall rise first: Then we which are alive and remain shall be caught up together with them in the clouds, to meet the Lord in the air: and so shall we ever be with the Lord. Wherefore comfort one another with these words.

The Second Advent of Christ **will affect** the Christians who are alive on earth, for mortals will put on immortality and the challenge will go forth — *"O death, where is thy sting?"* The Second Advent of Christ **will affect** the dead in Christ, for corruption will put on incorruption, and another challenge will go forth — *"O grave, where is thy victory?"* What comforting words! What a *"blessed hope"* for those who are in Christ!

171

The Second Advent will inaugurate an Age, in which all the effects of the first Adam's disobedience will be wiped out and all the benefits of the last Adam's obedience will be enjoyed in a new heaven and a new earth. Listen to the prophetic voice in Revelation, chapter 21, verses 3 and 4:

And I heard a great voice out of heaven saying, Behold, the tabernacle of God is with men, and He will dwell with them, and they shall be His people, and God Himself shall be with them, and be their God. And God shall wipe away all tears from their eyes; and there shall be no more death, neither sorrow, nor crying, neither shall there be any more pain: for the former things are passed away.

When our Lord returns He will not find a converted world, He will find a world in rebellion against Himself and His people; a world suffering from the greatest time of trouble it has ever known. Let me read from Matthew, chapter 24, verses 21 and 22:

For then shall be great tribulation, such as was not since the beginning of the world to this time, no, nor ever shall be. And except those days should be shortened, there should no flesh be saved: but for the elect's sake those days shall be shortened.

It is the Second Advent of Christ, with power and great glory, that will shorten this time of great tribulation. Only the manifest power of God from Heaven will be able to destroy the manifest forces of evil then on the earth.

The lowly Babe of Bethlehem's manger, the humble Jesus of Nazareth, the Crucified Christ of Calvary, will be seen in that day clothed with power and great glory, shortening the time of tribulation on earth for the sake of the elect.

Preachers of the inspired Word of God faithfully warn us that the time of the end is upon us. Leading scientists, historians, philosophers and statesmen also warn us that we are living at the time of the end.

Listen to Einstein, the scientist —

"Annihilation of any life on earth has been brought within the range of technical possibilities. The ghost-like character of this development lies in its apparent compulsory trend".

Listen to Wells, the historian —

"The end of everything we call life is close at hand, and cannot be evaded...there is no way out of, or through, or around the impasse, it is the end".

Listen to Joad, the philosopher — He had found Christ as

172

Saviour just before he came to the end of his earthly life, and very soon afterwards he asked the question:

"Will God once again intervene with one of His mighty acts to arrest the drift of mankind to destruction?"

Listen to Churchill, the statesman —

"We and all nations stand at this hour before the portals of supreme catastrophe. Well may we humble ourselves and seek for guidance and mercy".

The question might be asked by someone listening to me this evening: Are persons **elected** to be saved? The question is best answered thus: On the outside of the door into life eternal are the Bible words: *"Whosoever will may come".* When once the convert is inside, he can read over the inside of the door the Bible words: *"Elect according to the foreknowledge of God the Father".*

Are **you** one of the elect, one who has accepted the Lord Jesus Christ as their own personal Saviour? If not, accept Him **now** on the authority of God's Word in Romans 10:13 — *For whosoever shall call upon the Name of the Lord shall be saved.*

FIFTH MESSAGE — GOD'S PLAN OF SALVATION FOR SINNERS AND GOD'S PATTERN OF LIFE FOR BELIEVERS

The Bible teaches that all are under condemnation because *"all have sinned and come short of the glory of God."* But believers in God's plan of salvation have not only had their sins forgiven, they have had their condemnation removed. Listen to God speaking of believers in the opening words of Romans, chapter 8:

There is therefore now no condemnation to them which are in Christ Jesus...

Again, in Romans, chapter 5:

Therefore being justified by faith, we have peace with God through our Lord Jesus Christ.

Throughout almost 50 years of continuous revival ministry my soul has been stirred to its depths again and again as I have listened to thronging crowds singing with sanctified fervour the words of Wesley's well-loved hymn:

"No condemnation now I dread;
Jesus, and all in Him, is mine!
Alive in Him, my Living Head,
And clothed in righteousness Divine,

173

Bold I approach the eternal Throne
And claim the crown, through Christ my own."

God's Pattern of life for believers emphasises that they should become members of the local churches. Listen to the writer of the Epistle to the Hebrews instructing believers in chapter 10, verses 24 and 25:

And let us consider one another to provoke unto love and to good works: Not forsaking the assembling of ourselves together, as the manner of some is; but exhorting one another: and so much the more, as ye see the day approaching.

God's Pattern for the local church is given in Matthew, chapter 18, verses 15 to 20. Each church is seen as a centre of practical holiness, verses 15 to 17:

Moreover if thy brother shall trespass against thee, go and tell him his fault between thee and him alone: if he shall hear thee, thou hast gained thy brother. But if he will not hear thee, then take with thee one or two more, that in the mouth of two or three witnesses every word may be established. And if he neglect to hear them, tell it unto the church: but if he neglect to hear the church, let him be unto thee as an heathen man and a publican.

Each church is also seen as a centre of supernatural power, verses 18 to 20:

Verily I say unto you, Whatsoever ye shall bind on earth shall be bound in heaven: and whatsoever ye shall loose on earth shall be loosed in heaven. Again I say unto you, That if two of you shall agree on earth as touching any thing that they shall ask, it shall be done for them of My Father which is in heaven. For where two or three are gathered together in My name, there am I in the midst of them.

Thus in words that came over the sacred lips of Christ — The Living Word — and which are recorded in the Bible — The Written Word — Christ Himself established the sovereignty of each local church. There is no hint anywhere in the New Testament of central control over a church or a group of churches.

"Tell it unto the church" in verse 17 of Matthew, chapter 18, cannot possibly mean the Universal Church, part of which is in Heaven and part on earth. **It can only mean the local church.**

Implicit obedience to these commandments of Christ would mean churches free from malice, guile, hypocrisies, envies and evil speakings. These stunt spiritual growth and hinder revival, and it is a tragedy when local churches are legally deprived of this Divine Pattern for cleansing and power.

The registered members of the local church can only be assured of their Scriptural right to obey the commandments of Christ in their church building, by having a legal right to a voice and a vote in the conduct of their own church affairs.

In the practical outworking of Matthew 18, verses 15 to 20, **each local church should have at least four essentials:**

(1) An up-to-date membership register in which no name can be added to, or taken from, except by a resolution passed at a church members' meeting.

(2) A minute book in which the decisions of its church members' meetings are recorded in resolution form.

(3) A copy of its constitution for each member, clearly stating the working arrangements of the local church.

(4) A Trust Deed, or a lease, or a rent book, as advised by a solicitor, to ensure that the church property is held in trust for the registered members of the local church.

Because formal Protestantism has neglected or ignored Christ's Pattern for His Churches in Matthew 18: 15 to 20, one of the most powerful promises in the Word of God has been surrendered to a false centrally-controlled priesthood that has no foundation whatsoever in the New Testament.

All preachers of the Gospel are commissioned by Christ to teach **all** things He Himself has commanded them. Listen to His words in the 28th chapter of Matthew, verses 19 and 20:

Go ye therefore, and teach all nations, baptizing them in the name of the Father, and of the Son, and of the Holy Ghost: Teaching them to observe all things whatsoever I have commanded you: and, lo, I am with you alway, even unto the end of the world. Amen.

SIXTH MESSAGE — THE ISRAEL KINGDOM

In this broadcast Principal George Jeffreys dealt with four important phases of Bible teaching, including his belief that the Israel Kingdom is God's chosen servant nation to the world, according to Isaiah 41: 8: *But thou, Israel, art My servant, Jacob whom I have chosen, the seed of Abraham My friend.* He maintained that Israel would continue to function as a nation on earth as long as the sun, moon and stars were in the heavens.

Jeremiah 31: 35—36: *Thus saith the Lord, which giveth the sun for a light by day, and the ordinances of the moon and of the stars for a light by night...If those ordinances depart from before Me, saith the Lord, then the seed of Israel also shall cease from being a nation before Me for ever.* He taught that the Kingdoms of Judah and Israel (separated since the captivities) will be reunited on earth in the end—time, according to Ezekiel 37: 16—22: *Moreover, thou son of man, take thee one stick, and write upon it, For Judah, and for the children of Israel his companions: then take another stick, and write upon it, For Joseph, the stick of Ephraim, and for all the house of Israel his companions...And I will make them one nation in the land upon the mountains of Israel; and one king shall be king to them all: and they shall be no more two nations, neither shall they be divided into two kingdoms any more at all.*

In his pamphlet entitled "Three Schools of Thought on the Israel Question" in which he deals with The Jewish School, The Church School, and the Israel School, he shows that the Jewish people comprise only a small section of the whole house of Israel. The multitudes of Celto-Anglo-Saxon peoples of the British Commonwealth of Nations, the U.S.A., Scandinavia, the Netherlands, etc. (as yet partially blind to their destiny) comprise the much larger section, and he quotes from Romans 11: 25: *...blindness in part is happened to Israel, until the fulness of the Gentiles be come in.*

A further quotation from this pamphlet reads: "The indisputable fact that, although all Jews are Israelites, all Israelites are not Jews, gave me the right premises that led to right conclusions. The truth is demonstrated in my own experience. All Welshmen are Britishers, but all Britishers are not Welshmen."

In his broadcast message he went on to say: "To every one who is listening to my voice over the air tonight, whether you be Israelite, Jew or Gentile, **let me emphasise that there is only one way of salvation for all** and that is by accepting Christ as your own personal Saviour, on the authority of the Written Word of God. Listen to God speaking to you from the 1st Epistle of John, chapter 5, and verse 13: *"These things have I written unto you that believe on the Name of the Son of God; that ye may know that ye have eternal life, and that ye may believe on the Name of the Son of God."*

176

Conclusion

...Hitherto hath the Lord helped us — 1 Samuel 7:12

ONE is moved to read of what was reported of George Jeffreys and his pioneer co-workers of 1915 onwards, such as:

"Though many a time well-nigh overwhelmed, they staggered not through unbelief, but were strong in faith, giving God the glory, and being fully persuaded that what God had promised He was well able to perform. These great-hearts had, like the Apostle Paul, learned in the school of the Divine Spirit how to be abased and how to abound. They were willing if need be, to go anywhere and to be anything for Jesus; the master impulse of their lives was to please Him. To them to live was Christ. All things were possible through Him."

It is a far cry from that first Minute recorded by the Elim Evangelistic Band on January 7th, 1915, when they declared: "We agree that God promises to supply the temporal needs of every Evangelist that would be called by Him into the work, and that through prayer and faith in His promises He would prove Himself to be to each one Jehovah Jireh," to 1962 when Principal George Jeffreys' Will was made known. He had proved this beyond measure, so much so that I believe he would have been surprised at the amount of his personal estate, yet modest as it was. For years until the end he took only a very nominal salary, being a man of simplest tastes. Some five years before his decease, however, he benefited considerably under the Wills of two good friends, which accounted for approximately half his estate, the larger donor in particular insisting that he was to use this personally in his old age. His estate would have been larger still had he accepted all gifts offered personally because of the blessing grateful donors had received through his ministry; but he saw to it that they were used to help further the work of God, to which cause indeed he bequeathed all his formal assets, a clear indication that the work was very much on his heart to the end.

After leaving legacies to his last surviving sister who bore thankful testimony to her brother's goodness to her over the long years, myself and another, he named as the residuary legatee of his Will the World Revival Crusade, through which, since 1935, he had pioneered for Elim and then for the Bible-Pattern Church Fellowship.

The Divine promise in the Name Jehovah Jireh — "The Lord who provides" — never failed him in over half a century of ministry, his Lord and Master faithfully supplying before the world the needs of His servant who in turn gave back to God's work that which had been so graciously provided. This was in the sum of £14,300, contributing towards the help the World Revival Crusade has been able to give Bible-Pattern Churches in obtaining places of worship of their own.

It is fitting that reference should be made here to Pastor Darragh, co-worker with Principal Jeffreys from 1915-1959. On the day which saw the Principal's 70th birthday, February 28th, 1959, R.E. Darragh, having been conversant with the congratulatory telegrams and letters from those in many parts of the world, and sharing in the birthday luncheon which he had arranged, suddenly received his homecall as we were about to retire for the night. And so that long and fruitful earthly companionship was broken. Principal Jeffreys gave a powerful appeal for souls at the graveside at Streatham Cemetery, Garratt Lane, Tooting, London, a grave he was himself to occupy almost three years later.

It is a remarkable fact that they both died suddenly when in harness and without lingering illnesses or pain-wracked bodies, and considering their extensive travels through life, each in their own home in London, both at 72 years of age, the cause of death being given as coronary thrombosis in both instances.

Significantly, just two weeks after having made his Will, R.E. Darragh was gone. After remembering myself and another, he left the residue of his modest estate, as did Principal Jeffreys, to the World Revival Crusade.

Pastor Darragh also had a ministry in the gifts of the Holy Spirit, to which this extract from a letter testifies: "I remember, too, the wonderful convention meetings in Belfast at Christmas time, and there is one in particular which stands out in my mind most vividly. It was an ordination service, and truly waves of glory swept over the place, and it became hallowed ground. On that particular occasion Mr. Darragh gave a message in tongues, the thrill of which I still catch. It seemed to me then just like a voice from heaven, and we knew that God was in the place."

Many testimonies came in at the time of his death, some touching on the long association of 44 years together. Six words in one of them says it all, "It has been a wonderful partnership."

As regards George Jeffreys' decease in 1962, he had been conferring only the day before with a few of us Bible-Pattern ministers at the house, and out in the car in the evening. I had been with him as usual sharing the same room through the night hours and had talked with him the next morning before 8 o'clock. Just before I left him he saw the bold headline on the morning newspaper, 'Atrocities in the Congo,' and commented to me, "What a state the world is in!" something that can surely be repeated today. When Pastor Eric Marsh entered the room by 9 a.m. the homecall had come to God's servant when he was alone.

In the foregoing chapters we have endeavoured to portray George Jeffreys for what he was — a man of God who stood true at all costs to what he believed God had revealed to him from The Written Word. His worthy life, unsparing ministry and labour, and indomitable courage challenge us to go on contending, as he did, for the whole Counsel of God with its emphasis on the restoration of true Primitive Christianity in the whole Church. This is no easy task, especially as it means stressing the autonomy of each local church according to the New Testament Pattern. This ancient but revolutionary doctrine cuts right across organised formal religion in this country with its powerful secular and carnal grip on the people of God, who must be freed.

Pentecostal people and others often sing the 'Old Hundredth,' used as it is at times on stirring State occasions in our country —

For why? the Lord our God is good;
His mercy is for ever sure;
His truth at all times firmly stood,
And shall from age to age endure,

bearing in mind it was our Lord Himself who said: "...If ye continue in My word, then are ye My disciples indeed; And ye shall know the truth, and the truth shall make you free" (John 8:31—32).

In bringing this biography to an end I quote these expressive words in memoriam:

A servant of the living God is dead!
His errand hath been well and truly done,

And now hath he gone to his reward:
He shall come no more forth, but to his sleep
Hath silently lain down, and so shall rest.

Would ye bewail our brother? He hath gone
To Abraham's bosom! He shall no more thirst,
Nor hunger, but for ever in the eye,
Holy and meek, of Jesus, he may look
Unchided, and untempted, and unstained.

Would ye bewail our brother? He hath gone
To sit down with the prophets by the clear
And crystal waters; he hath gone to list to
Isaiah's harp and David's, and to walk
With Enoch and Elijah, and the host
Of the just men made perfect. He shall bow
At Gabriel's hallelujah, and unfold
The scroll of the Apocalypse with John
And talk of Christ with Mary, and go back
To the last Supper and the garden prayer
With the beloved disciple. He shall hear
The story of the Incarnation told
By Simeon, and the Triune Mystery
Burning upon the fervent lips of Paul.
He shall have wings of glory, and shall soar
To the remoter firmaments, and read
The order and the harmony of stars;
And, in the midst of knowledge, he shall bow
In the deep pauses of archangel harps,
And humble, as the seraphim, shall cry —
"Who, by his searching finds Thee out, O God!"

There shall he meet his children who have gone
Before him; and as other years roll on,
And his loved flock go up to him, his hand
Again shall lead them gently to the Lamb,
And bring them to the living waters there.

— *Willis.*

When this remarkable occurence took place in the life of this leading present—day Pentecostal Evangelist, George Jeffreys may have appeared aged to a young man of 21, although perhaps not to those in general who still knew him publicly and privately: and at this time he was ministering at Kensington Temple, London, as is shown in this biography.

This extract is reproduced as it was sent to the biographer early in December, 1988, and read with much pleasure, having first been mentioned by *New Wine Ministries*. Singularly enough, a saying of George Jeffreys was, "We serve our day and generation."

Extract from the book on
HOLY-GHOST EVANGELISM
by Reinhard Bonnke
with George Canty

The Great Commission
To Each Generation

PASSING ON THE FLAME

IN 1961, at just 21 years of age, I completed my studies at the Bible College of Wales in Swansea, the UK. I could go home to North Germany. The route took me via London. My train was not due to leave until the evening, so I spent the time doing some sight-seeing. I went where I pleased, and somehow wandered on to the nice avenues of Clapham, South London. Then, on one pleasant road, I saw in front of me a notice on a panel — "GEORGE JEFFREYS." I had just read a book by this evangelist and could hardly think I had chanced upon the very house where the same man might be. George Jeffreys came out of the Welsh Revival and, with his brother Stephen, introduced the flame of the full Gospel message publicly to the people of Britain. His work shook cities, and tens of thousands saw mighty miracles. He planted not only churches, but an entire movement. Here was a man worthy of the name of apostle. Eagerly I ventured up the path to the door and rang the bell. A lady appeared and I asked, "Is this the George Jeffreys who founded the Elim Pentecostal Church?" The reply, to my delight, affirmed my hopes. "Could I please see Mr. Jeffreys?" The reply was a firm "That is not possible." But then that deep Welsh musical voice, that is said to have held thousands spellbound with its authority, spoke from inside, "Let him come in." Thrilled, I entered, and there was George Jeffreys, looking to me like a man of 90, but then 72.

"What do you want?" were his words to me. I introduced myself and then we talked about the work of God. Suddenly the great man fell on his knees, pulling me down with him, and started to bless me. The power of the Holy Spirit entered that room. The anointing began to flow, and like Aaron's oil seemed to run over my head and "down to the skirts of my robes," so to speak. I left the house dazed. Four weeks later, like Elijah, George Jeffreys had been taken to glory. He died soon after I saw him. But I knew I had picked up something from this former Holy-Ghost, fire-brand evangelist. I am sure the Holy Spirit had arranged my meeting with him. How else was it possible that I should stumble upon this one house in a city of ten million people when George Jeffreys wasn't even on my mind?

Whatever this happy event did for me, one thing I can claim — seeing this man made me understand that we build on the people who went before. It is like a relay race. One man runs with the baton, another grabs it and runs, and then another and another. They share in the race. If one drops the baton, or even runs badly, the efforts of all are spoiled. The team cannot win. We read about "the cloud of witnesses" from the past cheering us on as it were from the battlements of glory. We must do a little more than they, not a little less, because it is the last lap before Jesus comes. The Great Finish is already in view. Do you see what the following Scripture means?

"And the Gospel of the kingdom shall be preached in all the world for a witness unto all nations, and then shall the end come (Matthew 24:14)."

The theme of the hour, **God's** theme, not our slogan, is HOLY-SPIRIT EVANGELISM, the first item on God's agenda for today. The Holy Spirit's power is the only way to reach our generation effectively with the Gospel. We have only one generation to reach our generation. The original Gospel is impossible without the original power. The perfect plan of God is there, and we are part of it. He enmeshed us within it from the start. If we know that, then we can do it...go it...weather it...finish it...no matter what.

Appendices

Appendix 1

AN OPEN LETTER
TO MINISTERS AND PEOPLE OF THE ELIM
MOVEMENT, ASSEMBLIES OF GOD AND
THE BIBLE-PATTERN CHURCH
FELLOWSHIP
25th July, 1986

From: PASTOR ALBERT W. EDSOR
(Principal George Jeffreys' Private Secretary, Secretary of his
Revival Work and last Member of his Revival Party)

A REFUTATION OF
MISREPRESENTATIONS PUBLISHED IN
RECENT BOOKS ENTITLED 'THE GREAT
EVANGELISTS' BY PASTOR DESMOND W.
CARTWRIGHT AND 'RESTORING THE
KINGDOM' BY DR. ANDREW WALKER

'Touch not Mine anointed, and do My prophets no harm'
— 1 Chronicles 16:22/Psalm 105:15,
with other Scriptures making it plain as to the penalties which
God exacts on those who either wilfully or carelessly cast
doubts upon His own works through His servants.

To
  The Reader,

HAVING read these books I have been left with a choice — either I allow these grave misrepresentations about Principal George Jeffreys' life and work to go unanswered or else put the record straight. I feel before God that the decision I have come to is the right one, hence this Open Letter.

I would ask you to bear with me if you have not had a copy of either of the books. Obviously I have to send this out at random but such an action serves this purpose: it helps to turn back that which has so grievously clouded vital issues in Elim's history as they relate to George Jeffreys for almost 50 years.

MY CLOSE ASSOCIATION OF 34 YEARS

I must first introduce myself and give my background before dealing with these pressing matters. The new biography of Principal George Jeffreys on which I am engaged in anticipation of reaching a much wider public will take time to produce, whereas this Refutation needs urgent attention.

I maintain no one is more qualified to undertake such a biography of Elim's Founder and greatest pioneer for the following reasons: A member of the C. of E. I was brought to Christ through George Jeffreys' ministry at Brighton, Sussex, in June 1927 and 15 months later, when 18 years of age, I became a member of his Revival Party as pianist-organist and driver of the car. This led to my very close association with George Jeffreys as his private secretary and secretary of his revival work (known as the 'World Revival Crusade' from 1935 on and of which I became the director, at his wish, following his decease in 1962), living, working and travelling with him wherever his ministry or leisure time, rare as this was, took him here in the homeland and abroad.

On the day of the funeral his last surviving sister Chrisley said to me under deep emotion when I met her and other members of the family at Paddington Station, "I am so thankful the Lord did not take you before my brother," which I took as a spontaneous generous tribute to my years of service to him in his lifetime and which has helped inspire me to further service in his honoured memory.

POWERFUL FOURSQUARE GOSPEL MESSAGE

Those 34 years, from 1928 to 1962, beginning for me as they did just 13 years after the founding of the Elim Pentecostal Movement, cover all the great revival and healing campaigns and conventions of George Jeffreys at home and overseas during that long period, as well as the administrative side of his work and, too, his traumatic severance from the Elim Movement he loved and faithfully served for 25 years, on the issue of *Church Government and that issue alone.* To the end of his life he preached *the same* glorious Foursquare Gospel message he had always preached, viz. Jesus the Saviour, the Healer, the Baptiser in the Holy Spirit, and the Coming King.

I was ordained in Elim in 1934 at Kensington Temple, Notting Hill Gate, London, W11 with 23 others including the late Pastors P.S. Brewster and Douglas B. Gray, the latter being conductor of the London Crusader Choir. I remained a fully accredited minister of the Foursquare Gospel Churches of the British Isles, afterwards the Elim Church Incorporated, until my renewal certificate was withheld at the end of 1940 by the Executive Presbytery of the Elim Church Incorporated. This was because I chose to stand with George Jeffreys and others for the reform policy of government advocated by him for the Movement. *This will be gone into in the biography,* as well as other issues including the happy association with Stephen Jeffreys, in my case from 1933 when I first met him in Sunderland in company with his brother George, until his death 10 years later, George Jeffreys' charitable stand *when in Elim and after* for freedom of conscience and expression on all schools of prophetic interpretation provided fundamental truths were faithfully maintained, and the present-day position of the Bible-Pattern Church Fellowship and its relationship with the Elim Movement.

HISTORIAN WITHOUT FIRST-HAND AUTHORITY

The 'Elim Evangel' of April 19th, 1986, official organ of the Elim Pentecostal Church, in announcing the publication date of Desmond Cartwright's book entitled 'The Great Evangelists' (Marshall Pickering), advertised it as tracing "the history of the two brothers from their infancy in Wales, through the great crusades *to their subsequent obscurity.*" (My italics). It is with this latter aspect I am mainly dealing in this my emphatic refutation of what Pastor Cartwright has written of the last 20 years of George Jeffreys' life and ministry — 20 years no less! With all his 'qualifications' as listed at the beginning of the book plus researching the Elim archives as official historian, and despite my contacts with him over 6 years since 1980, even loaning him early volumes of 'The Pattern' magazine, he has signally failed to tell the truth on vital issues. Following his conversion in 1949 he entered the Elim Bible College at Clapham Park in September 1952 and became an ordained Elim minister in September 1957, *some 18 years after the division in the Movement,* but this should not have prevented him as an historian from stating the facts surrounding this and other issues of importance even though he was not present in person.

'PICTURE POST'

He devotes the merest reference to these last 20 years towards the very end of his book, beginning by writing, "It saddens me to have to record the details of the last years of George Jeffreys life: things might have been different" (page 157). And what are these 'details' he intends to 'record'? one may well ask, when he goes on to add, after giving his own absurd ideas about the outcome of the Stockholm Pentecostal Conference of 1939 (at which I was present), which in no way tally with the facts as they concern George Jeffreys, "We pass over the remaining years of George Jeffreys life in a few words. After he left Elim he spent a time in the wilderness" (page 158). Then, after a few derogatory remarks about his latter achievements and a brief reference to his 'greatest success' in the post-war years, again not factual, he proceeds to cite 'Picture Post' by way of confirmation presumably of this 'wilderness' experience, by writing, "When the 'Picture Post' wrote about him in May 1946" — he had the date wrong until I corrected him, for which he thanked me! — "they called him one of the last great revivalists. Yet their report and pictures could *only* show him ministering to a small group of elderly ladies: things might have been so different" (page 158. My italics). Clearly the impression is being conveyed that George Jeffreys' ministry was finished, Mr. Cartwright having added by way of emphasis, "We regret the way that things turned out in his later years" (page 158). *Such an intolerable misrepresentation is unbelievable in the the light of the facts,* as Mr. Cartwright knows as well as I and others do from the paper as published. A Pentecostal minister telephoned me being unaware that I had a copy of Mr. Cartwright's book, to say he had read it and viewed its general tone with distaste; but more particularly he was in possession of 'Picture Post;' of May 1946 and was appalled at Mr. Cartwright's presentation of this.

THE TRUTH

Now let me give the truth. The paper published a lengthy article by A.L. Lloyd*, its own representative, on George Jeffreys' life and ministry, the Elim Movement and the division, and the formation of the Bible-Pattern Church Fellowship of free, self-governing churches, together with no less than 9 excellent pictures, large and small, showing sick ones being prayed for, newly-won converts being baptised in water (32 passed through the waters in two such services arranged by Principal George Jeffreys, baptiser, assisted by Pastor R.G. Tweed in the baptistry, within a fortnight in March-April, 1946), and part of the enthusiastic congregation entering into the singing and waving their hymnsheets at these Kensington Temple meetings in London, in which Pastor R.E. Darragh was the song-leader as ever and I was at the piano.

* See Appendix 2

METROPOLITAN THEATRE, LONDON

Immediately prior to its publication George Jeffreys had preached in the notable Metropolitan Theatre in the Edgware Road, on Sundays, March 3rd, 10th, 17th and 24th, afternoon and evening, with the weeknight meetings being held at Kensington Temple. These revival activities had obviously attracted the attention of 'Picture Post', hence the exceptional publicity given through their representative having attended there and witnessing at least one of the two baptismal services held on March 31st and April 14th respectively.

That issue of the paper went to different parts of the world from the publishers, letters being received by George Jeffreys from such countries as far apart as Australia and Greece, the latter being a desperate appeal for prayer from one who had read a translation of the article as published in a Greek newspaper and who went so far as to affix a photo of Principal Jeffreys on the air mail envelope inadequately addressed (which I still have), that it might be sure to reach him in London!

A REMARKABLE SEQUEL

It had a remarkable sequel: George Jeffreys was talking to a stranger when passing through a town in the North of England. She was from a Staffordshire town and told him she had ordered a copy of the book 'Healing Rays' referred to in the article. She was amazed to discover she was talking not only to the author of the book but to the one who had figured so prominently in the paper. He had the great joy of leading her to Christ for salvation.

INVALUABLE COMMENTS IGNORED

In strongly remonstrating with Mr. Cartwright over his false presentation of the 'Picture Post' article and the last 20 years, I enumerated to him in writing, in an eight-paged foolscap letter, having seen a rough proof copy of his manuscript just shortly before he had his final proofs in January, 1986, a catalogue of other unprecedented 'details' he had left out or misrepresented, a proof copy on which he had written, "I would welcome your comments, any correction on detail or facts"!

What tremendous years they were in revival power and blessing and soul-saving ministry!

GREAT PUBLIC HALLS CROWDED

Mr. Cartwright makes no reference at all to the fact that in these 20 years George Jeffreys continued to engage great public halls and fill many of them, even during the Second World War, 1939—1945, such as the famous Ulster Hall, Belfast, the Wellington Hall and Royal Hippodrome, Belfast, the equally famous Royal Dome and Pavilion, Brighton, the Guildhall (then newly opened), Southampton, the large hall of the Caxton Hall, London, the Metropolitan Theatre, London, already referred to, the Theatre Royal, Brighton, the Lyric Theatre, Glasgow, the Albert Hall, Nottingham, the Grand Theatre, Halifax, the City Hall, Sheffield, the Empire Theatre, Bristol, the Palace Theatre, Southampton, the Royal Assembly Hall, Plymouth, Town halls at Bournemouth, Hove, and elsewhere, to name some of them, often with queues forming and waiting outside for admission, besides ministering in many, many churches including the well-known Westminster Chapel, Buckingham Gate, London, taken for the purpose, conducting great Tent campaigns and conventions, and preaching to crowded meetings on the

Continent, in Scandinavia and Finland, being engaged fully in the ministry of healing, seeing to it that the converts were taught to follow the Lord through the waters of baptism, to seek the baptism of the Holy Spirit, and to look for the Second Coming of our Lord and Saviour Jesus Christ.

WESTMINSTER CENTRAL HALL, LONDON

Mr. Cartwright makes no mention whatever of the Great Hall of the Westminster Central Hall in London which George Jeffreys took every Easter Monday for 20 years, morning, afternoon and evening each time, from 1942 to 1961, filling it more often than not, and which was booked for 1962, the trustees being prepared at the time to let the Hall to him as long as he and the Bible-Pattern Church Fellowship wanted it on Easter Monday, after which it would not be let out again that day. I drove George Jeffreys to Victoria Station in London, with Pastor James MacLeod, then minister of the Glasgow Bible-Pattern Church, to collect the posters sent by train from the printers at Brighton, on the January evening before George Jeffreys was so suddenly and unexpectedly called Home the next morning. He saw himself announced to conduct THREE GREAT MEETINGS at the Westminster Central Hall on Easter Monday 1962.

I was at the organ for these 60 ever-memorable occasions, and afterwards, attended by those from all parts, Elim people amongst them, and even from overseas — one lady coming from Neuchatel, Switzerland, for at least 10 years and recording many of the services. I also dealt with the arrangements for the meetings each Easter Monday, as well as for the follow-up meetings annually held there that day of the Bible-Pattern Church Fellowship for the next eight years after 1961, including two occasions when I organised Easter Saturday demonstrations in Trafalgar Square.

The three meetings on Easter Monday, 1962, were in the nature of Memorial Services in the Principal's honoured memory in which his voice was heard, one of his IBRA radio recorded messages being movingly relayed over the loudspeaker equipment in the Great Hall.

THOUSANDS OF DECISIONS FOR CHRIST

Mr. Cartwright writes nothing of the thousands of souls George Jeffreys led to Christ, with results in the healing ministry, in these 20 and more years right up to when God's servant was preaching at the Kensington Temple in January 1962, just two weeks before his passing.

Before elaborating on what has been so basely omitted by Mr. Cartwright, let me say that, although being so much engaged in the governmental struggle in Elim, George Jeffreys never neglected his evangelistic call. Even in 1939, when matters were coming to a head, he was fully engaged right up to when the Big Tent was erected in Worthing that summer, with the campaign concluding a week before the British declaration of war by Neville Chamberlain on September 3rd. That Sunday morning and evening Principal Jeffreys was preaching in the Elim Tabernacle, in Union Street, The Lanes, Brighton (my home church in which I had found Christ in 1927), when the sirens were heard sounding almost immediately after the declaration at 11 o'clock. It was later said that an unidentified aircraft had crossed the coast. My vivid recollection is of the Principal preaching with fervour to that large congregation, only one person getting up and leaving the Tabernacle.

COVENTRY TENT CAMPAIGN 1940

Throughout the war years George Jeffreys preached in many cities and towns, even erecting his Big Tent in Coventry in the summer of 1940 which seems to have been God's last call to so many to repent before the city was blasted by German bombers in November of that year. When the civic authorities asked for the tent to be taken down on the site in the city centre because it was not camouflaged, we went into the Corn Exchange and completed the greatly-blessed campaign there. This building and surroundings were devastated in the air raids.

Prior to this he was in Southampton's centre, preaching in the Above Bar Congregational Church and Palace Theatre to crowded congregations, buildings soon to be bombed and destroyed in the war. Here a Chief Petty Officer who, together with his wife and mother-in-law, had been converted through the Principal's ministry in the Big Tent at Portsmouth in 1938, gave testimony to his miraculous escape in October, 1939, at Scapa

Flow, when the British battleship 'Royal Oak' was torpedoed and sunk by a German submarine. For two hours he swam or clung to crude rafts, sounding out the Gospel to drowning sailors around him in those icy oil—covered waters, urging them to call on the Name of the Lord for salvation. His joy was to know that at least one did so.

YEARS OF INTENSE REVIVAL ACTIVITY

I could go on enumerating other places visited in 1940 towards the end of which the final 'break' with Elim came, such as the campaign at the City Temple, Nottingham, with two crowded gatherings in Nottingham's magnificent Albert Hall, of Methodism fame, with further meetings that year at Kensington Temple and Orange Street Congregational Church, London, in Upper Norwood, Croydon and Barking, Glasgow, Greenock, Dundee, Aberdeen, Carlisle, Kenfig Hill in South Wales, Brighton, Portsmouth, Lincoln, Blackpool, Mansfield and Normanton.

Moving on into 1941 the Principal and Revival Party began the New Year as was customary for many years with the New Year Convention at the City Temple, Glasgow, followed by meetings at Scarborough, Stockport, Portsmouth (twice visited), Southampton (twice), Worthing (twice), Brighton, Petersfield, Barking (twice), Barnsley, Blackpool, London (Fulham), Nottingham (twice), Harrow, Grays, Bristol, Aberdeen, Bradford (twice), London (Caxton Hall), Hanley, Newport, Pontypool, Bournemouth, Carlisle (twice), Southport, Mansfield, Cardiff, Edinburgh, Dundee, York and Newbury

1942, 1943, 1944 and 1945 present the same story, with no less than over 120 cities and towns visited (some twice) including a Big Tent campaign at Cardiff in 1945 — preaching, preaching, preaching, leading souls to Christ, such was the burning passion in the heart of this man of God, of whom it was said he no longer preached the Gospel, besides being a sick man, in constant ill-health! What a lie!

TREMENDOUS SCENES IN BELFAST

When the European war had ended in 1945 we crossed over to Belfast, Northern Ireland, not having been able to get there during that time, when 2600 people packed the Royal Hippodrome from floor to roof on a Sunday afternoon and again in the evening, with hundreds being unable to get in. At one of the meetings in the Ulster Stadium, a large boxing and skating rink used as well at that time, it was reported nearly 100 stood to their feet to testify to having received divine healing in that campaign. Here again hundreds were unable to gain admission.

During the war, when our house in London was badly damaged by a flying bomb, with half the roof gone and windows shattered, with ourselves then campaigning at the Royal Pavilion, Brighton, we came up in haste to make the house as secure as possible, with the Principal also bending himself to the task, then went back to Brighton to continue the campaign. Two others and myself (Pastor Tweed being one of them) returned from Brighton to get as many unbroken tiles as we could back on to the gaping roof!

Like so many others in those grim years we drove with shaded headlamps through the streets of London and other cities and towns, or when the petrol allowance was curtailed we travelled in trains with windows darkened, to fulfil an incredible number of engagements all over the country.

UNREMITTING LABOUR AND SERVICE

It is the same story in 1946 and in all the years that follow, as I can show from our archives, a story of unremitting labour and service plus intensive travel, sometimes driving over snow-covered and fog-bound roads, yet getting through and rarely missing out on the arranged meetings, always with journeying mercies in the hundreds of thousands of miles covered so that in all our travels at home and abroad we neither harmed ourselves nor others by the mercy of God.

Continuing with the record ignored by Mr. Cartwright: before certain German prisoners of war were repatriated, and with war—time restrictions still in operation in our country, a contingent of them were permitted to attend in the fine Town Hall at Lewisham, London, and in the course of the service they gathered around the grand piano on the platform to sing 'Silent Night' in their own language, Christian believers being amongst them. As a result of this the Principal was able to visit the P.o.W. camp at Beckenham in Kent and preach the Gospel in a recreation hut put at his disposal which was packed to capacity with many standing at the back, the message being interpreted into German by a British Army Officer.

In advertising this campaign at Lewisham I had large

bold-lettered placards fastened to the sides of the car. Driving back to Clapham on a bleak winter's night after the meeting, the Principal, Pastor R.E. Darragh and I had the extraordinary experience of being caught up in a hold-up by gunmen at a house not far from our own in Clarence Avenue. After having extricated ourselves, we read the next evening under a large type heading in the London 'Star' newspaper, that the 'bandits' on that occasion had got away 'in a placarded car'!!

FORTITUDE AND STAMINA

I make particular mention here of the campaign in the Regal Theatre, with its 1200 and more seats, on the South Pier at Blackpool in 1947, in the coldest winter of the century as was then reported. The fuel crisis and intense wintry weather conditions did not prevent the Principal and Party from beginning the campaign on schedule, March 1st, and going through with it to the end. In my account I headed it 'BLIZZARDS! BOLDNESS!! BLESSING!!!'

BIG TENT CAMPAIGNS AND CONVENTIONS

In the years I am now dealing with, from 1946 on, arduous Big Tent campaigns were held, which usually meant meetings every night, except Friday, with two on Sundays and several afternoons in the week, for weeks on end, with the Tent erected at times on bombed sites. I list these campaigns: a site in the North End Road, near the Olympia, London (1946); Halifax, Yorkshire (1948); Stockport (1949); Brighton and Hove (1949); Stockwell, London (1950); Frampton Street, Edgware Road, London (1951); Elephant and Castle, London, Coronation Year (1953); Birmingham (1955). In most instances the Tent used was considered to be the largest Evangelistic Tent in the country, some 150 feet long by 80 feet wide, demanding a large site, otherwise we hired a Tent to suit the size of the site available. The Big Tent was also used in these years for greatly-blessed summer Christian Conventions in the Lake District of England. One can imagine the souls brought into the Kingdom through this ministry alone plus the blessing experienced and enjoyed by thousands of God's people.

In between campaigns and conventions we stored the canvas at a well-known Tent makers' works at Kingston-on-Thames, with the large centre poles, quarter and outer poles deposited with the forms for seating in the basement at Kensington Temple. After 1955, and only seven years before the Principal's decease, Tent work having become very demanding on one's strength by then, the Tent and all appertaining to it, such as forms, platform, electrical and loud-speaker equipment, was sold at a modest figure to another Pentecostal evangelist.

CONTINENTAL CAMPAIGNS

Before the 'break' with Elim, George Jeffreys had had tremendous meetings on the Continent and elsewhere abroad, which in themselves were quite apart from his ministry in and for Elim. Now let me give details of the ministry overseas immediately following the war years, again necessitating much labour, effort and travel, *and which have been omitted by Mr. Cartwright:*

In 1946 the Principal and Party were in France, ministering in Nice, Cannes, Marseilles in the South, and Lisieux, Evreux, Le Havre, Dieppe, Lille and Calais in the North. Thousands received blessing in these inspiring revival meetings and over 800 conversions were recorded.

1947 — Geneva, Zurich, where George Jeffreys was a prominent speaker at the 1st World Pentecostal Conference held there, Montreux and Yverdon: further crowded gatherings and 574 souls saved in eight days.

1948 — Neuchatel, Lausanne and Saint Etienne: over 1,100 decisions for Christ and the Full Gospel message broadcast over Radio Lausanne, Switzerland.

1950 — crowded meetings in Le Havre, St. Etienne, Evreux, Paris, Lausanne and Bienne, in public halls including the magnificent Pleyel Concert Hall inthe city of Paris, May 10th to 14th; in churches and evangelistic Tents. Over 1,500 decisions for Christ.

The meetings in France included preaching in the Threatre in the Casino at Nice where compulsive gamblers gather daily to satisfy the urge to gamble in the various forms available. What a venue this proved to be for the Foursquare Gospel message as preached with power by George Jeffreys! No wonder the Pastor at Nice later testified to how many of the converts, mainly Roman Catholics, he had baptised in water on the confession of their new-found Faith!

We crossed over to Monaco and visited the Monte Carlo Casino where an official there who had attended the meetings in Nice told the Principal he wished he could hear him preach his message in the Theatre in the Casino, into which he took us, but such public Protestant meetings, he said, would not be permitted in Monaco.

SCANDINAVIA AND FINLAND

I can also personally testify to the revival meetings he addressed in *Sweden* (Stockholm), *Denmark,* where Copenhagen's fine Concert Palace Theatre accommodating 2,000 people was crowded to capacity, *Norway* (Oslo) and *Finland* (Helsinki and Pori).

I feel it is worthy of note that the 'revival' car which took us on most of our journeyings, a Chrysler, DLP 963, capable of carrying eight persons apart from the driver, and much equipment used in the campaigns, purchased for less than £500 with the exchange in 1937 — a gift to the work from a grateful convert in the Scarborough Campaign of 1933 — was as well known on the Continent and in Scandinavia as ourselves as a Party! We had the use of this car in the Lord's work for 32 years until 1969.

As I had the task of co-operating with Principal George Jeffreys in the organising of these and our other engagements in conjunction with those at the 'other end', one can imagine the immense amount of correspondence involved as well as our other work, with much pressure upon his time and energy in responding as well to thousands of prayer requests and attending to administrative responsibilities. It was the same with the typing of his letters in connection with his extensive correspondence in Elim with Elim H/Q, and of his books which were published in the years prior to the 'break' with Elim, so that no matter where we went here and overseas, even if only for a brief respite at the home of his sister in Maesteg, South Wales, the typewriter was an essential part of our equipment to meet the demands of correspondence sent on. A full time job, together with the meetings, not made any easier by reason of the fact that for so much of the time we did not have the advantage of occupying comfortable office quarters!

In this summary of the crowded activities of a man of God in the last 20 years of his life, having a passion for lost souls which remained with him from the beginning to the end of his long ministry, *I have given an emphatic and positive refutation* of Mr. Cartwright's base references to those years in his book, which has so saddened him and which he passes over 'in a few words', expressing 'regret for the way things turned out'!

'Picture Post', Dr. Bryan Wilson's book 'Sects and Society' (Elim section), well documented as it is, and Noel Brooks' book 'Fight for the Faith and Freedom' all scornfully dismissed or ignored by Mr. Cartwright. Who then is to speak for George Jeffreys?

PERSONAL MINISTRY

The week which saw George Jeffreys' passing he visited two homes at Twickenham, Middlesex, to be of help to those in need, the second and last he was ever to visit being that of a cousin of mine whose wife had been ill over a long period of time. As we stood with the Principal he prayed for her as she lay on the couch. She made a remarkable recovery, living an active life for many years after that until the family called on me to conduct her funeral service when in her 80s. I recall my cousin saying to him as we were leaving the house, "That was a beautiful prayer, Mr. Jeffreys." How true it proved to be!

WHAT PRICE TRUTH?

As George Jeffreys was awaiting burial at our hands in London in 1962, a leading Elim minister at Clapham, J.C. Kennedy by name, was reported as saying of him in the Press, "Although he had been in bad health for about 20 years, he still managed to visit the churches periodically, especially around Easter and Whitsun." My authoritative refutation of this was published in the same London newspaper by courtesy of the Editor, with my letter headed 'A noble life spent in God's service.' It doesn't take much imagination to know what the Elim people were being told then and subsequently, seeing a challenge I made to Mr. Kennedy to call at my address, when I would give him proof of what I had written in reply to his false report, was ignored. *One may well ask:* if our leader was so incapacitated for the last 20 years of his life, what were we as members of his Revival Party supposed to be doing all that time, remaining with him at home and emerging mainly at Easter and Whitsun?

Now, some 24 years later, the same glib propaganda is

published in Mr. Cartwright's book, *this time for posterity to read,* plainly indicating that, in the eyes of these Elim men so blinded by prejudice that the truth counts for nothing, George Jeffreys' God-given ministry was dependent on the Elim Movement and therefore came to an end after he left it! In the same breath, as it were, Mr. Cartwright extols the heights to which he claims Elim has climbed today, without any regard as to the solid foundations established by its spiritual founder and greatest pioneer, continuing by expressing his regrets for his later years, *those 20 years of intensive soul-saving ministry which he has denied him,* and ending by writing piously of him by way of a sop (page 158) as "the finest and the most successful British evangelist since the time of John Wesley or George Whitfield." What adequate comment can one possibly make on double standards as this?

LETTER TO THE PUBLISHERS

Besides writing at considerable length to certain ministers on the Elim Executive Council, *I also wrote in the same vein to the Publishers,* Marshall Pickering, pointing out the errors, misrepresentations and omissions of facts in the manuscript, urgently and earnestly hoping that as the publishers "there may yet be time for him to think again and revise his MS. accordingly." To this they briefly replied, "Having received approval from the Elim Church on Mr. Cartwright's manuscript we see no reason to delay publication."

Apart from anything else (and there is much other material misrepresenting George Jeffreys' life's work, coupled with the lowering of his dignity which he always had), I would ask in view of what I have written so far: WHAT CREDENCE CAN BE PUT UPON MR. CARTWRIGHT'S BOOK OVERALL BY THINKING MEN AND WOMEN?

FALSE PRESENTATION OF B.I. CONTROVERSY

Having dealt with the 20 years there are other matters I must deal with here. In the multiplicity of words used by Mr. Cartwright as regards the British Israelism controversy in Elim, which he uses in common with that propagated by Elim H/Q to cloud the far more important issue of what George Jeffreys was striving for in his reform governmental policy for the Elim

Movement, he makes it clear that E.J. Phillips considered this prophetical viewpoint to be *false* (page 121), hence his opposition to it, whereas no where does he state that George Jeffreys' position *in Elim* was this, viz. he believed it to be *truth,* yet he had the commendable attitude of wanting all schools of prophetic thought to be propagated, whether Futurist, Historicist, or National Historicist, as he termed the B.I. school, *on condition* that the great basic fundamental teaching of 'Ye must be born again' was preached as it applied to all men everywhere irrespective of nationality, whether Jew, Israelite or Gentile. *What a lot would have been saved the Movement had this charitable attitude been adopted!*

The correspondence between the Principal and E.J. Phillips from December, 1936, to March, 1937, relating to certain issues including B.I. and the World Revival Crusade, touched on by Mr. Cartwright, embodies on the Principal's part the aforementioned charitable attitude regarding B.I. and the other schools of prophetic thought. *This Desmond Cartwright has deliberately omitted to state* (page 137), again demonstrating his half-truth tactics. I have it all on my files, with George Jeffreys' own hand-written notes alongside.

LEWI PETHRUS AND GEORGE JEFFREYS

Lewi Pethrus, the great Swedish Pentecostal leader, who was not a B.I. had an article published in a paper he edited called 'Herald of Faith' under date June, 1941. I quote from this: "We have learned that the opponents of George Jeffreys within the Elim Foursquare Movement have tried to assert the opinion in private letters to others in America that the reason for his resignation was based on a theological question, namely that of 'British Israel'. This is absolutely wrong, even if such a reason is given...What is far more important to me in this matter, are the reasons which George Jeffreys himself says are the cause for his resignation. For my part, I have so much faith in George Jeffreys that if the question concerning 'British-Israel' had been the reason, then he would have so stated in his own letter of resignation. Instead he writes that the real reason for his resignation is the unscriptural form of government exercised over the various churches, and that these same churches have lost their spiritual freedom through this; and when George Jeffreys says this — I believe him!"

'PEARL HARBOUR' SUNDAY AND LEGAL CHAINS

Furthermore, nowhere does Mr. Cartwright make it clear that George Jeffreys, heavily burdened as he was by the command he had received, 'Set your house in order,' was endeavouring against great odds to break the legal chains binding pastors, people, property and church finances to the Movement under its rigid central government system which he freely admitted he had unwittingly helped to establish. On the contrary, he is portrayed as a man who did not know his own mind (page 153), whereas his opponents led by those at Elim H/Q are seen as paragons of virtue, yet not above taking over a church building at Portsmouth by surprise and intimidation, accompanied by a detective in tow, and appointing another Elim minister on the spot on the Sunday morning, December 7th, 1941 ('Pearl Harbour' Sunday), thus depriving the church congregation of their godly pastor had they remained and of their building. All this was done in war-time, with Headquarters having frozen the funds of the church at the local bank! They had the legal power to do this under the system if not the moral right, as well as the legal ownership of the property, and they saw to it it was enforced in this shocking manner rather than resorting to law which they had resolved to do in their Conference of three months before! *None of this is mentioned by Mr. Cartwright in his 'history', nor* the disgraceful 'disfellowshipping' of George Jeffreys by the same Conference based on a claim that the Conference had done all to meet 'the demands of Mr. George Jeffreys,' deprecating his 'continued and persistent attacks upon the Movement and its Constitution', and his 'deliberate attempt to split the Elim Churches after his most solemn pledge to the Ministerial Conference of 1939 not to disturb these churches. It therefore has no choice but to disassociate itself entirely from him according to the teaching of the Word of God,' a pretext dismissed by the late Commander D.H. Macmillan, M.B.E., R.N.E., F.R.I.C.S., in these words:

"We have already seen that George Jeffreys' converts were deliberately prevented by certain anti-publicity devices from having any clear picture of the several causes that made his resignation inevitable from the entire Elim work he had so assiduously founded and built up. As he was also prevented from entering any Elim Church it was most natural that his converts should anxiously engage public halls on their own initiative (as in Dundee, York and Bournemouth), to hear first-hand the account of this serious event from their charismatic leader under whose ministry they had learnt to know Christ. Even on these occasions members of the Elim Executive Council and local Elim Ministers were not above attending such proceedings and interrupting them of set purpose, to muzzle the truth, amid scenes of indescribable confusion."

(I was there in each case, also confirmed in writing by the late Edwin Scrymgeour, ex-M.P., who was present at Dundee).
Commander Macmillan goes on:

"It is therefore abundantly clear that the withholding of the full facts surrounding his resignation, coupled with such unfair tactics, fully released George Jeffreys from any undertaking he may have made in good faith in the 1939 Conference. Accordingly the reason given by the 1941 Conference for casting off the undoubted leader of Elim and finally separating him from his own spiritual community can now be assessed for what it is worth."

WHAT A BACKING!

Mr. Cartwright uses James McWhirter's word 'illusion' as applied to George Jeffreys' 'vision', to back home his own expressed contempt for the latter as a reformer (page 144). James McWhirter, once a valued and well-used member of the Revival Party, but Mr. Cartwright does not say of him, that, amongst other matters such as an agreeable 'deal' by him with Elim H/Q, he has become the friend of Jesuits, with a re-thinking of theology, having newly discovered what Roman Catholicism really is today, according to his book entitled 'A World in a Country' published in 1983. One would hardly expect Mr. McWhirter to have supported the Scriptural teaching of the sovereignty of the local church, with the ownership of the property under control of the church members, as advocated by George Jeffreys, Reformer. The word I would use in his case as an Ulsterman, originally and firmly steeped in old-time Protestant belief, would be 'deluded' or 'delusion'.

As for "THERE WAS NO FINANCIAL CRISIS IN ELIM IN 1937" (page 142), I will say equally 'loud and clear' that this is another half-truth, as I know full well. What if the assets of the Elim Movement at that time were "valued at some £200,000 at least", as stated by Mr. Cartwright, George Jeffreys was well aware that church buildings could not be sold over the heads of the people, with the people on the street, to meet debts that might be called in!

A CATEGORICAL DENIAL

I categorically deny that "reconciliation", as Mr. Cartwright expresses it, (page 156) "was not possible during the lifetime of the Principal". He made a magnanimous OFFER to this end as late as 1958 which was turned down by the Elim Executive Council. Mr. Cartwright has seen this in print! Furthermore, I was present when George Jeffreys freely forgave E.J. Phillips (Elim's Secretary-General) who had so grievously opposed and hurt him, by saying to him, "I've nothing in my heart against you." Such was the Christ-like spirit manifested by this servant of the Lord just five weeks before he so unexpectedly died. If Mr. Phillips had made a move then in response, even at that late stage, who knows what the outcome might have been?

A FALSE DAMAGING ASSERTION

He makes a most damaging assertion regarding the book 'Fight for the Faith and Freedom' by Rev. Noel Brooks, B.D. (page 139). I have a letter from Mr. Brooks dated 7th April 1986, in which he tells me through a copy attached of his letter of the same date to Mr. Cartwright, "First, you make a comment upon my efforts to have the book withdrawn from circulation. I need to tell you that this was for purely personal reasons, not because I had come to consider that the book was defective in its factual content. To this day I have not been able to find any factual inaccuracies in the book. When I corresponded with Principal George Jeffreys during 1952, he agreed to withdraw the book from circulation if I could produce factual inaccuracies. I could not do so. In 1955 I corresponded with Pastor E.J. Phillips on the same issue. In a letter he had charged me with such inaccuracies, but when I asked him to give me a list of these in order that I might put pressure on Brother Jeffreys to withdraw the book he refused to do so. I could only conclude that he could not produce them."

"SO MANY ERRORS OF FACT..."

Rev. Brooks continues, "Second, your brief review of my own life contains so many errors of fact that I wonder what your

202

sources are. In your own interests as a historian let me set the record straight," which he proceeds to do, and ends, "I hope that these comments will help you to correct the paragraph in your forthcoming book before you publish." As we know, this has not been done — another case of unverified 'facts' before publication.

I emphasised several times to Mr. Cartwright, *"That the truth regarding the division and why George Jeffreys left Elim, and the fundamental basis on which he founded the Bible-Pattern Church Fellowship, might rightly and justly be given, is my main purpose in writing as I do."*

Mr. Cartwright makes no reference to the impressive funeral service of Elim's Founder at Kensington Temple, London, on February 1st, 1962, when representatives of established Pentecostal Movements at home and abroad were present to pay their respects. The great number of letters I received, some of which were published in the Memorial issue of 'The Pattern' and in my book, 'George Jeffreys — Man of God' (1964, now out of print), give their own revealing personal testimonies to what his ministry had meant in the lives of all classes of people. Both this issue of 'The Pattern', a magazine I edited for some twenty years, and my book are not referred to at all by Mr. Cartwright in his 'history', although he has them.

Thus God's faithful servant was laid to rest. Essentially he was a soul-winner, both in Elim and out, yet when he founded the Bible-Pattern Church Fellowship of free, self-governing churches in 1940, with its 'Free Churches Bible College', it was not to be wondered at that the build-up would be slow and painstaking in the war years and subsequently, with the intense opposition as it was, even as we have seen after his death, plus failure on the part of some who started out but who did not go on. It has ever been the same. Did great men of God in the New Testament and in our Nation's own history whom we honour today as Christian reformers see only failure when they ignominiously died, some of them, in ditches? And yet we can freely read, write and speak in our land because of such faithful men and women, and the freedom they stood for. It takes a man of courage and deep conviction to give up a life's work and begin all over again, but this has ever been the way of the true reformer. With it there is a peace of heart and mind which nothing can disturb, and in the end it is the Truth that will stand.

After Mr. Cartwright states (page 157) of the Advisory Committee of the Bible-Pattern Church Fellowship and the Elim Executive Council, that they meet together from time to time and that a number of Bible-Pattern Churches have joined the Elim Church Incorporated, he goes on to say, "Many of the things that George Jeffreys wanted are now a regular feature in Elim Churches", unspecified as these are and open to question, yet in writing thus he contradicts much of what he has written in vindication of the opposition to George Jeffreys and his stand for reform. One might well ask: why then were these many 'things' not granted in his lifetime and thus have prevented the traumatic division? The answer is of course that these do not include such as Government of the Local Church Members, by the Local Church Members, for the Local Church Members, with the ownership of the church property in the control of the registered church membership, as is the case with the *individual* local church of the Bible—Pattern Church Fellowship. The fact that the Advisory Committee of the Fellowship have gone the way they have does not alter this but it does blunt their own weapon of protest against the Elim Church Incorporated, that which Principal George Jeffreys so decisively renounced as they know full well.

So I could go on, but must leave the rest for the biography on which I am engaged.

WHERE THE RESPONSIBILITY LIES

I wrote to Mr. Cartwright stating that if he was bent on having his book published, following my adverse criticism, it would be to the detriment of himself and the Elim Movement. Elim H/Q had a similar letter and must therefore share in the responsibility.

Before ending this Open Letter there is something of a far more damaging nature I need to refer to. Last year (1985) saw the publication of a book entitled 'Restoring the Kingdom' by Dr. Andrew Walker (Hodder and Stoughton), with its section devoted to Elim and Assemblies of God,and to George and Stephen Jeffreys, recommended to me by Desmond Cartwright in a letter in December last but not brought to my attention until I read a review of the book by Tony Sargent in the 'Evangelical Times' of April, 1986. The author, the son of an Elim minister now deceased who was known to me, *relies heavily on Desmond Cartwright and the Elim side of the Elim story* without ever having approached such as myself as the one so closely associated with it on the 'other side' in order to have his 'facts' confirmed or otherwise, more especially when he has basely attacked George Jeffreys in his personal life and as regards his godly character. He writes:

"This whole story has still to be told, and as Elim have a first-class historian, an open and honest account will eventually emerge. Pastor Desmond Cartwright," he adds in brackets, "who is writing a book on Stephen and George Jeffreys is proud to be an Elim pastor, but he is not afraid of the truth; his work is genuine history, not hagiography."

This, his work "is" genuine history, I suggest is significant written as it was in 1985 before the publication of Mr. Cartwright's book in 1986.

Readers of this Open Letter can judge for themselves as to Mr. Cartwright's ability as a "first-class historian", his desire to give "an open and honest account", and regard for "the truth" and "genuine history".

As I have shown, J.C. Kennedy (Elim) pictured George Jeffreys as a 'write-off' after he left Elim. Desmond Cartwright has done precisely the same thing, supported by Elim H/Q and the 'Elim Evangel'. Now we have Andrew Walker, an outsider, repeating this completely false picture and going a step further by saying he "died a nonentity". He considers it "a shame" that George Jeffreys came to this sorry state, adding "History is cruel". I reminded him "So is lying propaganda…more so when a man is no longer able to answer for himself".

A SHOCKING ATTACK

I challenged Dr. Walker to give me proof of what he has further written in a far baser attack, viz. "George Jeffreys was a shy man outside the pulpit. He never married. Despite his rather effeminate looks in his early days (at least against his miner brother), and despite occasional whiffs of scandal surrounding his sexuality, there is not the slightest historical evidence that Jeffreys was homosexual." I also asked him to meet me, when I would produce the evidence showing what a mighty "nonentity" George Jeffreys was to the end of his life. He writes in reply he does not believe he has attacked George Jeffreys as I have claimed and states that, on the contrary, he refutes smears and allegations. He seeks to justify all that he has written, *pointedly adding*, "If you feel that Desmond Cartwright has led me astray, then you will have to take that matter up with him." My answer as to his being led "astray" is an emphatic "Yes, I do," confirmed by what I have submitted here in this Open Letter as factual evidence; but it is not for me to sort out the matter between these two men concerning what each has put into print.

Dr. Walker does not feel there is any point in our meeting but would be willing, if I send it, to put one short paragraph concerning Pastor George Jeffreys' work after 1940 and one short paragraph with my memories of him as a man and friend (not a great evangelist) in the second edition of his book. At the same time he urges me to write "a human and personal biography of the man...No one could do it better"! As for his own book, he believes it has "introduced thousands of people outside Pentecostal circles to a magnificent Christian and outstanding evangelist". The reader can form his own conclusions as to this.

BRITISH ISRAELISM — SAME OLD STORY

Such a contradictory story as he has published, again for posterity to read, has within it a re-hash of that falsely circulated by Elim H/Q concerning British Israelism ('Israelitism', as Dr. Walker terms it) as a blind hiding the real reason for George Jeffreys' resignation which, sad to say, was believed and propagated by such as Donald Gee and according to Dr. Walker, J. Nelson Parr, both of Assemblies of God and now deceased. A case surely of 'The voice is Jacob's voice, but the hands are the hands of Esau'! George Jeffreys contended with Donald Gee over this issue as late as 1953 but had no redress, and even after his death in 1962 Donald Gee still propagated it in, if I remember well, the A.o.G. magazine, that he (Jeffreys) had resigned from Elim ostensibly over church government without mentioning B.I.. The word "ostensibly" was enough. I wrote to Mr. Gee asking him to remove it when the reason given for the resignation would have been correct. I had no answer.

That there has been a great deal of accord between Dr. Walker and Desmond Cartwright cannot be doubted, but as the latter as official historian has made no such statement impinging on George Jeffreys' moral character in his book, who originated it in the mind of Dr. Walker? What is plain from Cartwright's book is his studied attempt to *justify* Elim then and now *at all costs*. One thing is sure: our Lord Himself was not immune from false reports, He who said, "The servant is not greater than his lord..." and who encourages such with His own Word.

One of George Jeffreys' faults, it seems, besides his "doctrinal deviation, and even personality disorder", was "spiritual pride" which led to his "fall" (later referred to as his "downfall"), so Dr. Walker describes older Elim members (clearly taken in by propaganda) as thinking, the last thing anyone knowing George Jeffreys would charge him with. A more self-effacing man in the public eye, as he was throughout his ministerial life, would be hard to find, yet Walker writes in complimentary terms of Pastor Cartwright as being "proud" to be an Elim pastor..."! It was Rom Landau, renowned author, who wrote of George Jeffreys at the Royal Albert Hall, in his book entitled 'God is My Aventure':

"The man whom ten thousand people from all over the British Isles had come to see and to listen to had mounted the platform quite unobserved. Though my eyes had rarely left the platform I did not see the entry of George Jeffreys, the founder and leader of the Elim Evangelists, and I only discovered later that he had been sitting for some time among his friends in the front row."

He goes on:

"I saw through my opera glasses a strong face with rather a soft mouth, dark curly hair and a fine presence in which there was nothing calculated to play upon the emotions..."

As for being a "pragmatist" (both Walker and Cartwright use this word in relation to George Jeffreys), if he had not been such in the best meaning of the word, Mr. Cartwright would not have become the minister of the three Elim churches in the six years I have known him, viz. Smethwick, Halifax and now Greenock, nor would the late Percy Brewster, to whom Mr. Cartwright's book is first dedicated, have been the minister of the City Temple, Cardiff, for some 30 years.

The distorted picture given plus, in my view, the character assassination of a truly great and good man, now deceased, without the slightest justification, warrants not just short paragraphs but a complete withdrawal in the second edition of Dr. Walker's book, of the falsely written passages in question. In claiming to be a Christian believer Dr. Walker is left with no alternative before God.*

The 'Elim Evangel' of April 19th, 1986, to which I have referred at the beginning, after having condoned what I can only

* We understand that Hodder and Stoughton have withdrawn the second edition due to comments made about the House Churches (May 89).

term as contributory to the calculated attempt to blot out George Jeffreys as a powerfully used evangelist to the end of his life, supported as this attempt is by an outsider such as Dr. Andrew Walker, goes on to state of Desmond Cartwright's book, "It will also stir the spirit of those who, today, are yearning to see the power of the Holy Spirit at work in the Church". God who is the Righteous Judge expected to use and bless such a book in this way? NEVER!

"For by thy words thou shalt be justified, and by thy words thou shalt be condemned" — Matthew 12:37.

Such teaching as given in the Movement's official magazine by Elim H/Q ministers regarding the precept of honesty, as for example, "...nothing must be allowed to obscure the need to obey scrupulously the principles of Scripture in every area. Honesty is not only the best policy, for God's people it is the only one. It is also the rewarding one. God has promised to honour it." (Tom W. Walker, 8/2/86) and "You shall not bear false witness against your neighbour. Exodus 20:16" (John C. Smyth, 22/3/86) cries out for Mr. Cartwright's book to be withdrawn from sale.

By way of conclusion let me add: in the last year of George Jeffreys' life (1961) he had the joy of seeing Mrs. Margery Steven at the Easter Monday meetings at the Westminster Central Hall, London, to publicly testify to her miraculous healing of multiple sclerosis in July, 1960. Mrs. Steven is still with us and her testimony will be given with others in the biography.

Yours in Christ,

Albert W. Edsor (Pastor)

17 Sumburgh Road,
London, SW12 8AJ.

Date 25th July, 1986

I make this public appeal to the members of the Elim Executive Council who, I am given to understand, have his framed picture in their board-room: in all conscience to take steps to have the injurious 1941 Conference Resolution 'disfellowshipping' Elim's godly Founder expunged from the Movement's records, a first step to their setting their 'house' in order.

A.W.E.
28th February, 1989,
George Jeffreys'
centenary birth date

Appendix 2
Extract from *Picture Post*
Vol.31 No.6, May 11th 1946
A Prophet Holds a Revival Meeting

Some say George Jeffreys has healing hands. Some say he has the power of prophecy. Thousands believe in him. Thousands deride him. He is one of the last of the great revivalists.

SOMEDAY, somebody will write a sober, scientific history of revivalism, and it will be an eye-opener to the theologian, the sociologist and the psychiatrist, too. The story is a strange and sometimes lurid one. There was 'Crazy' Dow — who wasn't so crazy, even though his appearance was 'more filthy than a savage Indian.' He set the Midlands ablaze with revival fire in the first years of the nineteenth century, and Primitive Methodism resulted. In the '70's, Dwight L. Moody (Mr. Sankey's friend) 'reduced the population of hell by a million souls.' Backed by Rockefeller, Billy Sunday fought the devil in public every night and twice on the Sabbath. Gypsy Smith bullied and blarneyed tens of thousands into salvation (though how many stayed saved after the shouting had died down and the sweat cooled off is not chronicled). Mrs. McPherson arrived with her curls and her angels, her spotlights and her trumpets, and (says an admirer) 'the Glory came down.' But somehow it dried up like the morning dew.

Of all the current soulsavers among us, only one is really prominent and worthy of close attention. That is George Jeffreys, head of the Bible Pattern Church Fellowship, a breakaway from the powerful Elim Foursquare movement. Jeffreys' Bible Pattern combines the benefits of mysticism, tongue-speaking, prophecy, and a good time for all. But its most striking feature, and its trump card, is healing. The extent of his following is not precisely known. But some idea can be got from the size of his congregations which, in good years, have exceeded ten thousand at a go (and on April 6, 1928, he baptised one thousand people in a single night, "the greatest number since the Day of Pentecost").

George Jeffreys — the Principal, as his followers call him — is a slight, dark, curly-haired man in his fifties. Every spring for years his face has been familiar on the London hoardings. On the posters he looks quiet and modest enough, and in the flesh that quietness and modesty is what strikes you first. The fanatic's gleam is not there. If you go to a Jeffreys meeting expecting the Bible-thumping and capers of the conventional hot-gospeller you will be disappointed. Even when he is preaching, Jeffreys speaks quietly and with restrained gestures. His appeal, say his followers, is to the will, not to the emotions. That is as may be. He is certainly a tête-à-tête man. He can take the Albert Hall and pack it, and when he speaks it is an intimate affair, everyone feels he is talking just to them alone. And without a lift of the voice he can rock them more surely than any other evangelist of our time. It isn't a subtle technique even. It is just a natural gift. But it can shake congregations. It can shake them into tongue-speaking trances and into dead faints. And sometimes it can shake them out of incurable illness into health, according to their own testimony.

Jeffreys comes from Maesteg, in South Wales. He was bent on becoming a Congregational minister, but creeping paralysis looked like cutting his career short. He was healed by what he holds was a miracle; and from then on, he was set.

In 1907 came the 'Latter Rain' revival. The fire of the Lord descended on an Anglican vicar in Monkwearmouth, and he began to cry out in a strange language not like any tongue known to man. That was the start of the Pentecostal movement.

Enthusiasts by the thousand, fired by this manifestation, were withdrawing from the ordinary ceremonial churches and going off into tongue-speaking huddles in little halls and backrooms up and down the country. The whole thing was in a state of anarchy. Jeffreys, who had his first personal tongue-speaking experience around 1912, probably did more than any single man to set Pentecostalism on its feet, when in 1915 he founded the Elim Foursquare Gospel Movement in Northern Ireland.

It was tongue-speaking that made Pentecostalism different from other forms of revivalism. When, under stress of

211

excitement in the course of a meeting, believers begin to cry out in what sounds like gibberish, Pentecostals hold this to be a means of glorifying God, and a miraculous sign to unbelievers. They have been much attacked for the exercise of this gift, though it is their custom to refer critics to the Acts, where there is evidence that tongue-speaking was a commonplace among the Apostles.

Traditionally, revival movements are a revolt against the power of the established Church. Originally the emotional excesses which attended them no doubt arose out of the exuberance of a people long oppressed and having their first fling of freedom. Nowadays, when there are excesses, they are more likely to arise out of the anxiety and emotional constraint of the bitterly poor. Certainly revivalism is always predominantly a poor man's religion. In this respect Elim ran true to type. The first Elim meeting hall was a disused laundry in a Belfast back-street. The second was a derelict slum cinema. But within twenty years Jeffreys had over 200 churches in the British Isles under his supervision. The movement had its own theological college, its printing works and publishing house, its own holiday homes, a youth movement, and missionary branches abroad. On his revival rounds, Jeffreys was packing the biggest halls in the country — the Albert Hall, the Crystal Palace, Birmingham's Bingley Hall, the Liverpool Stadium.

Then, dramatically, the Elim movement was split asunder as Jeffreys, always its star attraction, announced he was withdrawing. His grounds were good traditional dissenter's freedom-of-religion grounds. Till now, local Elim churches had been paying their own way and sending the surplus of money raised to the central body. Jeffreys branded this practice as 'definitely Babylonish,' and in 1939 he resigned and set out to build up a fellowship of self-governing churches, not answerable to him nor anyone except themselves. (Elim finances, by the way, are not wonderful. In 1937 the movement was £44,000 in debt. By 1939, the debt had been reduced to £14,000. But Jeffreys' withdrawal has no doubt hit the movement hard.)

Tongue-speaking distinguishes Pentecostals from other revivalists. Healing distinguishes Jeffreys from other Pentecostal preachers. He is the most assiduous and probably the most successful faith healer of our time. His procedure is simple. In the course of a meeting, when the congregation is 'set' and the atmosphere of faith is beginning to make itself felt, Jeffreys will ask for the sick to come forward. And while the congregation sings quietly and a young man lays out soft concert-party arpeggios on the piano, Jeffreys comes down from the platform and puts his hands on the heads of the sick (sometimes, especially in church meetings, he prefers to anoint them with olive oil), and murmurs a few words, "Pray to the Lord," or "Concentrate on Jesus Christ" or just "Glory." Some take it with tears, some with a smile, some go off into jerking or babbling fits, some just fall headlong and lie there. The whole thing is done without fuss or mumbo-jumbo on Jeffreys' part. He doesn't claim to heal. But the 'patients' commonly claim to have been healed.

The variety of cures performed can be gathered by cases listed in Jeffreys' own book, *Healing Rays*. The headings run: Helpless Cripple Walks out of Wheeled Carriage at Southampton, Dilated Stomach Healed at Brighton, Agonising Skin Disease Cured after Twelve Years Agony, Another Bath Chair Case at Wimbledon, Growth Disappears.

Jeffreys does not know how many cures he has effected — he only hears results when patients testify — but his followers reckon the figure runs into several thousands. Some believe the cures to be miraculous. Some believe them to be due to the therapeutic quality of autohypnosis, or to hysteria which might have a 'hair-of-the-dog' effect on illnesses with a hysterical basis. Whatever it is, the cures are there. The obvious danger, as with all sorts of faith-healing, is that simple-minded people may neglect the advice of doctors in order to try a miraculous cure. Jeffreys himself (unlike many faith-healers who lump doctors, drugs and devils together) is a believer in medical science. The way he looks at it, doctors do the same job on the natural plane as he does on the supernatural.

In some quarters this theory is held to be dangerous liberalism, like Jeffreys' views on prophecy. He believes in prophecy. But he is dead set against foretelling the future for personal ends. That he categorises as fortune-telling. He foresees the danger there, of a minister inducing a brother to sell up and hand over the proceeds, or persuading a sister to marry him. To Jeffreys, prophecy is merely a matter of interpreting Scriptures ("forthtelling not foretelling" is his phrase). Working on that basis he sees signs of a coming Revival, the formation of an Anglo-American bloc, a final great war in Palestine, and the return of Christ to earth. Jeffreys sees no future in organised religion. He thinks individual Anglican and Roman ministers may be fine fellows, but organisationally their churches are distinctly 'Babylonish.'

As far as the healing and the tongue-speaking and all the exuberant signs of revival enthusiam are concerned, it is easy for the sociologists and psychologists to dismiss the whole thing as a deplorable mass hysteria. The fact remains that Jeffreys means much to many thousands of poor creatures whose lives are emotionally starved. One of Jeffreys' helpers has said: "Meetings like this are the greatest impulses in the lives of these people. They are like an electric current that charges the batteries for months to come. When the batteries run down a bit, another meeting will charge them. People simply live for months in the memory of these days...when they return to their dreary surroundings in some London slum, to their work in factories in the black towns of the Midlands." Those who feel revivalism is something that needs uprooting will have to dig pretty deep.

A.L. LLOYD.

George Jeffreys had four double-spread pages and a run-over allotted to him in *Picture Post,* whereas a well known boxer of the time only had two in the same issue.

The nine excellent pictures with the article, large and small, taken at Kensington Temple, London, W.11, each with their caption showed a baptismal service, with one candidate at least receiving the baptism of the Holy Ghost, praising and glorifying God in other tongues, after coming up out of the water; the congregation in prayer: the sick being prayed for; and part of the congregation enthusiastically singing an old-time revival hymn.

This clearly disposes of the false account, as given in *The Great Evangelists,* that *Picture Post's* report and pictures could *only* show George Jeffreys ministering to a small group of elderly ladies.

INDEX